AS THE
ROMANS
DO

Also by Alan Epstein

How to Be Happier Day by Day
How to Have More Love in Your Life
Anything Is Possible

AS THE
ROMANS
DO

*The Delights, Dramas,
and Daily Diversions of Life
in the Eternal City*

ALAN EPSTEIN

William Morrow
An Imprint of HarperCollins*Publishers*

HarperCollins books may be purchased for educational, business, or sales promotional use. For information please write: Special Markets Department, HarperCollins Publishers Inc., 10 East 53rd Street, New York, NY 10022.

FIRST EDITION

Designed by Bernard Klein

Printed on acid-free paper

Library of Congress Cataloging-in-Publication Data

Epstein, Alan.
    As the Romans do : the delights, dramas, and daily diversions of life in the eternal city / by Alan Epstein.
        p. cm.
    ISBN 0-688-17272-5
    1. Rome—Civilization.   I. Title.
DG77.E77   2000
937—dc21   99-42763

00   01   02   03   04   RRD   10   9   8   7   6   5   4   3   2   1

For Diane and the *bambini*

Acknowledgments

Many people have contributed to the conception and fulfillment of this book. Ned and Debby Carroll, Alan and Cindy Sachs, David and Wendy Ginsberg, Hank and Phyllis Ginsberg, Eric and Margaret Burnette, Thom and Barbra Markham, Steve Antinoff, Alanna Nelson, Susan Page, Zack (the Mac) Edison, Julia Lord Kalcheim, Carl Haber, and Frank and Betty Avruch offered valuable suggestions, encouragement, and support.

Laura Trucchi, Cristina Sarmati, Ettore Fioravanti, Cinzia De Angelis, Susanna Negroni, Massimo Brozzi, Jo and Pino Donghi, Nancy De Conciliis, Maria Elena Vasaio, Franca Zambonini, Sandra Craig, Mourad Chaoch, Mats Carlsson, Gloria and Stefano Zatti, Monsignore Aldo Settepane, Maria Maddalena Uva, and Professore Ferruccio Di Cori were generous with their time and insights, thoughtfully—as well as playfully—considering my often complex queries.

My agent, Patti Breitman, has been her usual steadfast self, always assured that I would eventually write a book about my Italian experiences. And Toni Sciarra, my wise and wonderful editor at William Morrow, has not only been an enthusiastic supporter of this project from the beginning but has lent her understanding of the Italian way of life to every page.

Finally, words cannot be found to thank my wife, Diane, and my sons, Julian and Elliott, for their unwavering love and devotion. Diane's determination to make this work the best it can be, along with her indefatigable ability to read draft after draft, each time suggesting just the right word, phrase, or paragraph, has added immeasurably to the texture of the book. And the kids' wholehearted embrace of Roman life has both made this adventure worthwhile and deepened Diane's and my appreciation of this miraculous culture.

Contents

Introduction   1

1.   Just Another Day in the Piazza: The Show
Must Go On   7

2.   To Stay or Not to Stay: Summer in the City   13

3.   *Centro Storico:* Meandering Through the Heart of
History   27

4.   The Latest Martyr at the Colosseum: Will He or
Won't He?   35

5.   *Buon Compleanno, Giuseppe:* An Operatic
Celebration   42

6.   *Sciopero!* Rome Strikes Again   49

7.   Monte Palatino: The "City" on the Hill   57

8.   Business, but Not as Usual: Money Isn't
Everything   63

9.   *La Bella Figura:* The Flesh and Flash of Roman
Women   72

10.   *Buon Appetito:* The Tasty *Trattoria*   81

Contents

11. *La Famiglia:* Ties That Bind   91

12. Santa Pazienza: The Art of Waiting,
    a Metropolitan Pastime   102

13. Functional Anarchy: Who's in Charge of This
    Meeting?   110

14. *Che Bello!* Children Should Be Seen—and
    Heard   119

15. What Makes Romans So Sexy?
    Close Encounters of Every Kind   130

16. The Smallest Big City in the World:
    The Intimacies of Daily Life   140

17. Hanging the Wash and Other Joys:
    Romans Don't Trust Technology   146

18. For Men Only: Dinner After Eight
    (and You Don't Want to Be Late)   156

19. Sunday in the City: An Early Morning Run   166

20. Outsiders: A Jew in Rome Is Not like a Jew in
    New York   175

21. Breakfast in a Bar: The Coffee Culture   187

22. *Calcio:* The Only Game in Town   195

23. Retro Romans Still Do It All: Smoking,
    Drinking, Sex, Fur Coats, and Suntans   205

24. Breaking Bread in Rome: Hidden Bakeries   216

25. *Mi Scusi:* Romans Forgive—and Forget   223

26. Exodus: Weekends and Getaways   231

27. Latin Lovers: Real Men Don't Wear Sneakers   242

Contents

28. Not Only for Sale: The Artistic Approach
    to Life   251

29. James Joyce Slept Here: Everyone Who Is
    Anyone Has Passed Through   259

30. Rome at the Crossroads: Natives and
    Immigrants Through the Eyes of an Expat   268

31. The Many Faces of Rome: Getting Ready for
    the Party of the Millennium   277

AS THE
ROMANS
DO

Introduction

Imagine being three thousand years old. Suppose by some mysterious process you had managed to avoid the limitations of mortality, and year after year you keep going, adding more and more experiences to your life story until you have no choice but to repeat them because you have exhausted all possibilities.

You are the very essence of what it means to be human. You have had more than your share of victories and defeats, triumphs and tragedies, moments of glory and those of abjection, times when you wish you had never been born and times when you want to go on forever. You have loved and lost, have abandoned and been left behind, been rich and poor, skinny and fat, lived high on the hog and been forced to scramble for a few morsels of stale bread. You have seen it all, done it all, regretted it all, and then gone back and done it all again.

You are *la città eterna*, Rome, the Eternal City.

To live in Rome is to have the capacity to endure everything life has to offer—moments of timeless beauty followed by torrents of ugliness, the *bella* and the *brutta* mixed together in a bowl of hot minestrone that has left nothing out, that encourages you to live life from a completely different perspective. There is no more mature place on earth, and that maturity has something to teach you. Other cities may be older, but Rome still lives its past. Walk anywhere in the city or the areas surrounding it, and within minutes you are confronted with the remains of something that could be up to twenty-five hundred years old, that functioned and was vital to the daily life of the *romani*.

Rome is so old that its days of glory, when the empire stretched all across the Mediterranean and far into Europe, Asia, and Africa, ended well before the development of the Italian language. But by that time, history had already cast Rome in a leading role. Even if the stage on which it had starred had long since been taken down, its Latin culture was carried to the four corners of the earth by the establishment and dogged vitality of the Roman Catholic Church, whose theology came to dominate the everyday landscape of the world like no other institution. It was almost as if the Romans, in their infinite cleverness, came to see that they no longer needed to bear the costs of a far-flung empire but would invest their energy in a religion that would have more lasting effects. Rome would remain the *capo*, the boss, while its minions in nearly every other country would carry out the mission. Its position in the world secure (as it still is), the presence of the Church freed the *romani* to focus on and perfect the fine art of living well, leaving others to handle the historical heavy lifting while it devoted itself to the pursuit of pleasure.

The result is a strange anomaly, a sprawling metropolis that feels like a small town, simply because it no longer has any illusions of greatness. "Been there, done that" could be the motto of SPQR, Senatus Populusque Romanus, the name of the city government. Romans feel no need to prove themselves, to demonstrate to the world that they still have the ability to command respect, enact their wills, determine the course of history. Nobody cares about that any longer. The city's place in history is indelible, and now its inhabitants want to enjoy Rome's advanced age in a manner that befits someone who is three thousand years old. It's as if, had you lived to reach this age and had you realized every one of the dreams of your youth, you had no more worlds to conquer; that your drive, your ambition, your desire to impress had long since been satisfied, and now you were unabashedly devoted to the enjoyment of life's everyday pleasures—eating well, looking good, devoting time to your family, and accepting the inevitable ups and downs that human existence has no choice but to offer.

This is Rome and the Romans who live in it, a city and a people of contrasts and effusion, a place that has lived so many different lives, in so many different epochs, that all it wants to do is exist in eternity according to the wisdom of what it has learned. The lessons are obvious. Life is to be lived passionately, excessively, publicly—in bars, restaurants, streets, and piazzas—applying charm and style mixed with a healthy respect for tradition. Romans have big appetites, for theatrical experience as well as exquisite food.

Ever since I came here for the first time two decades ago, Rome has been a source of endless fascination to me. It does this to people. I am by no means the first to fall under its seductive spell. It offers itself to the *appassionato*, one who is impassioned, as would a lover who invites his or her suitor to find out every way in which the beloved can be admired, reviled, explored, cursed, caressed, rejected, made love to, and abandoned. I have heard it said on numerous occasions that it is

3

difficult to leave Rome, that once it penetrates your consciousness, all other cities, all other places, every other mode of living
is just so lacking, leaving one with the feeling that, for better or
worse, to live in Rome and to be a *romano* is to live at the apex
of what is most profound about life; that what it offers in the
way of beauty, of sensuality, of creativity, no other city can
match. Even if New York is more avant-garde, Paris more elegant, San Francisco fresher and more naturally dramatic, Rome
still holds first place when it comes to utter devotion to pleasure,
and to the sheer ability to survive. Its stories are older, more
truthful, more instructive and complex. Its spirit is still intact,
and it provides a new wrinkle on the ancient quest for everlasting
youth. As the Eternal City, Rome's eternity lies in its wisdom.
To live here now is to partake of the infinite, but to be in the
present. You learn to separate yourself from questions of status,
glory, ambition, and striving and live as the Romans do—in the
moment, with style, flair, and panache. The city has been host
to myriad lives since the days many, many years ago when a
nomadic tribe settled on the Palatine Hill, facing the Tiber, and
became the city of Rome. Not one of these souls has managed
to cheat nature. All have returned to the place from which they
sprung. Ashes to ashes, dust to dust. In the meantime, since the
same fate awaits everyone, why not enjoy the here and now
while there is still the opportunity?

If you walk down the Via Veneto from the top end of the boulevard, which borders the Villa Borghese, you will encounter
some of the most expensive shops, restaurants, and hotels in the
city—in fact, in all the world. The Via Veneto was the throbbing
hub of the fabled *dolce vita* of the fifties and sixties, when movie

stars, playboys, jet-setters, and their entourages came to partake of a party they hoped would never end, as indicated by the plaque that pays tribute to Federico Fellini for his role in immortalizing the street in the film *La Dolce Vita*. The Via Veneto, although long past its glory days, still retains the patina of a golden age. Friends of ours wandered unknowingly into one of its many tony sidewalk cafés one glorious spring day, sat down and ordered two *cappuccini,* four orange juices, and four small pastries. They walked away sixty dollars lighter than when they had entered. The same breakfast would have cost them ten dollars standing up—as the locals do—at any nearby coffee bar, and been just as delicious.

As you make the sharp turn past the U.S. embassy and continue down to the bottom of the inclined street, where the Via Veneto empties into the Piazza Barberini, you see evidence of the seventeenth-century Baroque artist Gianlorenzo Bernini, whose decidedly Mediterranean visage adorns the fifty-thousand-lire note. His artistic hand is as evident as anyone's in and around the city, and his version of Triton stands in a fountain in the middle of the square, where cars now gingerly ride around it. The piazza is so central to the city that if you continue down the Via del Tritone, you reach the Trevi Fountain. Go right on the Via Sistina, and you arrive at Piazza di Spagna. The Via Quattro Fontane takes you uphill to the gorgeous Renaissance Italian presidential palace—the Quirinale.

But tucked there on the left side of the Via Veneto is a small church, Santa Maria della Concezione, attached to which is a crypt of Capuchin monks (who, unbeknownst to themselves, lent their name to the famous coffee drink, which resembles the brown hood worn by the members of the order). The burial ground consists of a few small chapels, the pilasters, arches, and vaults profusely decorated with the bones of four thousand exhumed monks that were brought to the church in 1631. The designs are ubiquitous, creative, and macabre, once again pointing up the contradictory nature of Rome, and the Romans. Nothing is *only* what it is; it is that, *and more.*

While outside on the street millions of lire are being spent each day in the shops, hotels, and restaurants, in a quite successful attempt to convince oneself of one's immortality, inside the crypt, in one of the chapels, among the vertebrae, skulls, tibias, and patellae, a sign dangles from one of the long-deceased monks that most succinctly sums up everything one needs to know about the city—or about life, for that matter. It says, "*Quello che voi siete noi eravamo; quello che noi siamo voi sarete.*" "That which you are, we were; that which we are, you will be."

Benvenuti a Roma, where everyone, even those who have long since passed away, has something to say.

1

Just Another Day in the Piazza: The Show Must Go On

Not everybody who comes to Rome, either to visit or to stay, as we have, likes it. In fact, if you polled visitors arriving from other countries, asking them where their favorite places are in Italy or where they would want to live if they were ever to embark on just such an enterprise, few would list Rome as their first choice. Most of them would focus variously on some spot in Tuscany, either the cities—Florence, Siena, Lucca, Pisa, Cortona—or the delightful countryside that surrounds these beautiful places and gives new meaning to the words "bucolic" and "tranquil." In fact, there are so many people of British extraction living in the Florence-Siena vicinity that it has been dubbed "Chiantishire," in honor of the English way of identifying place.

Rome is considered too "Italian" for the tastes of many of the English and North Americans who come to Italy to vacation, recreate, sightsee, or indulge. Rome is too "other," too much like venues the average English-speaking traveler would never think to experience—Cairo, Beirut, Jerusalem, or other places in the Middle East, or Sicily, Greece, or Turkey, lands that barely qualify for being called "Europe."

What gives Rome this character, what makes Rome, Rome, is a sense of drama, of the theatrical, the exaggerated; a quality that pervades everyday life and distinguishes the city from most places one would find in the United States, Canada, England, and the other countries in the English-speaking world, as well as northern Europe. People live in these places precisely for the reason that nothing much happens, that nothing much should happen, at least not in a way that creates public spectacle. Rome is not like that. Every ounce of its soul is devoted to the art of being seen, to the show, to a way of being that opts for dramatization at the expense of understatement, histrionics that push aside silence. The ethos of Rome partakes of another culture— the Levantine, the Latin—rather than the European. The first thing I noticed on the way to my hotel after landing at Cairo, another Mediterranean capital, other than the fact that I was thinking that I probably wouldn't make it there alive, is that every driver, for no apparent reason, is leaning on his horn, creating a maddening cacophony that has only one purpose— to create a disturbance, to liven up the moment, to add a stupefying sense of dislocation in order to cancel out the reality that nothing much is really happening.

Although drivers do not use their horns much in Rome (in fact, it is considered bad form, a *brutta figura;* if you do hear a toot-toot, chances are someone is trying to acknowledge his friend on the street), the same principle of *commotion* applies. The other day, in the Piazza Santa Maria Liberatrice, in Testaccio, not far from Piazza Testaccio, one of Rome's most characteristic open-air markets, popular among the locals and near to where we live, an incident erupted that illustrates perfectly the sense of making the ordinary encounters of everyday existence a matter of life and death.

The piazza was crowded with people of all ages. The elderly were occupying the many benches, while children made use of the swings, slides, and climbing frames of the play areas as their parents watched and chatted with one another. Several young boys, including Julian and Elliott, our nine- and six-year-old sons, were playing soccer with a soft, light ball not far from a bench where four elderly women were sitting. The ball strayed often in the direction of the *anziane,* and, in fact, on more than one occasion glanced off their bench, bringing less than loving looks and sporadic admonitions. Finally, exasperated at her in-ability to carry on conversation—as she has done in the same spot for probably the last forty years—without the nuisance of having to dodge a harmless but definitely annoying ball, one of the *anziane* grabbed it and would not let go, placing the *palla* in a plastic bag she was holding.

The six boys crowded around the bench, engulfing the four steadfast matrons. Loud words and a million hand gestures began to fly—to no avail, as it turned out, because the woman would not budge. This brought into the fray the mother—obviously peeved that the conversation in which she was excitedly engaged on her *telefonino,* her portable cell phone, had been interrupted—of one of the offending *ragazzi.*

She was dressed *alla romana,* that is, as if she were on her way to an audition for a movie, TV show, play, commercial, or what-ever anyone would have for her. She was wearing heavy makeup, accentuating her deep blue eyes—a rarity for Ro-mans—with dark liner that extended past the sockets, creating a kind of catlike effect. Her long, full head of curly jet-black hair was flying in the breeze, as were her bronzed hands and arms. She wore a glowing orange sweater that crisscrossed in the front and revealed, here and there, glimpses of her bright white bra, made more obvious by her outsized body gestures—which forced her to become distracted now and then from her primary mission by having to pull together the folds of her sweater so as to avoid revealing everything—and by the dark skin of her killer tan.

Below the sweater was a pair of tight blue jeans and high-heeled boots that exposed a trim, curvaceous figure, a shape that would be the envy of most middle-aged women in the world. She had put herself together like this solely to accompany her seven-year-old son to the local park to kick around a soccer ball. But who knows, maybe she had heard the fabled story of the discovery of Lana Turner wearing an angora sweater in Schwab's Drugstore on Hollywood Boulevard and harbors deep in her shapely form the notion that it is still not too late for her.

Her sudden, electrifying presence, while adding more than a touch of raw sensuality to the heated scene, does nothing to ameliorate the situation. In fact, her insistence that the elderly woman give back the ball, *"La palla è mia, la palla è mia, la palla, Signora, è MIA!,"* only inflames it. The *anziana* was apparently waiting for just this opportunity to unload on the *mamma* of one of the *ragazzi* whom she considers *cattivo*, naughty, misbehaving, and even the attempt on the part of the would-be Sophia Loren, flashing white-white every which way, to wrest the ball from the old woman is of no avail. The *anziane* have decided to teach the *ragazzi* a lesson, and not giving up the ball is their strategy.

By this time, half the park has become the audience. Men,

women, and children have gathered from the far-flung corners of the piazza and are watching with obvious amusement as the sexy mother goes toe-to-toe with the four ladies in their golden years trying to sit contentedly on the bench, their natural-colored stockings rolled down to their knees. *La bella signora* goes off to make another call on her *telefonino*—presumably for help—as the boys begin to mildly insult the old woman and then erupt into a loud chorus of *"Palla, palla, pal-la, PAL-LA"* before Sophia reappears. She wades through the crowd, leans over, and—suddenly becoming aware that her dream has come true, that all eyes are on her now, that she is the show, and that maybe, *MAGARI*, someone will step forward and offer her a contract to be one of the showgirls who adorn three-quarters of Italian television programs, knockouts wearing low-cut evening dresses or skimpy bikinis, providing visual stimulation for all the boring talk-TV and sports shows that are piped day after day into the living rooms and bedrooms of Italian households—begins smiling and purring into the ear of the *anziana*.

Alas, there is no one in sight with pen and contract in hand, no one present but the audience, still content to watch from the sidelines as she gallantly does battle for her boy. Suddenly, unexpectedly, as if ejected by the blast of a cannon, the ball arches toward the heavens, landing thirty feet from the clump and rolling toward the other end of the park. The boys continue to taunt the four ladies as they get up to move to another bench, and all of us in the cheap seats, who have been entertained free of charge, let out a collective round of applause and genially begin to discuss with each other the parts of the performance that were most breathtaking.

The *bella donna* is the clear winner. We all agree that were it

11

not for her, the spectacle would have been dull, dull, dull; that it was her spirited performance that made the whole thing worthwhile. A few minutes later, the infamous ball rolls toward a man, a member of the former audience. He picks it up and makes a brief imitation of the *anziana,* clutching it tightly against his side, before smilingly rolling it back to the *ragazzi,* who triumphantly continue their play.

Once more, the Roman instinct for the spectacle, the dramatic gesture, the act that sums up all the frustration—and all the hope—wins out. Although the overall atmosphere was tense, charged, full of emotion, self-righteousness, and a sense of both sides having been wronged, there was never any ambient fear that the encounter would get out of hand. Underneath it all everyone knew—participants and spectators alike—that it was all for show; that not only would no one emerge harmed, but no blows would be struck, no threats made, no lasting damage done. It would be what it was—a frank exchange of position, *alla romana.*

2

To Stay or Not to Stay: Summer in the City

V*oi siete pazzi?*" "Are you crazy?" We thought we had put together a pretty good plan, but our Roman friends were telling us otherwise. "*È impossibile.*" To them, the way we had decided to coordinate our summer schedule with the big move into our own apartment in the center of Rome after living in a furnished villa outside the city for two years was too precise, too finely drawn, in the end *troppo americano,* too American.

When you live in Rome, you have to figure out every year what to do with your summer. Summer in Italy is not just an opportunity to take a vacation that might last two weeks; it is a state of mind, a complete break with the rest of the year, so much so that September 1 has a name attached to it—*rientro*—as if everyone who has any notion of living here knows that on or about that date all return to the city after being away during the month of August, the month that represents the entire summer, which sometimes begins as early as mid-June or, more than likely, sometime in July.

We know, because during our first summer after moving to Italy, in 1996, after a brief trip to the island of Ischia, off Naples, we were treated to the impossibly long, hot days, as we sent the kids to day camp and had absolutely no contact with anyone we had met during the year. It was as if summer were merely an excuse not to have to call, see, run into, or get together with anyone who is on one's regular circuit from September to June, as the bleached white light of the day drove everyone *a casa* or off to their traditional summer spots at the beach or in the mountains. Since here we have no relatives, distant or otherwise, with family property, there was no *villetta* tucked away on a cool hillside in Umbria or Tuscany; no *appartamento* at one of the many beaches along the Tyrrhenian or Adriatic coasts. We were pretty much limited to staying put with the kids, vowing that the following year would be different.

Yet there is another side of the summer question that has a completely different logic, a pretty seductive one at that. Rome is so crazy, so hectic, so often impossible to manage during the year that there is a strange temptation to hang around in the summer. Since most of the residents are gone, the city is easy to navigate, even to drive through, and at night, when the sun goes down and the heat of midday is a memory that will only be resurrected at dawn the following day, the city comes alive with street parties, outdoor concerts, and organized events that go on long into the night. People don't start to eat dinner until at least nine or ten o'clock, and the festivities continue into the wee hours of the morning. Traffic jams on the streets in the summer are not uncommon at 1:00 A.M., especially on the weekends, where there are outdoor *discoteche* and it seems that every park has set up a theater or stage for music or some other kind of performance. Sitting out under the stars in perfect temperatures at 11:30 P.M., listening to our friend Ettore Fioravanti's jazz band while sipping a beer after having just eaten a pizza, with the ruins of the Palatino in the distance, has its appeal, so it's not a foregone conclusion that spending the entire summer in the city is a terrible burden.

Then, the following spring, we were suddenly faced with a decision we had put on hold when we first devised our move-to-Italy plans. Our next-door neighbors in California had sent us an e-mail asking if we were interested in selling our house, a property they had always admired and perhaps now were in a position to acquire. Their missive prompted a major household discussion, and thank goodness we all felt the same way. We decided that our Italian venture was just heating up and that, after two years, it was unlikely that we would want to go back to the United States any time in the foreseeable future. Being absentee landlords was not easy, and so we decided to go back to California—in the summer—to sell our house in Marin County. Since my third book, *Anything Is Possible,* was also about to hit the shelves, the moment was opportune to leave Italy and spend time in the States.

But deciding to sell the house also induced us to think seriously about where we wanted to live in Italy. The longer we stayed in quaint but provincial Grottaferrata, the more we realized we wanted to live in the center of Rome, in our own place that we could furnish and make into a home. Every week we explored a different neighborhood, checked out the feel of the place—the schools, the bars, the trees (or lack of them)—and eventually we found that the Aventino best suited our desires. We gave ourselves enough time to find a place, contacted a couple of real estate agents, and basically gave them our wish list. One day, unexpectedly, we received a phone call from the noted agent Judy Allen, with whom we hadn't spoken for perhaps six months and whose properties we had never once seen. "I have just the right place for you. It will be available this summer, you can walk to the local Italian school, and it's in a great building." As soon as I saw the characteristic *palazzo*—the big shuttered windows facing the tall pines and spruces all around it; the large, elegant wooden door—I knew it was our place even before seeing the inside of it.

And it was. Lovely views, hardwood floors, lofty ceilings, unrestricted spacious rooms that opened up to one another, a rare eat-in kitchen, and a beautiful room in which I could write. The place was perfect, and we told the owners right away that we would like it to be ours. After more than two months of negotiating and revising the contracts over and over, with the owners never signing them, we were beginning to wonder whether they were serious about letting us move in. But the *padrona* finally, reluctantly, at the eleventh hour, signed the papers, as if she were renting us her firstborn son. I'm sure they were afraid we would never move out. The departing family, whose mother would become our landlady, would be gone as soon as school ended in June, leaving more than enough time to paint and repair the place so that we could move in when we came back from the States in early August, with our own house sold (we hoped).

In the meantime, we had some decorating to do. We had no furniture, since we had already sold most of it in California and really didn't want to ship what remained. My wife, Diane, whose family had been in the business of importing art and antiques from all over the world, knows how to choose and design beautiful interiors, and she swung into action. We had been living for two years in an intimidating villa in the Roman out-skirts. Although we had immediately been struck by the im-mense, luscious garden outside, inside it was dark, with clawed-feet antiques, cold marble everywhere, extravagant Ve-netian glass fixtures, and life-size nineteenth-century portraits of the unsmiling original owners. We'd felt as if we were trespassing in someone else's home, living in a different century and culture. We'd had to practically beg our previous landlords to take down the huge, three-dimensional Jesus dripping with blood, mounted above the master bed. It was only after we told them that we were *ebrei*, Jews—I'm sure the first this elderly couple had ever knowingly met—that they reluctantly allowed us to remove any of the religious paintings. All others were to stay.

We were now ready to create a lighter, warmer, more modern ambience. After ten years of marriage, it would be a gift to again start from scratch, to bring in a few precious objects from our past, and create each room, choose each piece, really design our spacious home in Rome. We selected a bedroom ensemble for the kids, couches and end tables for the living room, everything for our bedroom, a dining-room set of table and chairs, book-shelves, *tutto*. All this was to be delivered the day after we arrived back in Italy—August 6—because the following day we were due to leave for Sicily, where we would be staying with friends for ten days, and if we could not receive the merchandise on the appointed day, we would have to wait till at least *rientro*, since no one would even consider delivering anything later in August. The merchants assured us that the items would be delivered on the sixth, and our landlords assured us that the work on the apartment would easily be finished before then, by the third week in July at the latest.

17

"Yeah, right," said the *romani*. "You think that four different Roman vendors are going to deliver your furniture like they said, all on the same day? Keep dreaming."

But dream we did. We packed up what we had in Italy, put the boxes in our friend Alanna's garage, said a bittersweet good-bye to our fig trees, vegetable and flower garden, and balcony in Grottaferrata, and before long we were back in the U.S.A., doing what most people do in the States—hustling. Interviews, radio shows, book signings, in between heavy negotiations with our next-door neighbors, who convinced us of their seriousness and persuaded us not to put the house on the market. We agreed on a price, got the paperwork moving, and worked like pack-horses to wind down fifteen years of California living in my case, and thirty years in Diane's. What do we do with the ash rocker in which Diane had nursed both Julian and Elliott? "Sell it," I said. "I can't do that," replied my wife. She eventually acqui-esces. Score one for me. Or the delicately hand-painted red an-tique chest that didn't look to me like it would survive a transatlantic trip. "Sell it," I said. "Not a chance," said she. Score one for Diane. Or the record albums I had been collecting since 1965, and which had survived a serious paring down after my first marriage ended in divorce when I was in my early twenties. "Get rid of them," said Diane. "No way," was my swift reply. They are mostly gone, gobbled up by eager garage sale experts who bought them in lots—five, ten, twenty at a time—and complimented me endlessly on my eclectic taste in music. I still have six albums, waiting to be taped before they can be given away. Mission accomplished. Our life in California now consists of a single box of books.

A week before we were to leave the Bay Area, as the house

sale moved inexorably forward, our nerves were frayed and our fragile psyches were at the breaking point as we entered the final countdown on two intense years of ending our California life and starting our Roman one. The transition had proved much, much more difficult than we had ever imagined—lost luggage, car accidents, dealing with insurance companies and auto repair shops, to say nothing of the woman we hired to run our business in California, who turned out to be a thief and con artist. But all this did not deter us. We were hooked on the beauty, the thrill, the incomparable joy of starting over in a new land with a new language, as if we were just-hatched chicks who had no idea who we were or what the hell was going on. But our spirits were revived, and we were willing to endure whatever it took to make our dreams come alive. The emotion of selling the house where, in the backyard, we had planted the tree to remember Ethan, our first child who had died stillborn, the house we had moved into with our two-month-old Julian, where Elliott had come along three years later, where we had built fires to ward off the wet and cold of the damp northern California winters, where we had established ourselves as writers, relationship counselors and matchmakers, and where everything had blown up in our faces as soon as we left the shores of the New World and set sail for the Old, needed to be overcome, as we sorted through documents and personal papers, all the while thinking of the beautiful apartment in the historic Aventino, one of the original seven hills of the city, that awaited us.

With a week to go, we called Judy in Rome—just to make sure everything was going according to plan. "We should have known," we kept saying after the call, "we should have known." The apartment was not ready—and would not be ready. *Man-*

naggia, damn. All the assurances of our landlords, who were long gone and now living near Siena, had amounted to nothing. Our Roman friends had been right, but for the wrong reasons. Our plan had been too precise, too calibrated, too American.

No one would even estimate when the apartment would be ready. All they would say was that the workmen were working on it.

They should have said that the work*man was* working on it, because, this being August, there was no one around to help him. A cute, rather raggedy-looking old *romano* with thick glasses was all that separated us from a summer of grief, as he was *da solo,* left alone to paint a large apartment with fourteen-foot ceilings. *Madonna.* When I protested, when I started to complain, he raised his hand *alla romana* and basically told me it was of no use, that the crew that had been assigned to our place had at the last minute been plucked away to paint the *palazzo* of some American muckety-muck who was on his way to Rome and who obviously took priority. He led me to believe that the best thing I could do was not interrupt him any further, since he was all that stood between me and chaos.

The place was a wreck—dusty, dirty, dismounted doors and shutters everywhere. There wasn't a single clean spot where we could set down the eight duffel bags of stuff we had brought back from California, to say nothing of the fact that a household of valuable, brand-new furniture was about to arrive the next day. We stuffed the luggage in the closets and made room for the furniture, covering it with plastic when it arrived. It was all delivered *on time,* exactly as promised, probably a first for Rome, and, perversely, at the very moment when we would have settled for a delay. But the vendors reminded us that a delay meant a *delay*—sometime in September at the earliest, but undoubtedly later than that, since September was already booked with deliveries. They were all eager to make this last delivery and close down for the month. Better to take it now. We needed beds to sleep on, tables to eat on, chairs to sit on.

We threw together some things for Sicily after bringing over our boxes from Grottaferrata in the still-intense heat of 2:00 A.M., as that was when we could make use of a friend's van, (she was about to leave for August as well). Now the apartment was filled with our things—everything we owned—huddled on tables under huge plastic sheets, as if we had entered a morgue and our precious ones had been left for dead, looking like they were having second thoughts about having chosen us as their owners. Maybe, just maybe, we would be lucky and be able to relax with our friends in Sicily, before heading back to our painted, cleaned, beautiful apartment in the Aventino to assemble our new lives.

Not a chance. The island, a dry desertlike place that more resembles the Middle East than it does Tuscany, was experiencing a once-in-every-ten-years heat wave. It was unbearable. People had warned us that Sicily in August was not a great idea, but nothing had prepared us for this. Staying with friends near Erice, a beautiful hill town in the northwest corner of the island, we endured no air, no functioning indoor toilet, no relief from the crickets that played Beethoven's Fifth Symphony at full volume at three o'clock in the morning, and no hope. Even the sea was no relief from the white heat and humidity of the ancient land. The day after we arrived, the driver's side window of our car, an '83 Mercedes, fell inside the door, necessitating a part from the manufacturer that the cheerful fellow at the *carrozzeria*, the auto body shop, told me would arrive sometime in September, and two days later both Diane and Julian came down with terrible influenza. We were out of our minds, incapable of enjoyment, and close to delirium. We were approaching Ferragosto, August 15, the absolute ground zero of the national summer shutdown, but we were also determined to find an air-conditioned room. Anywhere on the island would do, since we couldn't get back to the mainland until the seventeenth.

Diane, being her usual resourceful self, found us a hotel room in the center of Sicily, near Piazza Armerina, a place that has the most intact, most beautiful Roman mosaic floors in existence. You walk on ramps through room after glorious room, viewing floors preserved for centuries under twenty feet of mud, excavated recently and in almost perfect condition. Then, just our luck, the heat wave was broken by a hundred-year storm; wave after wave of torrential rain soaked me as we were stuck in the car, and the window, which had been propped up, fell in again. At least it wasn't cold, and at least we had our remote-controlled air-conditioned room to go back to, where we could keep cool and eventually swim in the pool.

When we returned to the hotel, however, we could tell right away that something had changed. The odor was overwhelming. We went to the desk. "The rain backed up the septic system," the clerk told us. "It happens all the time." He assured us that there was nothing he could do about it, that the smell would go away "in about two weeks," and that if we didn't like it, we were welcome to find another hotel. Call after call produced nothing. It was stink or heat. We closed the bathroom door, which helped, and spent a lot of time at the pool.

Back to the mythical, ancient Erice to spend the last day with our friends before taking the ferry from Palermo to Naples, to be followed by the car ride back to Rome. The weather was bearable, the sky a beautiful blue, and Gloria and Stefano were congratulating us on our move, saying that all we had to do now, after the workmen were through painting and cleaning up, was have our things brought in, set them up, and not look back. "But our things are already there," I said.

For the second time in months we heard the same refrain. "*Siete pazzi?* Tell me again, you didn't leave all your new furniture in your apartment—unattended—with WORKMEN? *Mamma mia.* You'll be lucky if anything is there when you get back." Rome is not a safe place for possessions. There are thieves, pickpockets, marauding gypsies and car heists, aside from the clever ways in which people infiltrate, and betray, another's trust. Burglaries are common, especially in August, when people are away and there are plenty of open windows around. Ground-floor apartments rent for much less than their upper-floor counterparts, and a common method of cleaning out someone's place at ground level is for thieves to spray a sedative into an open window, wait thirty minutes for the occupants to fall asleep, and then spend the next hour doing their thing. Our new apartment has an armored door with nine dead bolts that would keep any stranger out of reach, unless, of course, he had a *key*. Workmen are notorious for disappearing without further notice. Gloria and Stefano gave us no better than a fifty-fifty chance.

We raced home in our big, lovable, but less than perfect old Mercedes. With no air conditioning and a window now permanently shut, the heat was once again stifling, and our hearts were pounding all the way as we sped toward our fate. Have our piles of diamonds-in-the-rough been excavated, stolen at the darkest hour—or will our possessions be safe, ready to be polished, shined, and exposed to the light?

We arrived to both pleasure and pain. What a relief! Everything was there, down to every last hand-carved chair lying upside down and sheathed in plastic, waiting to be resuscitated.

But there as well was Mario, the painter, still days away from being finished. He had taken his break at Ferragosto, and had only just returned. Staying at our place was impossible. We added to the plastic mounds several ceramic lamps, vases, and plates we had bought in a town called Caltagirone, and headed for the Hotel Domus Aventina on Via di Santa Prisca. In a few days, with Mario nearing completion, we pushed aside some things and spent a few nights among paint cans and dust and dirt. Finally, when Mario bid us *Arrivederci,* the cleaning crew came in. Again we were forced to the Domus Aventina, while fluids were applied and the floors cleaned and waxed.

On Saturday, August 23, 1997, having left our villa in Grottaferrata at the beginning of what seemed like an endless summer, having lived out of suitcases and slept in more than a dozen different beds, we returned from the Aventina to find our apartment transformed from a dirty, toxic, messy work in progress to a shiny, sparkling, pristine palace. Rays of afternoon light slanted down on our golden couches and comfy new armchairs, complete with a pile of handmade quilted pillows. Diane had chosen the blue silk and textured sea green, amber, and rich sienna fabrics, purchased at the Largo Argentina in Rome, after having been inspired by the exquisite mosaic tiles at the Church of Santa Sabina in the Aventino. Graciously, Alanna, a textile artist, had created patchwork pillows of various sizes and shapes and patterns that went perfectly in the new space.

The hand-painted lamps from Sicily were placed on our inlaid wooden side tables that we had picked up at a little antique shop behind Campo de' Fiori. As we smoothed out the Caucasus Kuban rug under the wrought-iron and glass coffee table that holds our vivid yellow Peking glass vases, I was reminded of how much each piece has a history, as someone lovingly transforms the flights of his imagination into something real and beautiful.

I recalled how, on our shopping spree, in search of an antique rug, we wanted something unusual, so we were taken by our friend Carl, an expert on antique rugs, to a quaint, overcrowded dealer on Via del Pellegrino, where the smell of incense instantly transported us to ancient Persia, where rug after rug was shaken and tossed, for our senses to absorb. Koukie, with his unforgettable smile, was a good businessman. We liked so many of the rugs. How do we choose just one? *"Non c'è problema."* He will pile the eight rugs on the back of his *motorino* and bring them to our *palazzo* to leave them for us to consider— *"Una settimana, due, come volete."* "One week, two, whatever you want." What is important is that we decide *"con calma."*

How perfectly the rug warms up our home. All the geometric designs—soft yellows, weathered blues and greens, reds and corals—each thread crafted with care, with the knowledge that not time—but rather artistry and workmanship—was of the essence.

The *tappeto* turned out to be the last piece of the moving-in puzzle. The hard part was over, and the wait had been worthwhile. We threw open the immense shuttered windows of the apartment and felt the late summer breeze. In the distance we could see the Church of San Saba, perched on the hill, its origins

25

tied to the monks who fled the Holy Land in the face of Islam in the seventh century. As Diane was preparing the table in the dining room for our first *cena*, I ran down to the corner to pick up a few delicacies—*spinaci, patate, melanzane, carciofi,* some *mozzarella* and *pomodori, pane,* and a bottle of *vino.* When I returned, the boys were eager to light candles for the momentous occasion, our first meal in our new home. The ordinarily delicious food was especially tasty, and it was comforting to be dining once again with familiar china and silver. Everything looked *bellissimo.* For us, life as *romani* had just begun.

3

Centro Storico:
Meandering Through the Heart of History

Romans build their lives around tradition. In fact, it is one of the things you immediately notice when you live here. Sunday *pranzo* is always at Zia Elena's house; every summer is spent at the same beach, at the same resort, under the same umbrella at the same spot with the same people; and you picnic outdoors every year on Pasquetta, the day after Easter, with the same friends. In fact, one of the reasons why I decided to come and live here, and why I like it so much, is that it holds on to a kind of year-in, year-out sameness that I associate with my youth, growing up in inner city Philadelphia, where the rhythms of life were predictable and most of one's daily encounters were in the neighborhood. When we moved to the suburbs, in 1962, the bonds of tradition on which our family life was based were pretty much broken, and I, along with most Americans who had made the leap out of the "old neighborhood," lost that feeling.

Rome is still the "old neighborhood." It has that immediate, postwar community, traditional, rhythmic quality that I fondly remember, and one of the customs that has developed in our family is the Tuesday jaunt into the heart of the city for my son Julian's weekly violin lesson.

The geography of Rome is fairly easy to understand, once you give up the American notion of the grid. Instead, think of a series of concentric rings that emanate from the very center of the city and continue indefinitely until you are completely out of Rome and into the countryside. If you stand, say, at Piazza Navona in the center, you are probably twenty to thirty minutes by foot from most of the places you'd want to see—the Colosseum, the Pantheon, Piazza di Spagna, St. Peter's, the Trevi Fountain, Castel St. Angelo, Villa Borghese, Trastevere—because they are all within the confines of the first ring. And, of course, even if the monuments did not exist, the many streets leading to and from these places are themselves worth the trip to the city, tightly packed, narrow, winding alleys down which one can meander endlessly, aimlessly, as if one had been transported to another time; tiny passages that enclose residences, shops, and services of every kind, in which real people are living real lives as housewives, teachers, bakers, restaurateurs, taxi drivers, and clothing designers.

We live in the next ring out, an additional fifteen minutes by foot to traverse, but still containing some of the richest historical sites and charming neighborhoods in the city—the Aventino, San Saba, Testaccio, San Giovanni, Prati, San Lorenzo, Monteverdi Vecchio and the Gianicolo—within easy striking distance, by foot or public transportation, of the places one would most like to visit, even repeatedly.

Julian's teacher lives in the center ring, and so every Tuesday after school our task is to arrive at the home of the *maestro* at 6:15 for the one-hour lesson. My son looks forward to the weekly tradition as much as I do, but for different reasons. For him, it is a chance to travel the streets of the Eternal City by bus. For me, it is an opportunity to spend time wandering through the *centro storico* alone, *senza impegni,* without any commitments, as if I had just arrived and was seeing the city for the first time.

At age nine, Julian is Mr. Public Transportation. Although we still have our Mercedes 230E, a rather large vehicle for the tight spaces of the city, it is usually parked, undriven, at our *palazzo,* for that very reason. Getting around the city, like doing anything else in Rome, is an unpredictable experience. I'm always amazed at the innocent travelers trying to maneuver their rental cars through the one-way, closed-off passages of the *centro storico,* their knuckles squeezed so tightly around the steering wheel that the blood drains from their hands. For the natives, at least, most of the time things go well, but one never knows when traffic will be so bad that you wish with all your heart you could just step out of the car, leave it where it is, and continue on your way by foot.

We always take the bus. It suits me because I don't like to drive in the city, and it works for Julian because he gets to check out different routes, as the public transportation plan of Rome, especially because of the Jubilee—a Roman Catholic Holy Year that brings millions of pilgrims to the city—is constantly changing. There are usually new ways to go, new routes to contemplate, new streets to explore. At the moment, there are at least six or eight different lines we could take, a trip that would require forty-five minutes by foot, ten by car if there were no traffic, and up to an hour if there were. But on this particular Tuesday, a day of heavy, humid thunderstorms that have continued unabated for days, we decide to take the 280 on Via

Marmorata, the street of marble, which will then go up the Lungotevere, along the river, and drop us off five minutes from the house of the *maestro,* who lives on Via dei Banchi Vecchi, the street of the old banks, in the *centro storico.* I suggest to Julian that we leave enough time so that if there are a lot of cars along the river, we will still arrive when we're supposed to. He agrees, reluctantly. For him, the most direct route is never the most interesting. We hop on, and for some reason, the Lungotevere is nearly empty, so the trip takes as long as it would have had we taken la macchina, the car. We have lots of time before the lesson begins.

Julian wants to go to his favorite pizza place, a hole in the wall just around the corner, for a snack. Eduardo knows us by now and also remembers that Julian likes his pizza *piccante.* This type of pizza is called *a taglio,* which means it is cut in pieces from huge sheets and you fold it and eat it like a sandwich. Our family calls it "walkaround" pizza, as opposed to "sit down" pizza, which you order in restaurants and which arrives paper thin, round, hot, large as a plate, and ready to eat. Eduardo heats up a substantial slice with *peperoni, rughetta, e peperoncini,* red peppers, bitter greens, and hot peppers, and we walk down the street to the Piazza de Ricci, where we notice that an old, large *palazzo* facing Via Giulia, one that had fallen into disrepair, is about to be made into condominiums, something we always thought would be a good idea.

The *maestro* lives in a fifteenth-century *palazzo* that is well used; so much so, in fact, that the stone stairs leading up to his second-floor flat (considered the third floor in America) are curved and sloped downward in the middle, like a tilted gardening trowel, where people have walked on them for more than four hundred years. The effect at first is disconcerting, but after a while you get used to the vertigo, and it becomes a charming footnote to the fact that something so old is still in use, day after day, year in and year out. I leave Julian in his teacher's capable hands, hearing the familiar sounds of his repertoire as I descend the ancient stairwell, pausing to exchange *Buona sera* with another of the residents of the building.

As I pass through the front door of the *palazzo* and out into the street, I realize that I have the entire *centro storico* to myself. Via dei Banchi Vecchi has Rome written all over it. During the Christmas season oil lamps are placed in small ringed holders that remain affixed to the *palazzi* the year round, providing a kind of preindustrial touch that reminds you—if, indeed, you ever needed reminding—that you're really not in Kansas anymore. The street is lined with all sorts of shops—a pharmacy, antiques dealers, leather goods, jewelry, grocery stores, bookstores, art galleries, bars, an *enoteca*—but tonight, my feet are carrying me across the Corso Vittorio Emanuele, a relatively recent main thoroughfare that takes traffic to and from the Tiber and on to other parts of the *centro storico,* to the Via dei Banchi Nuovi, the street of the new banks, where I make a right and find myself heading for Piazza Navona, one of the larger squares in Rome and a destination spot for all who come here. I remember well my own first trip to the city, traversing the wet streets and sidewalks of the ship-shaped piazza, thinking that I never wanted to leave Rome. Now, almost twenty years later, I want to partake of the recollection. The rain has stopped for the moment, and within minutes I am exactly where I want to be.

The piazza is nearly deserted but for pockets of mostly German tourists who occupy the tables outside the many restaurants and bars, sitting under *ombrelloni,* huge, white canvas umbrellas. They are oblivious to the wet weather, choosing instead to focus on the undeniably warm temperatures by enjoying a meal *fuori,* in the open air. Most Romans, more sensitive to the elements than we northerners, and more selective since for them the opportunities are greater, would not pick this particular moment, despite the balmy evening air, to eat outside. In fact, if they have to brave the elements at all, they wear multilayered outfits that one would more expect to find in the Arctic. Wind and water, even of the warm kind, are greatly feared.

As I head for La Galleria a Piazza Navona della Ambasciata di Francia, essentially the French embassy's art gallery, one that generally has interesting photography exhibits, I wonder how many of these people are seeing Rome for the first time. What must it feel like to be in the Piazza Navona, among the Bernini sculptures, the Borromini facade of the Church of Santa Agnese in Agone, in the elongated oval expanse of an open space in Italy that is famous all over the world? What is it like to drink a *cappuccino* in Italy for the first time, to eat a pizza, savor a plate of perfectly prepared *pasta al pomodoro,* and share a liter of *vino bianco* with a friend, spouse, or amorous partner that was made from grapes taken from the hills of the surrounding countryside, probably the Castelli Romani, only twelve miles southeast of the city?

For a moment I envy these people, coming from Hamburg and Frankfurt and Berlin, from cold places that do not by and large share the zest for celebratory life for which the *romani* are known, because they are seeing the city, experiencing it, feeling it, for the first time, something I can no longer do. But my invidious feelings are brief, because I realize that after they depart I will still be here, that I can see what they see, albeit not for the first time but rather any time, and also because I have not grown tired of what I see, have not grown accustomed to it, have not stopped noticing it. It doesn't matter that I have spent the last four years of my life amid Bernini, Borromini, and Bramante, in the presence of Michelangelo, Raphael, and Caravaggio. I still see them, still appreciate them, still think, even more so, that the city they created and adorned is the most incredible spot on earth, and I congratulate myself that Diane and I have braved everything to come here, to remain here, to put roots here, because it hasn't been easy, and in many ways still isn't.

By now, after quickly eyeing the exhibit, which had wonderful old black-and-white shots of Paris and other spots in France from the twenties onward, it is raining, and with each passing moment the rain gets heavier, finally becoming a sheer white sheet illuminated by the wrought-iron street lamps that looks remarkably like a curtain dropping on the final act of an outdoor performance. But I do not have the luxury of the travelers, huddled momentarily in the archways of the church and the shops and restaurants, waiting patiently for the rain to cease so that they may continue their exploration of a place they've never seen before. I must go and retrieve my son, rain or no rain, wet or dry. The rain in Rome, like almost everything else, is a paradox. There is considerably more rainfall per annum here than in London—28 percent more—but still there are 270 days each year of sunshine. There can be only one explanation. When it rains, it comes down in torrents. And then, like a repeated miracle, the sun comes out and the air is warm and soft.

Within minutes I am soaked, drenched, slogging through huge puddles and rivulets of water that go every which way over the cobbled streets of the Via del Governo Vecchio, as I make my way back toward the home of the *maestro*. Each step soaks me further, as my boots, umbrella, and trench coat are no match for nature's power. Julian is finishing up as I—dripping, moldy, clammy from the humidity—arrive. As we step back onto the street a few minutes later, the rain has stopped again. We discuss our route home. Julian has for some time been lobbying to take the 170 from Piazza Venezia. It is a new green bus, twice as long as the normal ones, and it would drop us off fifteen minutes by foot from our house. I urge opting for the 175, our usual bus and the one closest to home, but Julian is reminding me that last week I had "promised."

In any case, we must first grab the 64, reputed to be one of the worst routes in the city. It goes from the train station, the Termini, to St. Peter's, and is a new bus, but it is the favorite haunt of the city's many pickpockets, and is often crowded, which is the case tonight. We ride for a few minutes before switching to the sleek, nearly empty, bend-in-half 170, which lets us off in Testaccio, along with the necessity of walking home. I am complaining to Julian as the rain begins again—although not nearly as heavily as before—and he says, in his inimitable way, "Dad, would you rather be walking for a few minutes or be back on the hot, crowded, sweaty, stinky, slow 64, just to be able to take the 175?"

I put aside the fact that I am wet, clammy, tired, grumpy, and hungry and acknowledge to my son, who is busily searching out puddles and deciding the ones he wants to step into, that he is right, that Rome is best when you can be out on the streets, in this case among the *platano* trees of the Aventino, trees so old you can't put your arms around them, about to conclude another everyday episode in the ancient center of the universe.

4

The Latest Martyr at the Colosseum: Will He or Won't He?

Of all the monuments of Rome, the Colosseum is perhaps the most well known, the enduring symbol of the city. It is also in many ways the strangest, for the very reason that it is the prototype of the kind of sports stadium that stands everywhere in America, hosting the same kind of combat, albeit stripped of the gorier excesses that took place in ancient times when the arena was built. Proudly displaying its skeleton and its bowels, the oval arena's huge, hulking presence is a reminder that Rome lives in both the ancient and modern worlds, and in many in between. An English churchman in the Middle Ages, the Venerable Bede, said—although proof of his assertion has always been lacking—that as long as the Colosseum stands, Rome will stand, and as long as Rome stands, civilization will stand. Whether that's true or not will be left up to the judgment of historians.

The Colosseum sits just at the edge of the first concentric circle and is the most visited monument in Italy. Each year millions engulf the place as if they were a swarm of ants about to devour the drippings of a cone of *nocciola* and *stracciatella* ice cream, hazelnut and chocolate chip. Until the nineteenth century, years of decay had allowed a huge hole to remain in the side of the building that faces south, and engravings of that time show people wandering freely in and out of the many arches and especially through the opening. During the reign of Pope Gregory XVI (1831–46), the vacant bricks and marble were filled in, so that now the inner skeletal perimeter of the building is continuous all the way around. The outer perimeter, which generally wraps around the north side of the building, is two stories taller and considerably more spectacular, and gives the structure its fullest shape and perspective.

It is hard to look inside the Colosseum without imagining what went on there, the blood and guts and lacerated flesh that were spilled there, the animals that were slaughtered, the gladiators who fell for the glory of the empire and their allegiance to the emperor, the Christians who were martyred there, and the average Roman who enjoyed the spectacle as a way of reminding himself that his meager life might not be so bad after all, especially in contrast to the mayhem he could witness within the confines of its circular walls. If you look closely above the arches of the outer north wall, through the soot and grime that has accumulated—mostly in this century as exhaust from the engine emissions of cars, trucks, and buses and industrial pollutants—you can see the Roman numerals carved in the stone that indicate which gate one is entering. You can't help but imagine Lucius Civius and his friend Marcus Brontius managing to obtain tickets for the annual summer solstice slaughter of three thousand lions, tigers, elephants, and mountain goats at the same time as hundreds of gladiators are cut to pieces and an assortment of unrepentant Christians are dropped in hot oil, ripped limb from limb, burned alive, stoned, and otherwise dispatched in any way the authorities could conjure up to warn others of their fate if they chose to consider adhering to the outlawed, subversive sect. *Cristianus non licet est.* It is not legal to be a Christian. Alas, it was to no avail, but you couldn't expect that the Romans would give up their power voluntarily. Who ever does?

These days the show at the Colosseum mostly takes place, thank God, outside the structure, where there are all kinds of souvenir stands, tour buses, Africans displaying their wares on white sheets that can be gathered up in an instant so as to avoid detention by the police, who make a halfhearted raid on the illegal sales once a week or so, locals dressed up as Roman legionnaires who offer to have their picture taken with anyone who is willing to part with three or four dollars, and ordinary tourists milling about in every direction as they try to comprehend the awesome majesty of a still-imposing building that has stood on the very same spot for nearly two thousand years. On a given day, but mostly on the weekends, the casual observer is also treated to the sight of an assortment of brides, in full white or off-white regalia, along with their grooms and the various components of their retinues—in-laws, friends, chauffeurs, video and still photographers—taking hundreds of pictures of the most memorable day of their lives, with the Colosseum as the backdrop. Limousines, Rolls-Royces, and open horse-drawn carriages are everywhere, and tourists, if they have the nerve, are busily snapping away as the brides are pulling up the taffeta, organza, chiffon, or tulle to show off a shapely, sheer white leg, or bending forward—especially if nature has endowed them in this direction—to display a bit of cleavage for all to see, pretending to the end that later they will perform for the first time in their lives *the act,* something they have been pointing to for months, maybe years, although everyone knows by now that it is unlikely that Francesca or Veronica or Lucia or Bianca will stain the sheets. Virginity until marriage is as rare in Italy as it is elsewhere, although the fact that Roman men and women do not wait does nothing for the national birthrate, which is the lowest in the world, perhaps the lowest in all of history.

What's really strange is that from time to time the bridal couple will be Japanese. Just think of the logistics of flying everyone in the family halfway around the world, just to be photographed in front of the Colosseum, a place whose past is somewhat less than romantic. It's easy to see how for the natives the Colosseum as a backdrop fits in with the history and bloodthirsty spectacle that is woven into the very fabric of their own culture, but when I see a Japanese bride, the juxtaposition is jarring. Yet to top off the scene, right in the middle of the shoot, a *telefonino* goes off, and it turns out to be that of the bride. *Ma com'è?* Who in the world could she be talking to now? Her boyfriend? Her agent? A rich Middle Eastern client? The sight of this young Japanese woman walking languidly away from the scene while talking into the phone is so disconcerting that I gently pull Diane away from our voyeuristic pleasure and insist that we move on. There are some times when even I, a jaded Roman by this point, am still jolted into senselessness by something not quite being what it appears to be, and this is surely one of them.

But what has just transpired is nothing compared to what comes next. The edge of the aforementioned north wall of the Colosseum has been draped with scaffolding for God knows how long, probably since the Middle Ages. This is, of course, nothing new for Rome, where the restoration of the magnificent Villa Borghese, which finally opened in June 1997 and houses the majority of the Bernini creations in the world, took *fourteen* years. Time is long here. Scaffolding is also everywhere in Rome these days, as the city continues its preparations for the grand Jubilee of the year 2000, which is intended to celebrate the third millennium of Christianity but what might turn out to be the mother of all disasters if predictions are true and the world's computers break down, creating a particular kind of Roman chaos that would either prevent the pilgrims from arriving or from leaving once they got here. I've been saying lately that the best business to be in right now is the scaffolding business, but everyone waves their hand at the obvious joke and says that it is controlled, like all lucrative businesses, by a consortium. In Italy you never know whether the problem of consortiums' having a stranglehold on the economy is not as bad as people say and is merely a convenient hook on which to hang every economic shortcoming, or the opposite, in which case it would be a good idea to forget about the scaffolding business. Anyway, true to both its conformist nature and to the idea that everything one sees has to be adorned, the scaffolding sites all have wooden barriers at street level, all painted the same color red, presumably from the same source. Another "bureaucratic" operation? It's anyone's guess.

As I am about to pass the Colosseum, only fifteen minutes by foot from my house, I say to myself—which I do every time— "maybe today is the day the scaffolding will be gone." There is a sign on the amphitheater with a date on it, indicating when the work of restoration on the ancient facade is to be completed, but no one who knows anything about Rome pays the slightest attention to what it says. You'll know that the scaffolding is down when you don't see it anymore.

Today turns out to be a normal scaffolding day, but then I notice that something has, in fact, changed. Everyone is looking up into the mottled blue sky, and soon it is clear that an event is taking place. The police have cordoned off the area, and up, up, way up at the top of the interlocking metal, it is easy to make out the figure of a man, standing alone and leaning out over the uppermost railing. How he got there no one seems to know, but soon, a fire truck has deposited a rescue worker two-thirds of the way up, and the Italian Dudley Doright is slowly, nonchalantly making his way up the stairs to see if he can ameliorate the situation.

My stomach is dropping by the second. We come from San Francisco, where the Golden Gate Bridge has been the site of roughly a thousand suicide attempts, most of them successful. I cannot bear the thought that from this moment on, my image of the Colosseum will be forever marred by the sight of another martyr plunging dramatically to his death, hundreds of feet below. I am American. I expect the worst.

I cannot watch, but at the same time I also cannot turn away. As the rescuer is just two flights from his target, the man at the top leans over but then pulls back as he is being greeted by his fellow Roman. They are talking. They are gesticulating. We look through the telephoto lens of the camera to get a bird's-eye view. My heart is still pounding, my stomach is still in knots. Then the two men begin to walk down together, and it is clear that the danger has passed. We turn away and are met by the eyes of a grizzled, middle-aged Roman with a three-day growth, who has also been one of the spectators. We lock eyes for a moment, as he shrugs his shoulders and says, "Just another guy out of work, trying to make a point. They never jump."

"We come from San Francisco," we say, as he nods in recognition, "where they almost always jump." He manages a smile. "It's different here," he says. "No one has ever jumped from there." "Never?" we say. "Not once." He sounds so sure of himself. Maybe he's much older than he looks.

5

Buon Compleanno, Giuseppe:
An Operatic Celebration

I have long been a fan of Italian opera, so I felt myself on familiar ground as the lights dimmed, the first few notes came forth from the piano, and the sounds emanating from the singers made it apparent why they consider their voices to be musical instruments. The duet was familiar: Alfredo and Violetta from Verdi's *La Traviata*. It takes place just after the famous toasting song of the first act, as Alfredo is making his feelings known to Violetta, and she, as a courtesan, is both intrigued and mocking as she tells Alfredo basically to look elsewhere. The opera sounded clear and refreshing, just as I had heard it twenty-five years before in the Kennedy Center in Washington, the first time I had ever been in the audience when grand opera was being performed on stage. Only this time I was not at the Kennedy Center nor at the Metropolitan Opera in New York City. Neither was I in La Scala in Milan or at the Rome Opera Theater. Nor was I sitting on a blanket in San Francisco's Golden Gate Park, listening to selections from various opera crowd pleasers to kick off another fall season.

I was in the living room of a friend's house, not far from ours, and the occasion was a birthday celebration for the incomparable composer of *La Traviata,* Giuseppe Verdi, who would have turned 185 on this particular October 10. Our friend is more than just a fan. Verdi is his life, and this was the fourteenth such event he had hosted.

As is usually the case with parties, especially ones given by foreigners, I didn't know what to expect. By now I have come to see that party giving could have been invented by the Romans. Theirs are often lavish affairs, with much to eat, drink, and look at, beautiful women dressed to the nines, with earrings of shimmering gold, strands of pearls moving every which way, and perfectly fitting dresses and suits to go along with tinted hair the color of straw, platinum, copper, or henna, or shiny black and flowing past the shoulders. They are displaying the characteristics that *le donne romane* are known for—flesh and flash.

Then there are the men. They all seem to look like they have just stepped off the pages of a glossy magazine—handsome, coiffed, and well groomed. They have easy smiles and a kind of insouciance that one always associates with Marcello Mastroianni, the kind of men you have to watch out for, who seem always to be looking for a new *amante,* a lover, and are usually interested in women who are themselves married because they are more of a challenge, and there is less to fear, since a young *ragazza* might actually fall so head over heels in love with her lover that she would want them to run off together, hence breaking up the family.

This was not promising to be one of those parties, but a rather more staid, more sedate affair, with a seemingly endless supply of American and British expats who still, after five, ten, twenty years of Rome under their belts, cannot shake an appearance that recalls the town meetings of New England, the silos of Nebraska, or the open terrain of California and the West. Even when they are well dressed, and many of them are, they do not pull it off with the kind of instinctual flair or genetic predisposition that defines Italians, that makes you think when you look at them that they were created to adorn their bodies.

Even before we left for the party, I was telling Diane that we didn't have to stay if we didn't like it, that we could always duck out early and walk a few blocks to Testaccio to grab a thin, delicate pizza with a sprinkling of *mozzarella* and mushrooms or perhaps topped with *rughetta* at 10:00 or even 11:00 P.M., just to make sure that the evening would not pass without the opportunity to avail ourselves of another round of typical food in one of the incomparable food capitals of the world. She smiled and reassured me, but when we arrived at the party, and the only edibles visible were an assortment of small bowls with olives and walnut pieces and party mix, I was preparing myself for the worst. *Mannaggia,* I said to myself, I should have known better. I should have eaten before I came because, of course, an 8:30 P.M. invitation from an American is not the same as one from an Italian. With the latter, the message is clear: *cenone,* a huge, multihour dinner that probably will not start until 9:00 or 9:30, after glasses of *prosecco,* sparkling wine, and that will go on until hours past midnight. I remember the first time we accepted an invitation for a party beginning at that time, and I was already feeling little pain from two or three glasses of the bubbly wine as the host was still cooking dinner—in the fireplace—almost at midnight, and after-dinner drinks weren't served until two in the morning. Sometimes I forget that I ever lived in northern California, where a dinner invitation on a Saturday night was usually for 6:30 or 7:00 and you could be assured that you'd be snoring away by 11:00, regardless of whether you were the guest or the host.

But this was an American party, given by an American expatriate, and I'm thinking, "Eight-thirty means that you eat ahead of time, that this is going to be a musical event with a quiz on Verdi interspersed between carefully selected recordings, and we are not about to be distracted by anything so obtrusive as eating a big meal." I refused the olives, the nuts, the party mix. I'm holding out for pizza, later.

Suddenly, we are called to order. Our host, wearing a green Verdi T-shirt amid the suits, jackets, ties, and dresses of the guests, thanks us all for coming, and begins to explain that we will hear a few Verdi selections—*live*—before dinner, consisting not of frozen pizza, ham and cheese sandwiches, and diet Coke, but of real Roman food—two kinds of pasta, one *arrabbiata,* the "angry" pasta, with tomatoes, garlic, and parsley, and a liberal dose of hot peppers, and pasta with *porcini* mushrooms, the big, fat, tasty kind, since fall is their season. This course will be followed by roast chicken, potatoes and green beans, then dessert and coffee. It is to be a feast, the kind of meal one gets used to very easily in Rome and is difficult to find in any restaurant in the United States, even Italian ones, because the cooking here is at one and the same time both basic and delicious, and the rhythm, the order, the pace of the meal—long, slow, drawn out, like making love when you have all the time in the world and no other commitments—is just as pleasurable as the taste and variety of the food.

Suddenly, my mood has changed. I look at Diane, sitting next to me on the oriental rug in the living room with the forty or so other guests, and, still holding on to my snobbery, say to her, "OK, if I can endure the singing, I can then at least get to the food." Frank, our host, introduces the singers, and within a few moments, the tenor, a handsome Italian who is looking down in rapt concentration as he prepares to launch into his declaration of love for the "led astray" Violetta, begins to radiate.

For years, in the eighties, I was a season ticket holder at the San Francisco Opera, and I listened in gradual disappointment as the quality of the singing steadily declined, year after year, to the point where I often wondered why I was not at home in my own living room, listening to Maria Callas sing Tosca or Sherrill Milnes play Scarpia or Giuseppe di Stefano die ignominiously as Cavaradossi. When you strip away the theatrical part of the art form, *tutto sommato,* the bottom line is that opera is singing. Although the costumes and scenery add much to the experience, ultimately we do not remember the beauty of the sets or the composition as much as we do the way in which the music has been rendered and infused by the voices. As a listener, you want those notes pure, steady, clear, emotional. It had been a long time since I could say I'd heard them that way.

As soon as Alfredo let loose, I knew my wait had come to an end. His evocation was so good, so immediate, so real and unadorned by affectation or trickery, that my whole being was immediately transported to that place it goes when it is in the presence of the most astonishing beauty, the most perfect harmony. God gave us all gifts, every one of us, and this man was using his, both to express himself and entertain us at the same time. Then came Violetta's response, sung by Alfredo's wife, whose voice was beautifully lilting and facile, and suddenly the room was charged with the probability of erotic encounter. *"Ah, sì, da un anno! Un dì felice eterea mi balenaste innante"* ("Ah, yes, for a year! One happy, heavenly day your beauty shone before me"). Alfredo is making his move, and Violetta (*"Ah, se ciò è ver, fuggitemi,"* "Ah, if this is true, then flee from me") is responding in the only way she knows—coquettishly—and we in the audience, sitting on the floor and on couches all around the living room, are being treated to Verdi's genius, to his ability to put into musical notes the full range of human emotion.

I am transfixed, listening as the voices of the singers fill the room and perfume the air with the fragrant scent of artistic creation. I look to my right, up at Senator George McGovern, who is sitting on a couch. He is the United States ambassador to the United Nations Food and Agriculture Organization, and a friend of ours. He is weeping. In the afterglow of his illustrious career, he is here in Rome, away from family and friends, once again serving his country. Is he missing the familiarity of Washington, D.C., or his country home in Montana? Is he thinking of his disappointing presidential defeat of 1972, of his son who is in difficulty, or of his beloved daughter Terry, dead in the frozen snow of Madison, Wisconsin, passed out from overindulgence in alcohol one time too many? Tears are rolling down his cheeks as he leans forward to remove a handkerchief from his back pocket. He whispers to me that he can't remember in his whole life when he enjoyed a party more than this one. How is it that survivors find their way to Rome?

The arias continue with selections from other operas. The soprano and tenor are joined by an Italian mezzo whose voice is full and beautiful. Listening to her reminds me that we came to Rome for moments just like this one, that in all my fantasies I never dreamed I would be sitting next to George McGovern in the *salotto* of a house not far from ours, as semiprofessional opera singers were regaling me with luscious fragments of the work of the Italian patriot Giuseppe Verdi—*Trovatore, Aida, Falstaff, Rigoletto,* to go along with the familiar *Traviata.* The famous toasting aria led by Alfredo and Violetta— *"Libiamo"*—completes the first part of the performance, and it is a perfect lead-in to the appearance of delicious, perfectly prepared *al dente* pasta, and the *pollo, patate, e fagiolini* that follow. The food is as delectable as the singing, which is no mean feat to achieve for forty people sitting around a living room. I talk to the other guests, people from all over the world—Syria, Iran, Denmark, England, as well as Italy and the United States. The evening is international, or rather without nation, as the *insieme,* the "together," the ensemble, seems to blend in a different kind of party mix, one that could serve as a model for future generations who would seek to end the violence and hatred that our species seems not to be able to shake off.

Sated, we fall in once again to listen to the singers, and, as before, the creations of a musical genius fill the warm autumn night. After the final curtain, we sing happy birthday in Italian— *"Tanti auguri a te . . ."* (which literally means "Best wishes to you")—to the inspiration of the evening, Giuseppe Verdi, as a huge cake bearing his likeness is brought out and cut into pieces by the efficient yet solicitous staff. I ask for a slice that comes from his forehead, hoping that it partakes of the stuff that in real life stood inside his, wishing that by devouring a bit of his brain I will be animated by the same muse, that I, too, will be able to make music, if not with notes and scales, then at least with words.

6

Sciopero!
Rome Strikes Again

It is the dreaded word, one that strikes fear into the hearts of Romans, even more than *fame*, hunger, *brutta figura*, bad form, or *vergogna*, shame. It is the word that everyone knows will throw one's life into tilt, into a kind of chaos that only Rome can produce. It is the s-word, *sciopero*—strike.

In America there are strikes of public servants, but they are different. There the strikes are usually the product of failed collective bargaining agreements, as contracts run out and workers strike for lack of new ones. As a child I remember bus and subway strikes, garbage collection strikes, and newspaper strikes, and I especially recall auto- and steelworker strikes, which only affected me insofar as they were reported in grave tones on the evening news. Today in the United States there are strikes, but many fewer of them. When they do happen (my God, in these days even sports millionaires strike), they usually go on for a long time and affect only the families of the striking workers, usually for the worse. They don't penetrate into the lives of ordinary men and women who go about their own business, possibly feeling bad about the fact that the strike is happening but in reality not giving much of a damn because it has nothing to with them or their lives.

In Rome it is different. Strikes are common. Strikes are sudden. They are sometimes predictable, sometimes not. There are called-for, agreed-upon strikes, and there are wildcat strikes. At any moment the way in which life normally proceeds can be called into question by the sudden squall of a strike, sometimes even with comical results. In July a few years ago we had booked a trip to Sweden on the German airline Lufthansa. And then several days before our departure I saw it—the small item in the newspaper that immediately triggered fear, dread, and a sense of dislocation. There was to be a strike of air traffic controllers at Rome's Leonardo da Vinci Airport at Fiumicino on the day we were to leave for Sweden. It was scheduled to begin at 12:30. I rush to find our tickets. The time of our flight is clear. We are supposed to depart at 12:20. I call Lufthansa. With Aryan certainty, the operator assures me that the flight will leave. It *will* leave. Still, I am nervous. Although I am reassured by the cold efficiency of Lufthansa, we are not flying out of Germany, but out of Rome. We have to deal with Fiumicino.

At 12:10, on the plane, the captain comes on the intercom, speaking in English. He is urging us to take our seats, as we have only a few minutes to spare to taxi away or we will not be able to get out of Rome at all. Some passengers hurry; others, mostly Italian, do not. Italians in general are averse to displaying any signs that the untoward events in life merit moving any faster than they normally would. It is rare to see a Roman quicken his pace to avoid being hit by an oncoming car in the middle of the street. In fact, when we can't tell by the way someone is dressed if that person is Italian, which is usually a foolproof method, we can tell by the pace of the step. Non-Italians are eager to get where they are going, while the natives in general and Romans in particular are not. In this sense, Rome is the very opposite of New York.

But now the situation aboard is grave. The captain is reporting that the strike is going to commence within minutes, and that if we do not leave *now,* we are for all intents and purposes not going on vacation. While flight attendants are frantically urging passengers to take their seats, practically shoving them down and fastening their seat belts, the plane begins to move away from the gate. Perhaps fifteen people are still on their feet, putting bags in the overhead compartments or rummaging through the blankets and pillows as they try to keep their balance. Items begin to fall out of bins that have not been closed. We are moving faster now, as people scramble to sit down and the captain is telling us that even though we are the last plane cleared to leave, the job must be accomplished NOW! *MACHT SCHNELL! SUBITO!*

It is a rare event to see Germans in disarray, but this was one of them. If someone had told me that a Lufthansa flight would be taking off with people standing in the aisles, I would have not believed him. But this is different. This is a *sciopero,* and Herr Kommandant in the cockpit knows that this country, this city, this airport, is as capricious as his country, his city, his airport, is not. At any moment, instructions from the tower could send us all back home for the strike's duration.

It is only as we are idling for takeoff, our fingers and toes crossed, hoping that we will escape, that Herr Kommandant comes on the intercom to say that we have been cleared. Only when we leave the ground do we know for certain that we have avoided the worst. As the ruins of the ancient port of Ostia Antica and the blue, blue Mediterranean come into plain view, the inconvenience of a strike is already a distant memory.

But it is amazing how easily those memories can be rekindled. We are now in the midst of another *sciopero,* of public transport—buses and the two metro lines—that is scheduled to last two days, from 8:30 A.M. to 5:00 P.M. and again from 8:00 P.M. till midnight, followed the next day by a taxi strike. It is difficult to convey how inopportune a strike is in a city like Rome, where even when everything is running as it should, the city is on hair trigger, barely managing to function. One strategically placed, malfunctioning traffic light can turn life into a nightmare. With a *sciopero,* full-blown chaos replaces mere inconvenience. Even if one customarily takes the car, as most Romans do, the fact that everyone is taking the car makes for gridlock. Once, on the first day of the school year, when everyone was in serious motion for the first time in three months and no regular pattern had yet been reestablished, a wildcat public transportation strike materialized at the last moment, creating havoc and backing up cars on the Grande Raccordo Anulare, the ring road that surrounds Rome, for a distance of six miles.

Of course, the best way to get around town in these cases— in fact, in any case other than by foot—is by *motorino,* motor scooter, but we don't have one, Diane having nixed the idea repeatedly, informing me that I could not be trusted—not having grown up with them—to drive on the perilous streets. I protest, but not strongly. Perhaps she feels it is not in my genes. When we once visited the Mediterranean island of Ponza, about an hour away by hydrofoil, with my brother and his wife, we were all sitting on *motorini,* ready for a day's adventure, when

Perry suddenly took off like he was shot out of a cannon, heading straight for the bulkhead separating the street from the beach, about ten feet below. Luckily, he was stopped by the wall, unhurt, but at that point the *signora* renting us the vehicles made us return them, insisting that we take a Land Rover instead. So much for the *motorino* idea.

Even for those who work at home, as we do, the *sciopero* is a nuisance, as we often receive clients and guests who arrive frantic and out of breath, with horrendous stories to recount. The exhaust fumes and usually unheard blaring horns of cars, as drivers are stuck every which way and frustrated at their inability to fulfill the appointments they have scheduled—whether for work, study, or love—pollute the air and one's consciousness. A *sciopero* is a constant reminder that Rome is, in fact, a big city, when most of the time we fool ourselves into thinking that it is a small town, and degrades the usual *non fà niente*—it's really nothing—quality of everyday life. The irritability of the usually contented Romans, who find it a *brutta figura* to protest too loudly or display too strong a sense of disappointment or dismay, puts everyone in a bad mood.

In midafternoon we receive an invitation to dinner at the home of the McGoverns, who live about a mile away. What are our options? Is Luisa, our baby-sitter, available on such short notice? Luisa in many respects represents the true international nature of the city. She is a twenty-four-year-old daughter of a Roman father and English mother, and has a brother, Stefano, who also lives *a casa* with his Hungarian girlfriend. Luisa attended Italian public school but then went to St. Stephen's International High School, which has an American curriculum. She is perfectly bilingual, a lovely dancer, who lives, literally, five feet from us, as her family's *appartamento* shares the same floor in our *palazzo*. We don't know. As a single, young artist, she keeps hours completely contrary to ours and is often going to bed just before we are waking up. What do we do?

Diane has an appointment in the center, which she can reschedule for later in the week. This way she can avoid the chaos of the strike and meet the McGoverns' friends from Washington, who are visiting in Rome and will be the guests tonight at dinner. A taxi will be difficult to find in the strike, as they are not all that plentiful to begin with. (Ironically, that very fact has induced a wave of taxi strikes, as drivers resist the liberalization of their industry, which is intended to create more taxis.) Chances are that the cabs will be taken by people who are stranded or in desperate difficulty. We could always walk, however, and take a cab back, as at that time most of the inconvenience will be over and for a few hours Rome will once again return to its normally anarchic state, an anarchy that nevertheless functions.

Fortunately, we learn that Luisa is available, and when she arrives, she overhears Diane and me discussing the best way to get to our destination. Walk, cab, or car? The night is lovely. Perhaps a *bella passeggiata*? This is my preference. But Diane, normally a strong, willing walker, is this evening attired in her usual *bella figura,* and, looking down at her feet, comfortably ensconced—at least for the moment—in high-heeled pumps, suggests a taxi or the car. We suddenly remember that our battery is dead. We are now down to our last option, but Luisa is quick to interject. "You can take my car," she says. "There is very little petrol, but I think you'll get there and back." She is an angel. Not only do our two boys adore her, we do as well.

She is like the elder daughter we never had, as our twelve-year relationship would have been hard-pressed to produce a twenty-four-year-old offspring.

I look out the window. One side of our street, the side going in the opposite direction from the one in which we have to go, is completely blocked. *Mamma mia.* The other side, however, is clear. We kiss the kids, take Luisa's documents and car keys, and plunge into the unknown. On the way out of the *palazzo,* we run into a neighbor, who tells us that it's all a *casino,* a mess, out there. (Romans have lots of words for mess—*casino, macello, pasticcio.*) Everywhere is blocked, and the street lights are out in the center. *Mamma mia, che fatica!* How exhausting!

We are finally moving. Traffic is light, until we have to turn right a few streets ahead. Suddenly, cars and *motorini* are everywhere. Although we are not far from our destination, it will now probably take us at least thirty minutes to reach it. We fear being late, as we will be all *americani* tonight, but when we finally pull in, we find we have arrived before the other guests, who have taken a cab from the Hotel Hassler at the top of the Spanish Steps. They left an hour before, a ride that under normal circumstances takes at most twenty minutes. The senator is pacing, constantly checking his watch, and his behavior reminds me of the life in America I left behind. I try to reassure him that they are stuck in traffic and can do nothing about it, and intellectually he agrees with me, but you can see that viscerally he is nervous and impatient and is having difficulty accepting the inevitable. He hasn't been in Rome long enough to have assimilated the cultural differences emotionally. It does take time.

The other guests finally arrive. Their cab ride has taken them three times longer than usual. But now, all that is in the past.

Diane and I have already forgotten the inconvenience, the hassle, the persistent need to consider our options, and the senator is now relaxed as well. The dinner table is set. It looks lovely, and within minutes, we are dining. Another exasperating situation in Rome, something you cannot help but encounter over and over again, is being overcome by the pleasures of gastronomy. The skill of *arrangiarsi,* of making the best of a bad situation, something at which Romans are especially proficient, and that we are learning to incorporate *pian piano,* little by little, has once again tempered a potential catastrophe.

The *antipasto* and grilled salmon are tasty, the conversation lively, and *domani* we will once again face the vicissitudes. But as any *romano* will tell you, *domani* never comes.

7

Monte Palatino: The "City" on the Hill

I am standing on the Palatine Hill, the absolute ground zero of the city. It was here that the entire enterprise was conceived. On this spot, on April 21, 753 B.C., 2,753 years ago, the city was founded. Roman officials claim to have excavated and preserved the remains of the founder Romulus's hut, which stands on the west side of the hill, facing the river Tiber and the Isola Tiberina, but who knows for sure? The island served to encourage the crossing of the waterway, providing access to the north, to the Etruscans and the other tribes that were spread out over the Italian peninsula in much the same manner as the native Americans who inhabited the vast open spaces of the Western Hemisphere before the Genoan Cristoforo Colombo and the other Europeans came to forever change their lives, 2,245 years *after* the city of Rome had already been born.

It is a clear, limpid, luminous day, the kind that leaves you breathless. As I ascend the long grade that leads up from the entrance at street level to the Palatine, a few steps from the Roman Forum and the Colosseum, I cannot help but think that I am walking on hallowed ground. The deepness of the azure sky is made all the more vivid by the fact that it is set off against the brilliant red orange of the bricks that make up the remains of the baths of the Emperor Septimius Severus and the *palazzo* of the Emperor Domitian, built in the first and second centuries A.D. The contrast of the opposing sides of the color wheel gives the sky a purity and depth that would be difficult to capture on canvas or paper, let alone in reality.

The Monte Palatino is the ideal place to start an exploration of the Eternal City. It is the venue that was home to the original Romans, and as such, it is the purest of the seven hills. The others—the Quirinale, Esquilino, Celio, Aventino, Campidoglio, and Viminale—originally housed rival tribes like the Sabines and Etruscans, friendly enemies or hostile friends, depending on the time of year, the state of the harvest, and the disposition of the rulers. To the south of the Palatine lies the Circo Massimo, the Circus Maximus, where three hundred thousand people could watch the racing of chariots in an oval stadium that was nearly a half mile long, whose scant remains lie embedded in the accumulated dust, dirt, and soil of twenty-five hundred years, just enough of it jutting upward from Mother Earth to remind us that nothing lasts but, at best, the record of what once was. It was also here, on the spot that eventually became the Circus Maximus, that the infamous Rape of the Sabine Women took place, immortalized in art for centuries. An event shrouded in mist and myth, it was an early pass at the *furbizia,* the cleverness and trickery that Romans are still known for, when their ancestral forebears invited the Sabines from the neighboring hill to come and make peace and instead carted off their women when Romulus gave them the signal. A stream ran through the spot, and still does, although it has long been buried under fifty feet of fill, as repeated waves of civilization piled soil on the remains of what was before. Rome is a palimpsest, a piece of parchment that is used ad infinitum.

I wander up a little higher, passing under the spur of an aqueduct that extended from the Celian Hill across the street to provide water for the baths of Septimius Severus. Seventeen aqueducts fed the city at its height. Seventeen pipelines to civilization that employed thousands of Romans and provided the citizens of the city with the means to construct public baths the likes of which the world had never before seen and probably hasn't seen since; extensive hot- and cold-water pools spread out all across the landscape, providing sustenance and nourishment to the body and soul of patrician and plebeian alike. The aqueducts so defined the city and its empire that historians have dated its true fall from the time when the barbarian invaders cut them in the early sixth century, effectively ending Roman life as it had been lived for the previous one thousand years and ushering in what has been called either the Middle or the Dark Ages, depending on one's point of view.

I continue, higher, always higher, passing an assortment of Mediterranean pine trees, the famous *pini romani*. If anything, if it is possible, the sky is even bluer now than it was before. The ruins are extensive. Here and there a workman is making minor repairs to make sure that what still stands remains standing, and overhead two masons are topping off a wall to prevent water from seeping in and destroying it. All the world enjoys the splendor and richness of the city, yet Italians are the ones who have to pay for it. Romans constantly lament the high taxes they incur to keep Italy afloat, but deep down they know what it means to live in Rome, to know that the city is a gift they give to the rest of the world. The word *patrimonio,* that which has been inherited from one's forefathers, is often heard, so much so that even the ex–communist prime minister Massimo D'Alema used the term to refer to the extensive media holdings of his political rival Silvio Berlusconi, a sort of Italian Ross Perot, who was actually the head of the government for a time in 1994.

Nothing remains of one of the walls of Nero's palace but an arch, and through it in the blue beyond stands St. Peter's, Michelangelo's incomparably elegant cupola perfectly framed in the incongruous opening. Not only is it a sight that the ancient Romans never saw from atop their perch on the founding hill overlooking the Tiber, it is one they could never have even imagined. It would have been inconceivable that the scruffy, destitute, yet enraptured and determined converts to a mystical cult that came from that hardscrabble, inhospitable province called Palestine, the place the barbarian Jews called home, would one day—a day not too far in the historical future—not only subvert the mighty Roman Empire from within, but would also sustain the vision, the strength, the capacity, and the chutzpah to build St. Peter's in the very city that had sought—and failed—to annihilate them, to torture and eradicate them. The Romans succeeded only in sending them into the hereafter as martyrs whose example of serenity in the face of agonizing death by the most unconscionable means inspired thousands, and then millions, to follow the Gospel, resulting in an institution that is the most successful idea—in the sense of longevity and loyalty—the species has ever produced. St. Peter's is the grandest, most majestic, most commanding building in Rome—and perhaps in the world.

Suddenly, the smell of wild mint is everywhere, perfuming

the air with a sense of unreality. Can one truly be in the center of Rome, amid the noise and chaos of traffic, the fumes and crowded streets, and suddenly be in a refreshing green spot where the only thing one hears is silence, where the scents of nature abound, and where one can wander among the ruins of civilization, see the remains of temples and fountains and court-yards and small stadiums that held races and games and competitions of all types? From the promontory on the north side of the hill, the view of the city, of the Forum and the Capitoline Hill, which for a millennium formed the commercial and civic zones of the city to the Palatine's residential, is spectacular. One can only imagine what it must have been like to have been a patrician in the ancient capital, to have lived in a residence on this little knoll, to have been able to escape the stifling heat of summer by availing oneself of the cool breezes of the heights, and to have been able to look down and gaze upon the daily market of Rome and realize that one truly was a master of the universe.

Behind me, in another of the ruins, stand the remains of the large platform that served as the dining area for the Emperor Domitian. I can picture him, resplendent in his toga of the finest cloth, reclining on a divan as his servants provided entertainment and food and drink for the exalted one and his family. I imagine his spirit becoming incredulous, knowing that the Latin language, the tongue he employed to command, to execute, to dominate, was carried into the future, into history, only by the Roman Catholic Church, by that banned sect of wild Christians. What irony history brings.

I descend into the Forum to join the crowds. I pass the many evanescent items and T-shirts being sold for a few thousand lire to anyone who shows the slightest interest in buying them. Just outside the entrance of the ruins, business and commerce abound. In the crisp, brisk autumn air, it is clear that nothing much has changed in the past two thousand or three thousand years. There is buying and selling, good deals and bad, people with whom you enjoy doing business and those with whom you would rather not. The cast of characters is different, but the story stays the same.

8

Business, but Not as Usual: Money Isn't Everything

I remember well the moment. I was sitting on an airplane, waiting to take off from Rome's airport, after another Italian visit in the years before we finally moved here. I was glum and depressed that the pleasure of being in this country was about to end once again. Who knew at that point when I'd be back.

A group of Americans hovered in the aisle, eager to catch up on all the news they had missed while they had been immersed in their Italian adventures. Each bit of information was met with barely disguised indifference, as if the death of the ex–British prime minister Harold Wilson, the paralyzing injury to Christopher Reeve, or the breakup of CBS were nothing about which to raise an eyebrow. It was only when the raconteur mentioned that the stock market had gone up that the members of the group erupted in cheers and high fives—*all'americana*—as if life's joy were solely a matter of the state of one's balance sheet. Every people has its priorities, and I was once again reminded, microcosmically, what those of my countrymen are.

When you live in Rome, it doesn't take long to realize that business, money, and ambition are approached from an entirely different perspective. You learn quickly that the American way of life—based on buying and selling—is not a universal, but a value, and a relatively recent one at that. Although Italy is an advanced industrial country, its cultural proclivities and day-to-day habits were formed for the most part years before the "Protestant ethic and the spirit of capitalism" rose up out of the often-autonomous city-states of northern Europe to rule the world and spread the gospel of the market economy far and wide. Rome, like everywhere else today, has adopted these ideals, and Romans, like everyone else, appreciate money and the things it buys, not only ordinary things and luxury items, but also the psychological reassurance that enables one to master the struggle for survival and live at the upper reaches of evolution, in the rarefied air of self-actualization.

But the things Romans will do for money, the lengths to which a *romano* will go, to get or earn it, the level at which life is organized in the pursuit of ambition and career and the climbing of the corporate ladder—the rat race, as it is customarily called—is completely foreign to what we Americans are used to. It is a level that puts much less emphasis on pecuniary activity and much more on the work itself. To Romans the connection between enterprise and monetary reward is much less apparent than it is for Americans, who seem to regard money as the natural end result of effort. This is what is usually meant by the word "practical," when it refers to Americans, Germans, or Chinese for that matter, and why we could never attach this label to Romans.

Examples abound: the look of glazed incomprehension, directed at a spot in the far distance, on the part of Leonardo, my first *barista,* the one who makes *caffè* and other drinks at the Jolly

Bar in Grottaferrata, when I told him that one of the best qualities about America is that it is organized. He looked at me as if I had been mistaken, as if I had not understood that I was supposed to be listing the things that made living in the United States worthwhile. Being "organized" was not something that middle-aged Leonardo, who makes the best *cappuccino* in the world, could relate to. Or the ubiquitous *"torno subito,"* or "I'll be back immediately," signs that appear on the doors of the shops at the most inopportune moments, that are a constant reminder that holding down the fort at all costs is not something that needs to be done at the expense of going to the bar for yet another *caffè,* the local *forno* for a slice of pizza *a taglio,* or even to the shop across the street for a chat to catch up on all the latest gossip with one's fellow merchant and friend. The fact that a sale could be lost, a customer not served, an opportunity to open the cash register to deposit lire in exchange for an item leaving the store not taken, is beside the point. *Chi se ne frega?* Who cares? Life is just not organized around the principle that doing business and making money are the reasons why we were put here. Changing jobs in Rome is rare; changing careers is almost unheard of.

It is five minutes to two in the afternoon. The outdoor market in Testaccio is about to close. We are looking for a new bathroom rug and have not yet found something that pleases us. Suddenly, we see something in the back of a van not yet fully packed. It had just been removed from the tables on the street that minutes before had displayed an endless variety of choices. It is the perfect color, perhaps the one we are looking for. We ask to examine it. In fact, we are so close we can touch it. But the proprietor has other plans. "No, no, no," he says, nonchalantly waving us away. "It is too hard to get to, and it's time to eat." He makes the sign of hunger—the right hand, parallel to the ground, moving back and forth toward the right side of one's waist, where the liver is. "When I come back again, I'll show it to you." He continues loading the truck. We know and he knows that he visits many of the city's markets, and that it could be weeks before he comes back, and that there is no guarantee even then that the rug will still be part of his inventory. We wish him *Buon pranzo* and continue on. Ultimately, we find a rug in another place, and we're sure that the rug man at the market gives no further thought to the fact that he had failed to complete a transaction. Romans are philosophical about such things, and they regret very little.

Most of Rome still closes every day at one in the afternoon in order to take lunch *con calma,* in peace. I remember the first time I learned this. Exploring Rome as a neophyte, I wandered into the extensive expanse of the verdant Villa Borghese and did not emerge until well past the beginning of the *ora di pranzo,* the lunch hour. Everything was shut tight, and my first thought was that some terrible catastrophe—a nuclear exchange, perhaps— had taken place. The concept of the daily afternoon siesta had never registered. It is a custom that befits royalty, rather than the utilitarian way in which Americans either devour a sandwich at their desk, or use the lunch hour to make or break deals, introduce a new product to an old customer, or tell an expendable employee that he has been reassigned. Three hours every day, fifteen to eighteen hours each week, of unrecoverable time; precious, valuable moments that could have been spent lining their pockets with the lire of foreign tourists or of their countrymen, are given over to the pursuit of one's personal pleasure, be it eating, napping, or pursuing an amorous moment or two with one's spouse, lover, or someone with whom one could have *una bella scappatella*—a never-to-be-repeated fling with a man or woman who is similarly disposed and available. These classifications are important to Romans. One marries for family reasons, takes a lover in the same way as one would form a close friendship, and has a *scappatella* purely for sexual pleasure. All the energy Americans devote to the accumulation and management of money, the hours spent thinking about how to amass it, organize it, invest it, will it, spend it, keep it, share it or not share it, Romans instead devote to other things—to looking well, eating well, loving well, and spending time with their families.

Simple transactions that one gives not a second thought to in the United States are fraught with peril in Rome. The act of making multiple photocopies, for example, something that by now in America is so simple that one would be hard-pressed to find any difficulty executing it within minutes of one's home, is an altogether different thing in the Eternal City. Copy machines—the fast, clean, multiple kind—are still rare, and when one succeeds in finding a place that can make, say, three copies of a 240-page manuscript, something that you can do—yourself—at any Kinko's, at two o'clock in the morning if you so desire, is like trying to get into Fort Knox. The only thing, really, that is easy to take care of in Rome is getting a coffee at the local bar, which are plentiful and thankfully uniform. You walk in, say *"un caffè"* to the cashier, pay about a thousand lire, get a receipt, called a *scontrino,* place it on the bar under a *mancia,* a tip of one hundred or two hundred lire, ask for the *caffè,* get it within thirty seconds, drink it in the same amount of time, and then leave. I've come to the conclusion that the reason why Romans make endless trips to the bar to take a coffee is because

67

it is simply the easiest thing in the city to do. (Ironically, once you get the hang of it, making a phone call is also a breeze. Public phones are everywhere, and you simply buy a *carta telefonica,* a phone card, which are sold at some newsstands, most exchange places, and all *tabacchi,* tobacco shops, remember to tear off the perforated upper right corner, and *ecco,* you have five thousand, ten thousand, or fifteen thousand lire worth of phone calls at your disposal. There are even international cards.) Among the worst epithets a Roman can utter in your face is that you are acting like a Milanese, which means that you have devoted your life to the pursuit of money, the inference being that your general values and behavior must be less than genteel.

Merchants, moreover, almost never have change, and are loath to part with it even when they do. Look inside the tray of any cash register in America, and you will see gobs of coins neatly arranged in their bins, along with stacks of ones, fives, tens, and twenties, all ready, willing, and able to be given out in exchange for their big brother fifties and hundreds, which disappear under the tray when taken in and are counted up excitedly at the end of the day. The Roman cash register—or *cassa*— is pathetic by comparison. Because merchants want to avoid going every day to the bank, where they must endlessly wait on line, they have little or no change, perhaps a few 1,000- and 5,000-lire notes to accompany the lone 10,000. There are rarely fifties and—inconceivable—no hundreds (worth about sixty dollars today). If you are unfortunate enough to have to buy something at the beginning of the business day, you had better have close to the exact amount, or you will not be able to obtain what your heart desires. I know how I can bring a smile to the face of Maurizio, who owns the little cheese store where we shop, anytime I want. All I have to do is pay with the exact amount. He will grin, and exclaim, *"Perfetto!"*

It is also your responsibility to get the change, not the merchant's. Once, when I went to a film matinee, I wanted to pay the 8,000-lire price (less than $5) with a 50,000 note (around $30). The cashier dismissed me immediately. "You're only the third person who has bought a ticket," she said, as if it were out of the question that there should be any cash in the till in anticipation of an evening's worth of business. I said I would wait until she made a few more sales, but it was clear that the feature was not going to be well attended (Romans do not, by and large, watch movies in the afternoon). Finally, she told me to go across the street to the bar and get change. It was a good idea, but I didn't want anything, and if I asked for a coffee and offered to pay for it with a fifty, they would have given me the coffee and told me to come back another time to pay. In other words, problem not solved. I asked for a ten-thousand-lire phone card instead, something one can always use. "We don't sell them," she told me. "Go around the corner to the change place." I did. I resisted the temptation to just make change (they hate doing that), bought the card, got my needed change, bought the movie ticket to the satisfied smile of the cashier, and spent two hours in modern-day Bologna with the perfect, adorable wife who decided impulsively to run off to the south of Italy in search of amorous adventure with an old boyfriend instead of staying home and making Christmas dinner. The movie was called *Matrimoni*.

Another time, Diane had to go to a different part of Rome, two subway stops but another world away, to retrieve five shirts from a tailor who had agreed to shorten the sleeves. (When I tell the shirt merchant in the *camiceria* that in the United States you can buy shirts that have sleeves the same length as your arm, he stares back at me with incredulity.) The shirts had been promised the week before but were still not ready, another occurrence you get used to here. We called a few days later, and finally they were. It was summer, oh so hot, hot hot, city summer heat with humidity, and we were leaving for the States for six weeks the next day and I needed the shirts. Diane offered to retrieve them. The tab was to be 75,000 lire for the six shirts, $8 a shirt to shorten the sleeves. Diane arrives. She hands the woman a 100,000 note, and receives the usual reply— *"Mi scusi, Signora, ma lei non ha niente di spiccio?"*—"I'm sorry, ma'am, but don't you have smaller change?" "But what is smaller?" Diane replies. "This is the next highest denomination." Her nerves are frayed, the heat of the day having begun to gnaw away at her patience. The tailor's wife cannot be moved. If you wait ten minutes, she says, my sister will come with *spiccie*. Your ten minutes, Diane knows, is my hour. Said sister could very easily not show up at all. But the real point is apparent. This establishment does business only with people it knows. For their regular customers, the shirts would be tendered and the money paid another time, maybe even months later. But we are *stranieri,* foreigners, not, in this case, of the country, but more importantly of the *quartiere,* the neighborhood, and Diane must find the change. She goes next door to the *supermercato* to buy a few items and cash the hundred. She waits on line, but even there, the till is empty. "Go to the bar, Signora," they tell her. The bar is the same. This is a country without money, or rather, you realize in moments just like this one how plentiful currency is in America.

Exasperated, Diane returns to the tailor's shop to try again with Signora Proprietario. She is busy chatting away at warp speed on the telephone with her sister, who will come, she says, *subito*. Wonder of wonders. Miracle of miracles. In ten minutes she is there. She opens her wallet, gives Diane twenty-five-thousand lire in exchange for the hundred. Smiles and *mi dispiace*, I'm sorry, are uttered by all. The situation is resolved. My shirt-sleeves are now the right length, and within a day we will be out of the stifling heat of Rome and into the almost arctic chill of San Francisco in summer, where the tills will be full, and where, when we order a tea—never coffee—at the local café, we won't think twice about paying for it with a twenty.

9

La Bella Figura:
The Flesh and Flash of Roman Women

I knew a man once, an adventurer and world traveler, who claimed to have been everywhere and seen and done everything, and when he was asked who the most beautiful women in the world were, he answered, without hesitation, "The Burmese." Having never been to Burma, nor anywhere near Burma for that matter, I cannot say whether I agree with him. But I do know this. When it comes to choosing the most beautiful women in the Western world, I would answer, without hesitation, "The Italians," and especially the women of Rome.

It is difficult to know where to begin, because it is impossible to pinpoint any one feature, any one quality, any one particular aspect of the pulchritude that is *la bella donna romana,* and say, "This is it, this is the reason why Roman women make you never want to have to take your eyes off of them." Is it the hair, the complexion, the figure, the features, the way they carry themselves, how they wear their clothes, the way they not only don't mind that you look at them, but actually seek your gaze, your glance, your stare, your *"sguardo,"* as they would say in Italian, and return it with intensity, looking you straight in the eyes without a hint of modesty, as if to say, "It's worth looking at me, isn't it?" Beautiful women are a part of the landscape of the city. They pass by at every turn, at every moment, at any age.

If you sit at an outdoor café for longer than five minutes on a street that even comes close to being a main thoroughfare, you will see her. When the light is red, she will pull up on a *motorino.* Looking from the bottom up is like beholding a female who is half angel, half hooker. Black high-heeled shoes or boots blend nicely into fishnet stockings and continue up to a hemline that is very close, dangerously close, to being illegal. Depending on the weather, she will be wearing a jacket over her top or just the top, backpack slung over her shoulders, sunglasses wrapped round her face with her hair pulled back to keep it from flying all over as she begins to take off. Gold jewelry glitters in the sunlight—earrings, bracelets, necklaces, rings. All eyes are on her. She is the picture of classic, feminine beauty, and as the light turns green, dozens of men's hearts are shattered at the nearby tables in the instant she vanishes into the helter-skelter of Roman traffic. But the ache is short-lived. Within minutes, another *ragazza* appears. She looks nothing like her predecessor, yet she is just as beautiful, her tinted blond hair blowing sensuously around her shoulders. She laughs delightedly as the *ragazzo* behind her on the bike squeezes tighter and nuzzles her cheek and neck before it is again time to depart. In Rome, there is *sempre, sempre,* always, the show.

Everyone has the fever. Everyone plays the game. I go to the shoemaker to pick up a small repair, and his mother is there, in her eighties if she is a day, and she is all dolled up as if it were 1935 and she had to do whatever she can to attract a suitor. Her blouse and skirt are pressed, and over her wrinkled face her eyeglasses are something one would see in a magazine. Her fluffy white hair has just been cut and done, and her lips are ruby red, drawing my eyes to them, making me wonder for a split second if she still feels like she would want someone to kiss them.

In Rome images of women are everywhere. Statues and paintings of the Madonna are more plentiful than street signs. Figures of nymphs, nymphets, and voluptuous female figures in various states of undress adorn the ceilings and walls of the myriad rooms of the Renaissance and Baroque *palazzi*. Bernini's exquisite sculpture *The Blessed Ludovica Albertoni* in the Church of San Francesco a Ripa, accomplished when the genius of the age was already well into his seventies and close to his Maker, depicts a woman on the verge of spiritual rapture, but it is difficult to look at her face at the moment of her passing into the next life and not think of the other kind of rapture as well.

In Rome, to go along with the full range of artistic patrimony, images of nude or seminude women are ubiquitous, especially in advertising, and the way in which average women display their bodies as a matter of course would be considered indecent, perhaps even offensive, in the Anglo-Saxon world. Topless is common on beaches. In a print ad, a woman is jumping out of a bath, covered everywhere in soapsuds, her perfect breasts and erect nipples fully exposed, a smile on her face a mile wide, showing us the marvelous feeling that comes from immersing ourselves in water with no clothes on. Cleavage is everywhere— on television programs and commercials that are seeking to gain your attention, on billboards as you are in transit, and in the photos that greet you as you pass on foot by the many lingerie shops that adorn the streets. And then there is the latest in advertising chic—bisexuality—as gorgeous women are touching, caressing, gazing, whispering together, fulfilling in yet another way the need this culture has for the fine forms of female beauty to be seen, appreciated, and desired.

But it is in the day-to-day life of the city, as one goes about one's business, that the real story of the beauty of the Roman woman is there to behold. You can always see her, standing in sharp contrast to the tourists—the white sneakers and baggy khaki shorts of the *americana,* the flat sandals and socks of the *tedesca,* the heavy wool coat and functional walking shoes of the *inglese,* or the heavily made-up and overdone look of the *russa.* The Roman woman has spent a lot of time thinking about how to put herself together, how to please, to attract, to allure, to intrigue, even perhaps to seduce. If Americans are always dressed as if they could at the drop of a hat play a round of tennis or go on a five-mile run, Italians have other priorities. They are always ready to receive a special but unexpected invitation to dine in elegant splendor in a seventeenth-century *palazzo* without having to change clothes. As our friend Anneke told us after returning to the United States following three unforgettable years in the Eternal City, "In Rome, I was the worst-dressed woman. Here, I am the best-dressed woman."

The culture loves beauty, depends on beauty, is addicted to beauty. The single word to describe all good things, whether they mean great, terrific, wonderful, marvelous, fantastic, satisfying, or well done, is *bello.* The roots go way, way back. Even the Etruscans, the people who occupied the peninsula between the Arno (Florence) and Tiber (Rome) Rivers in the first millennium B.C. before they were ultimately conquered and wiped out by the Romans toward the end of that period, were lovers of beauty. Visit the Etruscan museum at the Villa Giulia in Rome and you will see their civilization, taken whole from the many burial grounds they left behind. There are perfume bottles, containers for makeup, rings that went into hair, and large baskets into which all the combs, brushes, ointments, and powders were put in an effort to please the gods, to make themselves beautiful in the eyes of the deities so that the beauty of their bodies would reflect the beauty of their souls. And that's how it stood until Judaism and then Christianity came along to break the connection between outer magnificence and inner purity. The one no longer had anything to do with the other.

But try telling that to a modern-day *romana*. Her beauty lies not in what God has given her, but in what she does with it. Anyone who wants to can be *una bella donna* in Rome, as long as one is willing to pay the price, or play the game, depending on your point of view. Make yourself beautiful. Use clothes, makeup, jewelry, accessories, whatever you can to accentuate your beauty, your femininity. Rome is still a place where men look *like* men and look *at* women, and women look *like* women and look *at* men. Their hair is thick, clean, lustrous, cut, permed, tinted blond or red or auburn, straight, wavy, but usually long, as that is what the picture of feminine beauty calls for. The women are shapely, and have large, oversize features, big faces with large brown, occasionally green, eyes, and strong noses and chins, large hoop earrings sticking through their ears and dangling along their jawlines. They wear sunglasses, the modern-day chador, to create the illusion of allure, of mystery, to make you wonder what kind of *sguardo* they are giving you, and what it would be like to look into their eyes, if only they were to let you into their most intimate thoughts and feelings. How ironic that you see nothing of a woman in the Islamic culture but her eyes, and almost everything of a woman in Rome but hers.

Their clothes are impeccable. Whether they wear jeans and a fitted parka with a fur collar or an expensive *tailleur* from one of the designer shops around Piazza di Spagna, the telltale signs of *la bella donna romana* are there. They, like a portrait of Louis XIV I saw recently, have great legs and know how to show them off with stockings of every pattern imaginable. Our friend Clelia, whom we have never seen in anything less than perfect attire, says, "I can tell right away if a woman is Italian just by her *calze.*" They wear skirts way above the tops of their knees, as their legs move down into shoes with heels, the shape of which changes with the style and is always an indication of whether the *donna* is *a stagione* (in season) or *fuori stagione* (out of season). Even when they wear pants, which they do, the length *a stagione* is short so that you always see their ankles (although we have heard rumors and seen evidence that the hems of women's pants are going down), giving the illusion of length, and the trousers are worn with a vast array of accessories—scarves, tight or low-cut blouses or sweaters, and blazers or coats over them. Their long hair is pulled into a ponytail with a huge, bright colored bow at the back to hold it in place, white teeth flash in frequent smiles, as the Romans, unlike their Parisian counterparts, have no qualms about showing their delight. And then there is the *telefonino,* into which they talk incessantly and which lends an even greater air of sexuality as you pass by and overhear snippets of what passes for conversation these days—*"Ciao, Paolo. Bene. Ma tu, come stai"*—all drawn out as if each syllable were its own world.

Like their bodies, their personalities, their movements, their clothes are worn to be seen. It is hard to imagine a more visually stimulating people.

So elegant and perfect and yet down to earth at the same time. How could women so beautiful be so accessible? That wasn't what we learned growing up. That wasn't the way it was. The pretty girls were snobs, "stuck up," uninterested in the boys their own age, but rather in those who were older and had cars. Roman women are so real, so "everyday," dressed like that to drop their kids off at school, pick up their dry cleaning at the *tintoria,* or buy a loaf of bread at the *panificio.* For a man, it is as if you've died and gone to heaven, and all because inside of them is the feeling, the knowledge, the *certainty* that they are beautiful, that because of their beauty they do not have to play it cool. Their grooming, their scent, their clothes, their *telefonini,* and their awareness of themselves as women is so high, so exalted, so solid, that you realize that their whole existence is based on being noticed.

Centuries, millennia of Roman life on the streets and squares—in the places people go, and have always gone, to escape the heat and cramped quarters of their houses, where *nonna* and Zia Franca and their cousin from Pisa who is a student at the University "La Sapienza" in Rome are all sleeping, and the only thing you have room to do is brush your teeth—have created the need to be out, where there is light, and air, and other people in the same predicament.

And as if by evolution, through some sense of the natural order of things, these people decided long ago that since they had no choice but to look at each other, to see each other, to pass by a thousand times a day and say *ciao,* that it made sense to give the other something to please his or her eyes. By now the tradition has become so refined, so mature, that you just cannot help but gaze, that you pass by dozens, hundreds of women each day who look like you would imagine a model or an actress to look, who carry themselves as if they made their living being looked at. And yet they are ordinary middle-class Roman women, working in stores or banks, or as doctors, lawyers, or architects, who call their mothers to find out if they need anything and pull their husbands' shirts out of the washing machine to be ironed. But they also think about what it means to be beautiful. By this time they take that part of life for granted. They are no more inclined to stroll down the street in a sweatsuit and white socks and tennis shoes than they are to be seen naked. I take that back. Less inclined.

Only in Rome does one find this happy combination of North and South, of a kind of Mediterranean eroticism that nevertheless partakes of the way in which northern, wealthier women look when they have the means to put themselves together exactly the way they want to. Occasionally, one is overdone, *esagerata,* but it somehow blends into the landscape, reminds you of a character in a Fellini movie, with big, platinum blond hair and heavy makeup and short knobby legs on wobbly spike heels that look like they are left over from the fifties. You see these women, and rather than feeling sorry for them, you think, "Way to go," for having the guts to go out like that, and you say to yourself that at least she is interesting to look at.

In Rome classic, feminine beauty still counts. Because crime against person is extremely rare and women feel safe, the streets are populated, wherever you go, with the chic, the swank, the high gloss, and the elegant, a veritable feast for the eyes, which gained prominence over the nose eons ago. We have been treated ever since to sights that make us thank God we can appreciate beauty, and the feminine form—the Roman variety— is certainly among the most beautiful.

10

Buon Appetito:
The Tasty Trattoria

Mangiare, eating, is the true passion of the city, the inviolable religion, at the same time sacred and profane. Food is everywhere. In markets both indoor and out are overflowing cartons of fresh fruits and vegetables, beautifully made display cases exhibiting layer upon layer of succulent meats and cheeses, racks of fragrant bread of varying shapes, sizes, textures, and tastes, ready to be cut and consumed to suit the proportion and contour of any palate; every square inch of tiny grocery stores, truly from floor to ceiling, is stacked with colorful boxes of pasta and rice, cans of tomatoes, beans, and tuna, and packages of every confection imaginable. Such a profusion of color, smell, and flavor, a true reflection of the bounty of Mother Nature and the miraculous yield of her fertile soil. No wonder Italy has always been referred to as the Garden of Europe. No wonder it is difficult to go anywhere in this country and find wilderness, true wild places, as every patch of land, every backyard and furrow where one can find green, every hillside or flat plain, is taken up with the cultivation of grains, grapes, olives, or fruit and vegetables, items with which to satisfy the *gola,* the particular tastes of the Romans and their countrymen.

Eavesdrop by chance on a conversation in the street and you are likely to hear talk about eating—*"Abbiamo mangiato tanto, troppo . . . , si mangia bene a quel locale . . . , c'era un piatto di . . . , no, no, no, è facile cucinarlo. . . ."* ("We ate so much, too much . . . , one eats well at that place . . . , there was a plate of . . . , no, no, no, it's easy to cook it . . . ") There is nothing quite like the quiet lull that descends on this otherwise crowded, noisy, chaotic city when the *ora di pranzo*—usually between one and four in the afternoon—is upon the populace. Suddenly, Rome seems empty. Most stores close. People vanish. And the only sounds you hear as you pass through the nearly silent streets are the particular rhythms of plates clacking, silverware clinking, and linen snapping on the tables outside the many restaurants and *trattorie* that line the *strade e vicoli* of the city, or coming from the open windows of the *palazzi,* where families have gathered as they have for more than two millennia to break bread before resuming the business of the day later in the afternoon. Then, refreshed, recharged, rejuvenated after a meal, a rest, perhaps more, they are ready to navigate the second part of the daily adventure, until 8:00 to 8:30 in the evening, when the next cycle of eating begins anew.

I am almost always asked, when I return to the States and friends and relatives want to know what kind of food I would like to eat—Mexican, Chinese, Japanese, seafood, Indian, Greek (never Italian; by this time they know not to mention it)—how it is that we can eat Italian food every day. Don't we ever tire of it? Is there enough variety, they inquire, as the sushi or the burrito or the plate of pad Thai arrives to put me in touch with a flavor that I cannot really anticipate because there is no real consistency from place to place? I smile, chuckle, and sigh, not knowing how to answer, not knowing how to make them understand. My mind drifts off to Rome, to the fact that in a city of three million people, there are only a handful of Chinese restaurants, one or two Japanese establishments, a few Indian, no Greek or even French ones that I know of (there must be some, I've just not heard anyone, since I've lived here, ever speak of them).

And yet when it comes to food, the Romans lack for nothing. In fact, the simple *cucina* of the city—its fresh, seasonal ingredients, perfectly prepared with techniques that have taken centuries to develop—is more satisfying on a day-to-day basis than the miscellaneous cooking that passes for the American variety at this point, or the vaunted, saucy French kind. (Mention French cuisine to a *romana,* and she will wave her hand and remind you that the French were still barbarians who ate with their fingers when Catherine de' Medici arrived in 1535 to marry the king, introduce the Renaissance, and teach the *francesi* how to cook at the same time.) Just give me a plate of delicious *risotto con zucca e piselli,* rice with pureed pumpkin and peas, or *spaghetti al pescatore* at Luna Piena in Testaccio; or *fettuccine* with tomatoes, basil, and *mozzarella* at Gran Sasso on Via di Ripetta near the Piazza del Popolo, where Mom cooks in her blue apron and slippers in full view of the diners, and her two sons deliver the food; or *linguine* with radicchio tomato sauce and a spot of cream at Le Grotte del Teatro di Pompeo near the Campo de' Fiori; or the *orecchiette* with broccoli or *fusilli* with eggplant at the charming Piccolo Arancio around the corner from the Trevi Fountain on the Vicolo Scanderbeg, where Mara, the friendly

redheaded owner, makes you feel right at home. The carpaccio
of octopus and the *zuppa di pesce* at Pierluigi are also divine. My
need for variety is more than satisfied by the various *antipasti* one
can eat for starters—cheeses, condiments, grilled vegetables of
every type or, if you choose, a smorgasbord of meats and seafood
(the *antipasti* at Grappolo d'Oro, also near the Campo de' Fiori,
is unparalleled), served with bread, followed by the *primo piatto*
or first dish, which usually consists of soup, pasta, or rice cooked
with your choice of tomatoes, every type of seafood, meat,
mushroom, or vegetable, depending on the season, the day of
the week, and what passes for the specialty of the house.

And if you can handle it, if you can still find room in your
stomach for more, after you've accompanied this delectable re-
past with wine and mineral water, you can then go to the *secondo
piatto* and order fresh fish or seafood, meat or chicken, accompanied by the *contorno,* a vegetable, salad, or potatoes. And just
when you think you will burst, when you swear you have in-
haled your last bite of food—ever—because, for all the quantity,
the taste has been so good, so flavorful, so incredibly strong and
delicate at the same time, your waiter will ask you if you care
for a *dolce,* a sweet, and you will first say, "No way," (*Macché!*)
and then, after a pause, "Well, what the heck, I have come this
far, I have already committed one of the seven deadly sins, that
of gluttony, so I might as well go all the way and preclude beyond a doubt the possibility that I might yet enter the gates of
heaven." In Roman *trattorie* there are few choices—usually *tir-
amisù, panna cotta,* and a *torta* or two—*mela, ricotta,* or *cioccolato.*
Of course, you can at this point still turn over a new leaf and
order a *macedonia*—a fruit salad, or a slice of pineapple or melon

in the summer, but it is easy to reject the temptation to withdraw from the ranks of the sinners and take up with the much less interesting saints, and so you order the *panna cotta,* cooked cream, with hot bittersweet chocolate poured over it, and swear you will never so much as think about food again.

You finish off the feast with a *caffè italiano,* a few drops of espresso that exists more for the taste and the experience than it does for the volume. (The coffee in Italy is much less caffeinated than its American counterpart, but most places now have decaf, ordered only by foreigners.) And if your host is a clever man, which he probably is, he will come over to your table carrying a bottle of *grappa* or *amaro* with which to wash your palate and help digest the food. You wave him off, but he pours a thimbleful in a small, elegant glass anyway and lets you know that the *digestivo* is on the house.

When you are ready, you must ask for the *conto.* It is the epitome of *brutta figura* to present the check to a diner who has not requested it, the polar opposite of some restaurants I've been to in San Francisco, where the *conto* is placed in front of you the moment you have laid down your fork after chewing the last morsel of food. You swear that they have prepared it for you in advance, that they have mental telepathy and knew what you were going to order even before you did. In Rome you can sit at the table till the cows come home, and they will never present the check until you ask for it, not even on a Saturday night or Sunday afternoon when every place is taken and others are waiting to get in. In Rome you never hurry a person who is eating, because even when he has finished course after course, he is usually nursing his *grappa,* lighting another cigarette, and talking animatedly with his friends or family. (The statistics are incon-trovertible—34 percent of men and 25 percent of women still smoke. The numbers are higher in the south, lower in the north, and it's difficult to find a nonsmoking establishment.)

And when you have finally had enough, when you know it is time to leave and you signal Mauro or Domenico that you are ready, and he puts down the folded piece of handwritten scribblings on your table, you will be shocked at what you must fork over to enjoy this once-in-a-lifetime experience, one that you can nevertheless avail yourself of anytime you cross the threshold of a Roman *trattoria*. If you've eaten it all, if you've ordered the *antipasto*, the first course, the second course, the *contorno*, managed to finish the *dolce*, had a *caffè*, consumed your fair share of *vino* and *acqua*, you are now—come on, guess, $50, $60, $70?—$35 lighter than you were before you crossed the portal of this particular bit of paradise that you can find on any ordinary street in Rome, including tip, tax, and cover charge, which are already calculated. (Beware of tourist traps—bad food and higher prices. You can usually spot them by the fact that the menu is in four languages.) What's more, you have eaten as you have never eaten before, like princes, pashas, and potentates of old, like the ancient Romans who feasted for days on end in between bouts of regurgitation brought on by skillful servants who knew just what to do with a feather. You leave a few thousand lire on the table—a *mancia*—just to acknowledge Carlo for having served you a meal that was everything you had hoped for—and more—and you stumble out into the soft, mysterious Mediterranean air wondering how you will ever again eat a tuna fish sandwich at the Gold Nugget Diner on the Miracle Mile in San Rafael, California.

In Rome you do not worship at the altar of the *trattoria* for the ambience, the decor, the snobbery, or the expense. You go for the food. *Trattorie* are simple, unadorned places, looking much the same as they did in 1953. No one will come to your table, introduce himself, and tell you that he will be your waiter that evening. Carlo will saunter over, not having shaven for two days, his ample belly stretching the fabric of his cotton polo shirt, a stained white towel slung over his shoulder, and ask what you want. If you request a menu, it will take him several minutes to find one, and then, when you have finally chosen, half the items will not be available. While he is still at your table trying to wheedle your order out of you, he will point his finger and direct his nephew Marco, telling him that the *bucatini all'amatriciana* (long spaghetti-like hollow straws of pasta, with tomatoes, hot pepper, and bits of *pancetta,* a kind of salty bacon, served with *pecorino,* not *parmigiano,* cheese) goes to the other table. When he asks you what you want to drink, you only have to say two things—*naturale* or *frizzante,* referring to the bottled water, and *rosso* or *bianco,* referring to the wine. The *vino* will arrive in a glass or ceramic carafe, corked. No one will pour a mouthful into your glass, put one hand behind his back while the other holds the bottle, and lean forward while you taste it and give your imprimatur, except perhaps at more upscale establishments like Alberto Ciarla and Checchino dal 1887. You wouldn't do that in your own home, would you?

Romans eat out to duplicate the experience of eating in, not to experience something new, exotic, or foreign. They have no need to try curried chicken or even something from some other part of Italy, like *pasta al pesto,* which comes from Liguria, or *seppie* and peas, which is a Venetian seafood dish. We are always

amazed at the communal way in which Romans eat in the restaurant, as if one of their own clan was doing the cooking in a
familiar kitchen and had carefully chosen what was about to be
served. Six, eight, ten people will arrive together and greet the
host as if he were their cousin. They are all dressed to the nines,
the women in hose and heels and dresses and scarves and
makeup. The clothes are freshly pressed and definitely *a stagione,*
with a look that matches their sister, daughter, or *nonna.* The
men are in jackets, sometimes suits and ties. The children look
like they are models for Benetton. The diners never hurry the
waiters, but the food arrives, huge plates of *antipasti,* firsts, and
seconds, from which the members of the party help themselves.
They all eat the same thing. They are the opposite of Americans,
who are individuals and want to be different from each other.
Italians are conformists and want to be just like the next person.

Until very recently, this family meal ritual was performed two
times a day, every day, at lunch and dinner. Breakfast as we
know it doesn't exist in Rome. If it is consumed out of the
house, as it often is, it is eaten in a coffee bar and consists of a
cappuccino and *cornetto,* a small sweet roll in the shape of a crois-
sant, only smaller and not as buttery. *Basta!* That's breakfast. I
have a friend named Mats Carlsson, from Stockholm, who came
here to work for a time and had a theory that in Europe, breakfast as we know it is eaten north of Brussels and skipped in all
points to the south. And my friend Ettore, the jazz drummer, a
batterista, who was born and grew up here, jokingly refers to the
Roman breakfast as a *caffè* and cigarette. I didn't laugh—I see it
all the time.

How can you eat at all at 8:00 A.M. when you didn't finish
dinner until well after 10:00 P.M. the night before, perhaps after

midnight in the summer, not having begun until 8:30 in the winter and later, much later, in July and August, when the days are hot and no one does *anything* between the hours of 1:00 and 7:00, much less cook. Not that everyone still eats a big meal two times a day. It's rarely done anymore, except among the elderly, who grew up that way and never gave up the habit, and even the *trattorie* have adjusted their expectations downward. When I first came to Rome and you set foot in a *trattoria,* you were expected to eat a first, a second, a *contorno,* and who knows what else. If you didn't want all that, you should have gone to a *tavola calda,* a hot table where there is a wide assortment of already prepared food, like the one we frequent, Cafe Notegen, founded in 1882, on Via Babuino near the Piazza del Popolo, or a bar, where you can pick up a *panino,* a sandwich, and be on your merry way.

The *trattoria* was for serious dining, not as expensive or upscale as a *ristorante* (where you can today easily spend twice what a meal costs in a *trattoria*), but, still, there were linen napkins and tablecloths, and serious, delectable, well-cooked food. Now, alas, those expectations are gone, thanks to the invasion over the years of foreign tourists with varying tastes and to the interest even on the part of the Italians not to eat as much as their parents do and their grandparents did. Although the prices of the first courses, the pasta and risotto courses, have gone up a bit since people stopped ordering the more expensive seconds, they are still a great value, and will fill you up and satisfy your desire for a sensual experience every time you sit down at the table.

We always wondered why Romans are not obese, why they can eat like they do and not show it (although they are not skinny, either). Now, having lived here, we know. It is because they are satisfied at every turn, at every meal, regardless of how much or how little they eat, whether it's a simple plate of *mozzarella*, bread, and fruit, a salad or *panino*, or a six-course affair that takes three hours to consume and transports you to another space-time dimension. Despite the fact that the city has been invaded of late by fast food, soft drinks, potato chips, and cheese puffs, mostly consumed by the young, more seasoned Romans simply have no desire to eat between meals, not when the ones they regularly prepare are so fulfilling.

Thank God eating is something you do every day, for in the temple of the Roman god of food, everyone is blessed, and no one walks away hungry.

11

La Famiglia:
Ties That Bind

As the years pass, old verities I once lived gradually fade away, like the worn-down yet illuminating frescoes at the Palazzo Massimo or the Church of the Santissimi Quattro Coronati. For example, the longer I live in Italy, the more I see the effort in America to promote and encourage "family values"—the idea that a strong family will in and of itself make a better country— as something romantic and futile. The reason is simple. It has to do with the inherent and inevitable conflict between loyalty to and preservation of the family on the one hand, and loyalty to and preservation of other ideals—economic freedom, individualism, patriotism—on the other. In this respect, the United States and Italy are at opposite poles. The world's only superpower constantly agonizes over what it means to be "American," whereas in Rome one hardly ever hears anything of significance that has to do with being "Italian." Loyalty in Rome does exist, but it is to *"la famiglia,"* which is the holy grail, the "the Lord, thy God," and will have no other gods before it. There really is no "Italy," because the common frame of reference is so much more intimate than that.

Romans don't need to talk about family values because they live them, personified in the oft-heard phrase, *tengo famiglia:* I keep a family. Here is a city with no nursing homes; where unmarried children commonly live with their parents well into their thirties and often forties; and where married children just starting out are given space within the bosom of the family seat or their own separate apartment somewhere close by that has been lying vacant for years, just waiting to be delivered to the *ragazza,* because tenant rights in this country are so strong and intractable that it is virtually impossible to evict a renter if he doesn't want to leave, resulting in the necessity of a lump sum settlement that can run into the tens or even hundreds of thousands of dollars. Why rent? Better leave the space free for the day—even years in the future—when it will be put to family use.

The apartment in which we live, now a condominium, is owned by the original *padrona* of the entire *palazzo,* a *principessa,* from a venerable Roman family. It was built in the early part of the century, and we are the first occupants who are not members of the family. Romans, in fact, love to rent to *stranieri* because people like us are used to paying higher rents, and we won't want to occupy their places for the next three generations. In our case, the daughter of our landlady has just moved to the Tuscan countryside near Siena, but wants to hold on to the option of returning to Rome when her sons are of high school age. Since Italians might not want ever to leave, renting to them is dangerous. We, on the other hand, are safe, i.e., law-abiding Americans who pay the rent on time and vacate when the lease is up.

In fact, Romans have such a strong attachment to family and

place that they end up owning property everywhere. The buying and selling of real estate in America is a vital part of the economy, and its sudden collapse would bring about an economic nightmare. In Rome property transfer is rare, as families seek to hold on to their familial patrimony and make it available as needed. And you don't have to be rich to make use of the *ville, palazzi,* and *appartamenti* available to the family. Our friend Pino, who organizes events every summer at the Spoleto Music Festival, is the son of a now-retired bus driver. But every August he, his wife Jo, their two school-age children, and his parents spend a month in their "summer home" in the hills of Le Marche, near Italy's Adriatic coast, which is the ancestral home of Pino's mother, who has lived in Rome for fifty years. Selling the place, aside from depriving themselves of an idyllic summer vacation, would be tantamount to erasing a part of one's very identity. When we decided to sell our house in Marin, which we had owned for all of eight years, our Roman friends thought we were getting rid of a place in which one of our family had resided for generations. They looked at us with total, uncomprehending incredulity. "You are selling your *casa,*" they said, a word that means not only house, not only home, but the actual *site* in which a family is based, rooted, tied, if possible, forever. Their incredulity had also to do with the buyers. Who would want to move into our place, become part of our identity, our past, and therefore our future? Finally, the *romani* also imagined that the result of the transaction would make us fabulously rich, that we would get to pocket the entire selling price, rather than the small fraction of that sum that actually accrued to us after the formidable mortgage was paid.

Family in Rome is the *cosa sacra,* the sacred thing, the bottom line. It trumps everything, even patriarchy. In a country notorious for its male chauvinism, which, when dissected, pertains by now to the work world, women keep their family names after marriage. No hyphens, no compounds, no legal changes. Thus, when Massimo Brozzi marries Susanna Negroni, both names appear on the intercom. Their child takes the name of *papà,* but how would Susanna's family feel if she gave up her name, and how is the rest of society going to know where she came from unless Negroni remains attached to her wherever she goes?

Rome, unlike America, is no melting pot. There are few people from elsewhere who come in and lend their particular ethnicity in ways that slowly but inevitably change the landscape. We are much closer to premodern here, where the tribe that lived on the hill 250 yards away lived in a world all its own. Take our friends Massimo and Susanna. The fact that we are friends at all is testimony to their unusual openness, at least for Romans. They travel. They have been to India—several times. They have in many ways broken the mold—Susanna, in fact, attended a French school here in Rome—but their living arrangement has *romano* written all over it. They live in a *villa* that sits at the very beginning of the ancient Via Appia, the Appian Way, opened in 312 B.C. to provide the Romans with a road that would first go south to Naples and then turn north to the Adriatic coast, the gateway to Greece and the eastern Mediterranean. The *villa,* built in the seventeenth century and purchased by Massimo's father, is called Horti Galateae, in honor of the statue of a maiden carved by Pygmalion, which then was given life by Aphrodite after he fell in love with it. In one section it houses Massimo, Susanna and their son; in another Massimo's sister Simona, her husband and son; and in a third Massimo's mother, the quintessential Italian mother-in-law who has a key to their apartment and doesn't hesitate to use it, much to the chagrin of Susanna. On the grounds, in a parklike setting with ancient Roman ruins mounted on the stone walls, are two other villas, available for weddings and corporate parties. Massimo's family also has a place *al mare,* which is rarely used.

Susanna's family is from Marino, in the Castelli Romani outside Rome, and she, too, has access to a place in the country and to another house at the sea, at the Maremma on the Tuscan coast. There they take their vacations, usually with her family. One day, as we were sitting on the terrace of the *villa,* overlooking the mountains and the sea, colorful tulips all around, Susanna was musing about spending the summer elsewhere to avoid the constant, inevitable enmeshment. Family is tied to *casa,* which is tied to place. Marriage is not only the union of two individuals, but above all of two families, who come together to hopefully produce a bond that is greater than the sum of the two parts.

Italians certainly don't come together primarily for love, at least not the kind of love that we in the Anglo-Saxon world would understand—the romantic kind, the kind that was born in France in the Middle Ages; the kind that speaks of troubadours and fair maidens and *Tristan et Iseult;* the kind that requires that you pledge your undying love to your one and only; the kind of love that combines passion, friendship, and domestic harmony in a kind of earthly yin-yang that resides in perfect resonance, a love of soul mates. For most Americans this ideal is something toward which to strive and aspire, and they feel bad and guilty when they inevitably fall short of the mark. The expectations of the Italians tend to be different. The males want to be pampered, well fed, and given free rein to play. The women expect to be the *capo della casa,* to run the household, and be able to express their emotions without restraint. Romans do not have a vision of marriage and family that was nourished at the cinematic breast of Hollywood. Theirs is rather closer to the European reality of not so long ago, when marriage was arranged and two people were lucky if they fell in love with each other. King Ferdinand of Naples, a member of the Bourbon family, did not see his betrothed, Princess Carolina of Austria, a Hapsburg, until the day of his wedding.

Although it is perfectly legal, divorce is lower here than in any other country in Europe, to say nothing of the stratospheric levels in the United States and the U.K. (In 1995, the United States, with five times the population of Italy, had *forty-three* times the number of divorces—1,169,000 to 27,000.) But this is not because Roman men and women are any more "in love" with their partners than in the north, or that the "death do us part" aspect of marriage impacts the feelings they may or may not have for their husbands or wives. It is because, to them, marriage is truly a vow, a contract, a commitment. A spouse is chosen because, all things considered, he or she would make a good partner for *familial,* rather than for personal, romantic, sentimental, or sexual, reasons, and to break up a family because a husband and wife do not have knockdown, drag-out sexual relations with one another, have had a fling, or even are involved with someone else, is considered just this side of madness. Our friend Franca Zambonini, who is one of the directors of the weekly newsmagazine *Famiglia Cristiana,* which is published by the Catholic Church, said that Romans used to laugh at Elizabeth Taylor because she had *"sei, sette, otto, non lo so, tanti mariti"* (six, seven, eight, I don't know, so many husbands). Having more than one husband is like having more than one mother.

This is why the Italians and the French could not find any part of themselves that understood how the president of the United States could nearly be removed from office for what he reluctantly admitted doing with someone not his wife. His taste in women might be questioned, as the Romans could not help but do, but never his right to have sentimental relations with whomever he chose, wherever he chose, under any circumstances, since it is his right to do whatever with whomever he chooses. These are strictly private matters. It was obvious that the president and the First Lady were together not because they couldn't keep their hands off each other, but because they were *"una famiglia,"* with a daughter who required both of them, and that their personal union was based strictly on political requirements—à la the Roosevelts and the Kennedys—and not on sexual attraction. You heard it constantly. Doesn't he, *doesn't she,* have the right to enjoy the pleasures of the flesh as much as the rest of us?

The statistics, which are as vivid and indisputable as the persimmon Roman ruins against the brilliant azure sky, back up the argument. When asked if they "betray" their partner, 70 percent of the coupled men responded yes, an indication of the fact that *gli uomini italiani* have never been and continue not to be a notoriously faithful lot. But the figure is almost matched by the women, whose positive response to the unfaithfulness question reaches 64 percent.

Talk about "family values." The religious Puritans in the United States would point to the depravity, the immorality, and the hypocrisy of the Romans, but what is really going on here is that marriage and family are not based on absolute notions of right and wrong, but on the fact that the family is sacrosanct, inviolate, unassailable, regardless of the sexual proclivities, arrangements, or partners a husband or wife may have. In fact, the "protection" of the family, the fact that so much of the psychic energy of an individual is invested in it—for the children, the parents, the grandparents, for economic and social survival, for respectability—gives free rein to what the Romans would call the natural sexual impulses that are held tightly in check in America, or when they are let loose, that produce mountains of guilt that both destroy families and create golden careers for therapists. When married or committed Americans "fool around," the relationship—which was based on moral and emotional absolutes—suffers the broken faith and trust, and more often than not, it ends in divorce and rampant recrimination. In Roman unions, everyone pretty much knows that they will last truly "until death do us part," so there is a kind of backhanded license to develop sentimental ties—if performed discreetly—outside the conjugal *camera da letto*. When the world first learned of the existence of Monica Lewinsky, and of the potential danger to Bill Clinton she then posed, Emanuela, a mother at our school, accosted me one day and asked if what was happening in the United States was "normal behavior." She then went on to say that if a guy is caught cheating here, the wife hits him on the head with a frying pan, tells him not to do it again, and domestic life continues. How can it be criminal behavior, and whose business is it but that of the individuals involved? Even for those who do choose to separate, the man almost always spends important holidays at home with his wife and kids.

Marriage makes the Romans powerful. It is first and foremost entry into society. The sexual part is separate, private, personal, not necessarily shared exclusively with one's spouse, but rather expressed as a function of one's particular erotic interests. A thirty-seven-year-old married woman who was interviewed recently about fidelity sums up the point of view. She opined that an occasional *"tradimentino,"* a small, insignificant betrayal, as only a *romana* could express it, was good for the marriage because it kept it fresh. To the Romans, vowing to be faithful and having only one partner might make sense if life expectancy were thirty-five years and people were together for the last fifteen of them. But when the ages that people reach extend into their seventies and even eighties, how can one expect two individuals never to stray when they could easily end up spending forty, fifty, or even sixty years together? Who would not confess to being interested in someone else, and even tempted to act on the impulse, with the prospect of such a long marital life in the offing? Why deny the pleasure, if it is conducted *sotto voce,* with discretion, tact, and, of course, taste? "Don't ask, don't tell," might be the policy of dealing with homosexuals in the American military, but it is also the age-old panacea, the secret of the long-lasting Italian union.

Strange things happen when an institution—in this case, the institution of marriage—rises up to dominate the life of a city, a country, a people, to such an extent that it forms the basis of society. The famous ability of the Romans to make the best of any situation—*arrangiarsi*—pops through like a wild, pale green weed that grows madly out of a crack in the stone wall of a two-thousand-year-old ruin. If you can't get around marriage, if you buy into it as a kind of necessary family obligation out of which you want the benefits but not the pain, then make love with whomever you want, stay married, and have no children. This is, in fact, what the Roman couple of today has apparently chosen, for Italy has the lowest birthrate of any country in the Western world, and perhaps in history: 1.2 children per woman, barely enough to replace the mother and nowhere close to replacing the couple. And it is dropping. In some places, like prosperous Bologna, it has dipped below one. By 2020 Italy will have more people over sixty-five than it will under twenty.

So while the family as an institution is revered and promoted, and while the species-saving impulse to be fruitful and multiply might be high on the agenda of the underdeveloped world, here in Italy, where men do not do housework, do not raise kids, do not get up to help with any kind of domestic chores, their spouses and partners, freed like their female counterparts all over the Western world from being second-class citizens, having attained the right to participate in whatever enterprise interests them, have responded in two ways—one, by delaying marriage and then not having children (or having one at most), thereby shedding forever the weight of domestic dependence, and two, by sleeping with whomever they want, since it is clear that they never got married primarily for love, but rather to fulfill the expectations of their family and the culture at large.

Modern Rome is a return to an ancient, pre-Christian past, before the God of Abraham and Moses, and then Jesus himself, infiltrated the Western world to spread the Gospel of guilt, renunciation, and expiation. If you want to see what life was like before the Emperor Constantine had a vision of the Madonna, was baptized, defeated Maxensius at the Battle of the Milvian Bridge, and then made Christianity the official religion of the empire in A.D. 313, come to Rome, a city so alive with erotic delight and possibility among people who are old enough not only to enjoy it but to do it well that even the Anglo-Saxon foreigners—much less overtly turned-on than their Roman counterparts—feel sexier, more attractive, more desired, and therefore desirable just knowing that the overwhelming number of people you pass and interact with on a daily basis can be persuaded to become someone else's lover, and are, in fact, conceptually open to the idea even while they are slipping the plain gold band on the fourth finger of the man or woman standing next to them, with the priest, at the altar, *in chiesa.*

12

Santa Pazienza: The Art of Waiting, a Metropolitan Pastime

I am having a *mattinata romana,* a Roman morning. Nothing is working. I'm out of kilter. When my father-in-law, who is in his seventies, can't remember a basic bit of information in the first instant he wants to recall it, he often says, "Oy, I'm having a senior moment." Well, when you run around the city trying to get something done, and you're in a hurry because you have to get something else done, or be at a certain place, and you want things to go smoothly, they often don't. At some point, you consciously have to tell yourself that you're no longer in the United States—where if you're lucky and you have the intention, you can accomplish in one day what many Romans get done in a month—and realize that you are having a *mattinata romana.*

It goes something like this. The first thing I must do, before ten o'clock because I am meeting a group of people for a four-hour guided tour of the Vatican Museums and cannot be late—these are North Americans; the tour must start on time—is find a certain piano book for Elliott, who has only the evening before begun his career as a *pianista,* having taken his first lesson at the home of *il maestro* of piano who shares the same *appartamento* as Martin Biggs, *il maestro* for violin. Danilo Manto is from Palermo and sort of resembles our son—diminutive, adorable, lively, cuddly. Watching the two of them sit side by side on the piano bench as Elliott plunked DEC DEC DEF E DEC made everyone's face light up—mine, Diane's, Julian's, and Danilo's—but especially Elliott's. He is a natural. *"Un genio, un genio"*—"a genius, a genius"—Danilo cries out in his effervescent, make-you-feel-good manner, as our *prodigio* is finishing. But now comes the work. Elliott must practice, and, of course, he needs a book. Danilo gives me the information as Martin and Julian take out their *violini*. Elliott's appetite is in full gear as he sits down with Diane and Danilo to indulge in some *panini* we brought in from the Silvano bakery, a ritual we all enjoy. I instead go off to Piazza Venezia, a twenty-minute walk to a large music store where I will certainly be able to procure the slim volume called *Me and My Piano* so that Elliott can begin practicing the very next day on the piano of Denise across the hall, who is also one of Danilo's pupils. Then, after a week or two, if it's clear that Elliott will stick with it, we will rent our own piano. "Ees a gud plan, *si, si"* Danilo says, *"tutto a posto,"* giving his stamp of approval in his usual mixture of English and Italian.

As I walk in the particularly cold air toward the geographical center of the city, the atmosphere on the streets is palpable. It's an ordinary weekday evening at the beginning of February in Rome, but to these American eyes it looks like Times Square on New Year's Eve, an event I experienced just once, almost thirty years ago. The sidewalks are teeming with people, traffic takes up practically every square centimeter of space, inching slowly toward and away from Largo Argentina, a large piazza where the ruins of four ancient temples from the sixth to the second centuries B.C. sit below street level as old orange and new green buses, taxis, cars, *motorini,* and people circle madly around it. Lights are everywhere, illuminating the stores, bars, streets, and the Teatro Argentina, built in 1731 on the site of Pompey's theater, where Caesar was murdered, right in the square. The pulse is unmistakable. It throbs, breathes, pumps life into the otherwise dead building materials that date back to the Iron Age. There is one hour remaining in the daily evening shopping routine, before the shutters and metal grates will be drawn and all of Rome will retreat behind closed doors—their own and those of the *trattorie e pizzerie*—for *cena,* dinner.

By now I have reached Ricordi, the formidable music store at Piazza Venezia. They have the book, but somehow it doesn't quite look the same. The songs inside are elementary enough, but I am unsure. The title is correct, but it lacks the appendage "Part One." The salesgirl assures me that it is correct, that there is no other known to her. I hop on the 64 to return to the *casa di musica* and can tell immediately by the look on Danilo's face that I have the wrong book. He says that eventually Elliott will have use for it, but still our son is without what he needs. Perhaps I can get it the next morning, as there are other music stores near the Vatican.

Diane and I take a quick *caffè* as the day begins. The weather has been ten degrees colder than usual, with daytime temperatures consistently in the forties, and our bar has long since removed the outdoor tables and seats from the sidewalk, so we stand inside in the coffee-induced aromatic warmth, spending the usual five minutes on breakfast. Diane and I place our order with the gracious *barista* Gianni. *"Il solito, per favore,"* the usual, please. One by one, our neighbors from the *palazzo* filter in, and we exchange a few words of greeting and updates. The rich brew goes down easily, as it nearly always does. We scan the patrons for the latest winter fashions. Velvet coats with fake fur around the hoods, collars, and sleeves, high black suede boots that fit tight around the foot, ankle, and calf, and hats that cover only the tops of heads, long, flowing manes spilling out every-where, moving sinuously. Heads are turning every which way as the women attached to these "looks" greet friends, acquain-tances, passersby, and even strangers. They enter, utter a word or two, and seamlessly begin a conversation, as the *bariste* prepare the *caffè, cappuccini, e caffè macchiati,* place them on the bar, and join in the simple human exchange for a moment or two before the exigencies of their profession require them to be elsewhere. They flit off, come back, and rejoin the repartee, all the while calling out orders to their colleague who stands squarely before the huge espresso machine, putting out custom-made coffee for each patron's particular desire.

The 23 bus will drop me off near the Vatican directly in front of MusicArte, the store that is my destination. I run to catch it as everyone already on board watches me, knowing beyond any doubt that I am not *romano.* To them, being late is the better option. I get a seat on the right side and gaze at the receding *palazzi,* piled up on one another like so many pastel-colored stucco Legos—the rusty pinks, sun-cracked yellows, rich corals—coming alive against the *celeste* winter sky. Every alley, every winding passageway that moves away from the river and dis-appears into the tangled maze of the *centro storico* greets me as I pass. The burnt orange rooftop *terrazze* whiz by, and now and then a woman—some old, some young, some with a cigarette, some talking, some silent—is leaning out her open shutters to take in the action on the street below. The bus must take a detour, as an eight-hundred-space parking lot is being constructed under the Gianicolo Hill to accommodate the Jubilee and traffic is being rerouted crazily, in every direction. I know I am close to where I need to go, but I lose the scent of Via Fabio Massimo, and my instinct tells me that I have passed it.

I ask a bike messenger, and he confirms my suspicion. But I am not far. I check my watch: 9:20. Plenty of time to find MusicArte, buy the book, and meet the other *americani* at the Vatican. I reach the store. The grate is down. I check the hours. It will open at 9:30. *Non c'è problema.* The street has five or six bars to choose from, and the one I select is dark and cozy. By the time I order and drink my second *caffè* of the day, the store will be open. The *barista* bids me a *buona giornata,* and I stroll out into the startling daylight. At 9:30 the store is still closed. I wander across the street. I need stamps, so I go into the *tabaccheria,* but the line is too long, and I can see as I look across the street that the grate has been lifted.

MusicArte does not have the book. Upon request, the employee directs me to another store, a different branch of Ricordi. If I hurry, I can make it there and still be at the Vatican at 10:00. If I can't buy the book this morning, the stores will be closed for siesta when I am finished looking at the Raphael rooms, the Sistine Chapel, the tapestry room, the map room, and all the other treasures contained within the smallest state in the world, and I will have to make a special trip back. I reach Ricordi. Its shelves are filled with teaching books for musical instruments, but they lack the one I need. I must give up not only the notion of getting the book this morning, but of even knowing where to get it, as the places recommended to me by Danilo have not proven out.

The Vatican Museums are incredible. It is perhaps the least crowded I have ever seen them, except for the first time, in 1981, when I was given a private tour by someone who worked there as a guide and had the pull to carry it off. The Nicolina Chapel is a revelation. Recently restored, its small size having the effect of enclosing you within the comforting hands of God, it tells the story of San Lorenzo in gorgeous frescoed detail, while the luminous blue of the ceiling, the heavenly color that covers your head with soothing clarity, was done by Fra Angelico. The grand proportions, each fresco telling its own tale, so intact, surviving centuries, has the effect of making me put my seemingly short life in perspective. Did these painters and sculptors become the artists we know today because they were driven, or was it that they were merely blessed by the angel of Santa Pazienza? Are they great because they were obviously more talented, or because they were able to endure disappointment, heartbreak, and failure, without ever giving up or losing faith in themselves and their creations?

Returning home, I am taken out of my reverie and put back into my simple familial responsibilities. I am still faced with the fact that Elliott lacks his first piano book. I pick up the yellow pages and call store after music store, but am repeatedly rebuffed. No one has the book. At first I try to avoid calling stores that are located in another section of Rome, but my search broadens, of necessity. Finally, I speak to someone who is at least willing to help me. He says that although he doesn't have the book, if I stop by we can call the warehouse together and see if it is in stock. If so, it will take two, three days to obtain. If not, then two or three months. I chuckle and tell him that the first wait is acceptable, the second not. I ask if he would be willing to call the warehouse, and again he tells me he would if I came into the store. I explain the problem. I live in the Aventino, I say, and your store is in the Parioli, on the other side of town. He gets it. He probably cannot conceive of anyone finding his shop through the yellow pages and just assumed that I lived in the neighborhood. He says he will call the warehouse if I fax him the information, which I immediately do. For the moment it is my only option.

When we return home later that evening and listen to our messages, there is one from the store. As soon as I hear the word, *"purtroppo,"* unfortunately, I know the news is not good. The warehouse does not have the book, so we are back to square one. When we pick him up from school, Elliott asks if he can go next door to Denise's to practice on her piano, and I tell him that we have to wait because I haven't yet found the book. He looks at me, shakes his head, and finally says, "You know, Poppi, you better get it soon, because I don't really want to practice on the weekend." Already the temperamental *artiste*.

I decide to be Roman about this and to forget about the book for the moment. The crush of the rest of my life takes over. A day goes by, another, and Elliott, we can tell, is feeling a little dejected. The weekend is approaching and still no book. We tell him that we might have to wait till Tuesday when we go back for his second lesson.

Our discussion is interrupted by the doorbell, which indicates that the visitor is local, within the boundaries of the *palazzo*. It is Denise, just returned from her weekly jaunt to the center for her lesson with Danilo. In her hand is the book, *the* book.

"Danilo told me to give this to you," she says. "It's for Elliott."
We call our son to the door, who from the look on his face
thinks that a miracle has just taken place.

In Rome the verses are many, but the song remains the same.
Patience is the key, not only to artistic endeavor, but to life itself.
It's an aspect of faith. You do what you can, practice your craft,
try your best, and let God or fate or happenstance determine the
rest. Ultimately, if you're willing to wait for things, the world
is yours.

13

Functional Anarchy: Who's in Charge of This Meeting?

I could tell something was up as soon as I reached the school, because the customary little clusters of parents huddled together talking to one another seemed to exude a more intense air than usual. Seeing them sometimes reminds me of the Renaissance portraits of the Florentines, intriguing all the way, clustered in groups in the Piazza della Signoria, where the Uffizi Galleries are, deciding the fate of one of their own, or calling in a loan that had long since gone bad and now the time having come to do something about it.

Although these groups of *mamme e papà* were without the historical prop of a famous Florentine gathering place, the garden of the *villa* that houses the school would do nevertheless. And there, amid the tall pines and oaks, bushes and playground climbing structures, they were plotting. As soon as she saw me, Emanuela, the class "representative," the liaison among the administration, the faculty, and parents, peeled off to inform me of the news. Diane and I are not usually part of the everyday discussions among the *genitori,* the parents, not so much because we don't speak the language as well as the others, but because our son came to the class in the third grade, and by that time, since these kids, along with the teachers, had already been together five years, all the relationships had been set. So, together with our foreignness, our lack of a common culture and relative newness have served most of the time to marginalize us.

But now we are needed, and Emanuela leans in close to my face and says, "There will be a meeting, Friday, 5:00." I need no further information. I know exactly what she is talking about. I say *va bene,* and she moves on to another group, to find out if there is any scuttlebutt that she missed in the seconds she spent with me. Information is Emanuela's stock in trade.

At the meeting we will discuss the problem of *"dopo scuola,"* the afterschool program. Enduring the many twists and turns of this situation tells me all I need to know about Rome and the Italians: how they think, how they plan, how they organize, how they identify villains, how they resolve matters. Until very recently, most Italian schoolchildren finished their day at one or one-thirty in the afternoon, six days a week. It is only in the recent past, as more mothers began to work outside the home and close relatives were not always at hand and available that schedules were changed and classes formed that offer the option for kids to stay at school all day. Our school a few years back opted for no classes on Saturdays, instead extending the school day two days during the week. But that left three days during which the kids were free at one-thirty. So they implemented a *tempo pieno,* a full-time program, but limited it to only one class, which filled up quickly and was therefore not available to most families. Then came *dopo scuola,* a program funded and staffed by the Comune of Roma, rather than the state of Italy, to watch the kids during the other afternoons while they ate lunch, played

111

in the *giardino,* and did their homework. During his first year at school, Julian loved *dopo scuola,* and especially his Maestra Maria, who was experienced and patient and wise, and had the respect of the kids.

Two weeks before the end of the school year, in June, we heard rumblings that there was no longer any money on the part of the municipality to fund *dopo scuola,* that it would end, and that parents would have to organize a new program themselves. A rally was called for in front of Rome's city hall, on Michelangelo's Campidoglio, but it was sparsely attended as parents were already beginning to think of their summer hiatus. *"Non ti preoccupare,"* "Don't worry," they assured one another, "they always talk like this in June, but in September they always seem to find a solution." But this September was different. They didn't find the funds, there was no *dopo scuola,* and three days a week for the first, second, and third weeks of school, our kids were around us more than we—and they—would have chosen. After the three-month summer break, our sons wanted a regular routine as much as we did, especially since Diane has a counseling practice and we both work at home. Thus we are around all the time, and it is convenient when they see one of us to ask to play Uno, or kick around the soccer ball, or cut open an apple—the kind of little requests that, when multiplied, drive parents over the edge. September was already turning into October, yet it seemed as though the kids were still on summer vacation.

At five o'clock on the day of the meeting, I am one of the only ones present, leading me to think, as I have done many times before, that there would be few in attendance. Once again I am wrong. By five-fifteen the room is filling up, as streams of parents solemnly come in, take seats, and caucus among themselves. Two sets of parents sit at the head of the class as the room is now lined all around the edges with people eager to know what will unfold, but even more intent on expressing their frustrations with the schools, their kids, and with life in general. The leaders have barely begun to introduce themselves and put forth their idea to organize a cooperative among the interested parents to privately fund the activities of *dopo scuola* when they are drowned out in a tidal wave of voices coming from every direction, which engulfs and overwhelms them. For three solid minutes, parents shout comments, evaluations, and instructions at them, hold private meetings directly on the floor, argue with one another across the room, the decibel level rising by the moment, the scene resembling nothing so much as the trading room of the Chicago futures market.

I cannot avert my eyes from the faces of the organizers, looking out over the sea of anger and frustration, knowing they are powerless to stop the venting, waiting for it to spend itself in order that they may continue with the meeting and their proposal, which we had still not yet heard. Suddenly, almost on cue, everyone seems to calm down, and the *capi* continue, explaining patiently, eloquently, cogently, that the SPQR, the municipal government, allocates its resources according to need, and there are schools on the *periferia,* the code name for "bad" neighborhood, like ghetto in America, that have greater need than we do in the wonderful Aventino.

The patient explanation produces the opposite effect. The mere mention of the political dimension of their problem sends the group into another round of shouting and gesticulating, their bodies and faces leaning forward as if to reinforce the point physically, as if they could bring the situation to a desired end if they could only get their hands and torsos on it. Their comments range all across the board. *"È troppo caro,"* "It's too expensive," "It's not expensive enough," "Last year my son's *dopo scuola* teacher didn't help him with his homework," "My daughter doesn't like the food," "I'm not paying fifty thousand lire a month if they don't have any organized activities, just to play *in giardino,"* "Give us some alternatives, at least."

My biggest fear is that the organizers, who are themselves only parents, who are not in any way to blame for the situation, and who are the only ones doing any real work, will suddenly say, *"Vaffanculo,"* essentially "Fuck off," and walk out, leaving the problem unresolved and all of us to contemplate a full year of school with our kids at home at one-thirty in the afternoon three days a week. But no, they are saints. They hang in there, making no move to vacate.

One of them is beginning to plead for order. In fact, she is beginning to plead for everything. I notice that every sentence, when she can be heard at all, starts with the words, *"Vi prego,"* "I beg of you." Finally, the parents begin to realize that what the organizers have proposed is the only plan that will work. The cooperative will legally constitute the association, hire the teachers, deal with the authorities over the use of the school building, set the rules, collect the money, keep track of the enrollments, deal with complaints, and essentially do all the things that must be done to keep 150 or so elementary school kids fed, educated, occupied, and happy.

Even as the situation diffuses, I find I don't understand anything. The language part is comprehensible to me, but the cultural part makes no sense. The *capi* are angels, saviors, heroes, yet no one is thanking them, applauding them, lifting them up on their shoulders in a display of gratitude after their assiduous efforts. Instead of congratulating them, which is what I feel like doing, the others are pillorying them for having had the guts to organize this motley group and present a coherent plan. I notice that the meeting, which has now lasted for more than an hour, has a certain rhythm that follows a regular course: five minutes of serious, if intense, discussion, followed by five minutes of free-for-all chaos, everybody talking at once, shouting louder and louder, people buttonholing their neighbors in a kind of "can you believe this?" mode, exuding disgust not at the organizers, but at the fact that this meeting is being held at all.

Italians do not have the natural instinct to turn to private enterprise to solve problems. The Family, the Church, and the State have always been there, and it strikes them as a kind of comedown, a failure of sorts, that they would have to form a private company to take care of something so basic to life as educating and diverting their children. This is the source of their outrage, their displeasure, their sense of betrayal. Really what they are expressing is their disappointment in the knowledge that the old way of life, the life they grew up with and once counted on, is vanishing. No longer can they rely on the old institutions to take care of them and their children. They now realize that they must take care of themselves, and they are pounding their fists in frustration that they have to pay for something that in their minds is a right, and should be free.

A mother, hair dyed blond, small, yet intense and powerful, can be heard above the din, *"PER FAVORE, PER FAVORE, SIGNORI, UNA PERSONA PER VOLTA,"* "Please, please, ladies and gentlemen, one person at a time." For the moment, she is heard, and the organizers move on to the final point of their agenda. It is time for the vote, which will decide once and for all the fate of the proposal. This prompts my friend and fellow father Manlio, who is standing next to me at the back of the room, to shout in his booming, basso voice, *"Se non mangia la minestra, salta dalla finestra,"* translated literally as "If you don't eat the soup, jump out the window," basically expressing the view that the organizers have presented us with a *fait accompli*. What choice have we? While I'm still thanking God that he has created these four brave, intelligent, dedicated souls, I'm now worried that the vote will be close, and might even go the other way. Then what? Will we be back at square one, and will the summer vacation of 1998 go down in history as the longest ever, the one that never ended?

By now I can see that the parents have had enough. We have been together a long time. The tension, which was so heavy just fifteen minutes earlier, is now beginning to dissipate, as these modern-day Roman parents—having had an opportunity to vent and having taken advantage of it, who just moments before were literally at each other's throats, turning around to argue with their counterparts in the back of the room, shouts of *"Che vergogna, che scemo,"* "What shame, what silliness," ringing off the blackboard and windows, have now been transformed from Mr. Hydes into Dr. Jekylls. They are smiling, laughing, kissing cheeks, holding elbows, obviously in group delight as the thought of *cena* and the weekend begin to filter into their lovely heads. I can barely hear what the Four Horsemen at the front are saying, but suddenly I look around and see every single hand in the room raised upward, as if they wanted to let God himself know that they were in favor. The smiles on the faces of the *capi di tutti i capi*—the bosses of all bosses, the organizers—are the only verifiable indications I have that the vote has gone well. Amid the noise, the confusion, the complete lack of Anglo-Saxon respect and order, I realize that the vote has always been an accomplished fact, that the meeting could have taken five minutes and would have taken that long in Stockholm, Amsterdam, or Minneapolis, but here, in the heart of the ancient empire, among people who live not out of their heads but their hearts, the opportunity to vent can never be passed up.

I ask Manlio if they know when the new *dopo scuola* will start, my thoughts racing ahead to perhaps Halloween at the earliest, Christmas at the latest. What he tells me could not be sweeter. *"Lunedì,"* he says. *"Questo lunedì?"* "This Monday?" I ask, incredulous. *"Sì, penso di sì."* "Yes, I think so." I am jubilant, relieved that seventy-five thousand lire (the second child pays only half, the third, if we had one, would attend free), forty-five dollars a month for both my sons, will solve the problem and cancel out my throbbing head and sweating armpits at the same time.

As I leave the school grounds, the air is sweet and mild. The bells of the nearby church begin to chime, as they have done for close to a thousand years. The twilight is perfect, the reddish pink sky in the west setting off the darker blue directly above it. In a few minutes my feet will have carried me home, and already my headache is beginning to subside as I pass the usual clump. A dozen men—past their prime, their parked cars all askew, left every which way in the piazza—are engaged in their daily ritual of card playing on top of a car trunk directly under a street lamp. They have spread a mauve velvet cloth that itself looks like it had been passed down from Siena in the fifteenth century, and their deck consists of Neapolitan cards, the meaning of which, of course, eludes me. It is hard to imagine a group of middle-aged men happier anywhere else in the world. They joke, laugh, rear back, drag on their cigarettes, and kid each other between discards, whiling away the time before *cena,* when their freshly prepared evening meal will be waiting for them. The insouciant merriment is a ritual they probably learned from their fathers, who, of course, saw *nonno* doing the very same thing.

My passage, just three feet from them, barely elicits a glance, an acknowledgment. They have nothing to hide. There is no shame, no guilt, no effort to conceal their pleasure. My mind returns briefly to the meeting, and I wonder whether the mothers and fathers of these characters ever had to organize a private cooperative to make sure they were taken care of at school, whether they even went to school, or if they did, for how many years. The world is changing, even in *la città eterna, bella Roma.*

14

Che Bello! *Children Should Be Seen—and Heard*

Just one more leg and the long airplane ride would be over. Within hours we'd be back in California with the kids, having completed yet another Italian trip that only confirmed that our dream to one day live in the *bel paese* was alive and worth pursuing. We had taken off from Fiumicino outside Rome and picked up the boys, who were then one and four, at the airport in Philadelphia, where they had stayed for two weeks with my parents.

Everything we had seen in Italy, regardless of city, province, or region, had demonstrated to us that children were the most adored commodities of the community. It was unmistakable. Even on our last day in Rome, as we were once again searching for the perfect *trattoria* to have our final meal before having to leave the land of *mangiare,* we witnessed a brief episode on the street that would have been unimaginable in the culture to which we were returning. Two scruffy skinheads, a rarity in Rome, were walking toward us in full regalia—black leather, Doc Martens, Mohawks, nose rings, other face metal sticking out at odd angles. In front of us, moving in the same direction, was an elegant grandmother—hair tinted and coiffed, *tailleur a stagione*—wheeling a small child in a stroller so pristine it looked like it had been bought just the day before. Not only did *la nonna* not flinch at the sight of what seemed to us potential difficulty, let alone danger, she kept walking straight ahead as the moment of encounter with the two semidesirables approached.

Diane and I held our breaths, as it seemed like the adolescents were about to make some kind of move toward the small child. We were perhaps three feet behind as the skinheads suddenly broke into huge smiles, leaned down to ruffle the thick brown hair of the *ragazzino,* and said at the same time: *"Che bello!"* The grandmother smiled as she moved on, obviously proud that her little *tesoro,* her treasure, had elicited the approval of her young countrymen, even if to us they seemed like an unsavory duo.

The image of this scene was still at the forefront of my mind as we took our seats on the plane in Philadelphia at 10:30 P.M. to return to San Francisco. All I could think about was going back to live in Italia. How could we do it? Could we do it? When could we do it? What would we do for income? Could we sell the business? How fast could Diane learn the language? Was this dream really possible?

It had been on my agenda for years, ever since I first came to Rome in the early eighties. As a graduate student in London in 1975, I relished my first taste of the cosmopolitan street life of a European big city, but the grayness of the northern capitals didn't please me. Paris was beautiful and romantic and seemed out of my reach. I had not been a great student of French, and the Parisians seemed to be traveling in different circles from the ones I normally frequented. Talk about intimidation. Over the years they have become much mellower, as they finally realized that the almighty dollar was almighty even in France. Their graciousness toward strangers has much improved, but back in the seventies, that didn't seem to be part of the culture. A small anecdote illustrates this difference between the French and the Italians. When President Khatami of Iran, in the first visit to a Western capital in twenty years, chose Italy, the Italians agreed to keep wine and other alcohol off the tables of the state dinner, stowing the bottles in a hidden corner of the banquet room. In the same situation, in Khatami's second Western visit, the French refused the request, and the trip was canceled.

It was only when I got to Rome that I realized that I had found my "spot," to use Don Juan's famous expression from the Carlos Casteneda books. Rome had characteristics that I felt were hard to come by in London and Paris—warmth, passion, fantastic, affordable food you could eat every day, great conversation, and treasures displayed before your eyes rather than neatly catalogued in museums—and yet it partook of the same Europeanness that was evident in the northern capitals. I was hooked. I never wanted to leave, and when I did, I thought constantly about returning.

Now, a dozen years later, married and with two small children, a successful first book, two more in the making, an *Oprah* appearance under my belt, and the years inexorably ticking by, I was sitting on the runway in Philadelphia trying to come up with a scenario that would get us to Italy. A four-month honeymoon in 1987 with Diane—whose parents had a time-share in a farmhouse outside Rome in the countryside, which acted as a base from which we explored the Continent, but mostly Italy—did nothing to slake my thirst to spend days and nights walking the streets of the Eternal City. The day I returned to San Francisco from that trip, six years before, was one of the saddest of my life. I had had to leave behind my beloved *città*. But there was also the joy of knowing that I would one day return and forever be with her.

As the ten-minute delay turned into fifteen and then twenty, our one-year-old Elliott began to protest. It was now 11:00 P.M. and everyone was tired, eager to get going. We knew that as soon as the engines revved and we took off, Elliott would fall asleep and stay that way for the rest of the trip. But while we idled in the darkness, he whimpered, not loudly, not aggressively, just steadily. As we waited, his whimpering began to upset the bored, tense, unrecovered equilibrium of the passengers seated around us. While no one came out and said anything directly, we could feel the "vibe" and hear the grumbling under their breath. Their body language was unambiguous. "Can't you shut that kid up?" accurately sums up the prevailing sentiment. The seat belt sign was lit, Elliott was snuggled up in his car seat, and we felt like aliens who were just returning from a completely different planet. Diane tried to explain to someone close by that he would fall asleep as soon as we took off, but our seatmates were not placated. We had just left the land of child indulgence—where every kid is *coccolato,* cuddled, coddled, and cooed at—and entered the universe where children should be seen and not heard.

Suddenly, the passenger sitting directly in front of Elliott, a woman, turned in her seat, got up, leaned over him, a demonic grin on her face, and hysterically shook a set of keys at him, which only, as one might imagine, made the situation worse. No one offered consolation. Not one person murmured "poor baby" or any kind of encouragement for his shell-shocked and tired parents. We were all stuck in a game with no winners, as the passengers could not accept the fact that they were being forced to travel with a small child. In their tired, restless, upset state, they wanted us to do something that we did not have the power to do. We could not pilot the plane. When we took off, moments later, Elliott fell asleep immediately and did not utter a peep for the rest of the six-hour trip. As we later disembarked in San Francisco, no one said a word.

Children in Rome, in Italy, are anything but a nuisance. They are a resource, a reflection, a national, cherished treasure. I could fill the rest of the pages of this book with stories describing how children not only belong to their parents, but to the community as well. They are an unmixed blessing, a benefit that everyone participates in tending. Two years after that unpleasant plane ride, we had thrown the dice, sacrificed all, and had moved to Italy. I was once again with Elliott, now three, at a bar in Frascati, a quaint, yet hopping village surrounded by vineyards in the Castelli Romani, the area in which we first lived before trading small-town life outside Rome for the city itself. Elliott was tired and thirsty and perhaps coming down with a cold that day. I spotted a table outside in the still-warm October air, and as there was no service at the table, I had to go into the bar, perhaps ten feet away, to order the few small items we wanted. I hesitated. Should I take Elliott with me? Should I leave him? He clearly didn't want to get up. He was perfectly content to sit outside basking in the sun while I would be away for a few minutes. In the States, of course, I would not have hesitated, not even for a moment—he would have accompanied me to the bar and then back to the table, if it was still free—but in Italy it seemed almost absurd to think that I could *not* leave him. People were continually passing by, and I could peek out every ten seconds to make sure he was OK. I then asked a well-dressed couple sitting next to me with their *caffè* long since taken if they would mind watching my son while I went to get something in the bar. *"Per carità, volontieri,"* was the reply, "Gladly, willingly." *"Non si preoccupi."*

I rushed into the bar and hurried back with a *cappuccino,* orange juice and two *cornetti,* only to find Elliott on the lap of the *signore,* playing with some small toy the man had managed to fish out of his pocket. The *signora* assured me that Elliott had been *bravo, bravissimo,* patiently explaining everything he had said and done during the three minutes that I had been gone. I thanked them profusely, but they waved it away, oblivious to the fact that to me, what I had just participated in was a scene from some version of parent paradise, where strangers you meet at the next table in a bar in a beautiful small town in Italy watch your kids and enjoy themselves at the same time. The event triggered a conversation between me and them about what we were doing in Italy, and, of course, they were both delighted and amazed to hear of an American family's decision to leave California—paradise in their minds, *"il mio sogno,"* my dream— and come to their country, *by choice,* to live and write and raise children.

Italy is kid heaven. Kids feel it. They know they are adored, protected, and pampered, not only by their parents and grandparents and aunts and cousins, but by everyone. The other day in a nearby *tabaccheria,* which sells the kind of things we used to buy at the local candy store when we were kids in Philadelphia, my guys were eyeing a sponge soccer ball and were having difficulty deciding between the red and the blue one. Back and forth, back and forth they went, as the man serving us went reaching into the counter twice while the kids changed their mind yet another time. The process exasperated me, as I am often witness to the intricate, sometimes tug-of-war, sometimes negotiations, between them to see who goes first, whether a shot was a goal or had hit the post, et cetera. In order to show some kind of sympathy with the elderly man, I said I was sorry, and mistakenly used the word *"pazzi,"* crazy, to describe them. His rebuke was swift and decisive. *"Non sono pazzi,"* he said, "They're not crazy," *"sono bambini,"* "they're kids," as if that was all he needed to say and that by this time I should know better. I got the sense that we could have stayed an extra twenty minutes deciding between the red one and the blue one, and it wouldn't have mattered a lick to him.

Children in Rome are indulged, spoiled, adored, and fussed over. They are treated like royalty. Since there are so few of them, the competition for their affection is great, unrelenting, all-encompassing. Our friend Paolo, who has a restaurant, says that Sundays, when huge extended families come in with three, four, five, six kids, are the worst. The kids run around constantly, and the parents, after a few brief, halfhearted, and unsuccessful attempts to control them, return to their plates, their cigarettes, and their conversation. The scene can often turn into almost mayhem, but an attempt on the part of Paolo and the management to impose order is useless—and even counterproductive. He says that if you say anything to the parents about keeping their kids in line, the families will walk out of the restaurant—*without paying*—and never come back. No one can afford to say anything. Basic training for any waiter in Rome is the ability to hold the plates level while they swing the lower parts of their bodies in this direction and that to avoid being hit by a four-year-old in full stride. When we go to a *trattoria,* we expect our boys to be mannerly, stay seated, eat well, and join in conversation. When we have gone out with Italian families with small children, the only expectation is that they return occasionally to the table for a bite or two, often shoveled in by *mamma.*

To Romans—with the possible exception of the teachers, who seem to have been assigned the role of community disciplinarians and who have a hard time carrying out these duties—children are the *innocenti,* in contrast to adults, who are the *peccatori,* the sinners. The Italian love of children comes out of the recognition that they are not like us, that they still exist in a state of grace that enables them to skip out on responsibilities and consequences. There is plenty of time for that, Roman parents say. They will eventually learn what it is like to be an adult, with faults and frailties. Why not indulge their innocence, why not enable them to experience the full panoply of childlike delight before the onslaught of reality makes its presence felt and introduces them to the complications and compromises, the disillusions and disappointments, that inevitably take over one's life and cling to it like ivy that spills over and covers up ancient stone facings. To deprive them of the state of sanctity in childhood strikes the Romans as cruel, perverse, severe, *troppo duro,* too strict. "Sure, *tesoro,* go ahead and stay up night after night in the summer, till eleven, twelve, one o'clock; you don't have to get up in the morning." "You want *biscotti al cioccolato* for breakfast, *amore mio*? OK, have chocolate cookies, but make sure you have a healthy *pranzo*." There was a scene in a recent movie where a woman, who was dropping off her four-year-old daughter at her mother's house in order to meet her lover, tells *nonna* that she doesn't want the daughter watching television. *"Sì, sì, cara,"* she says, *"non ti preoccupare."* The moment the door closes behind *la mamma, nonna* turns to her granddaughter, and, with a big smile, says, "Now, what do you want to watch?" a line that drew laughter from the audience, indicating knowing recognition—of both roles.

The desire to provide whatever pleasure kids sometimes want even compromises their safety, as you often see one or two bambini on the front and back of a *motorino* with *mamma or papà,* often without helmets, or jumping around wildly in the backseat of a car, waving to the driver behind, the way we used to do in 1957. Although it is officially against the law to drive unbuckled, only 10 percent of Italians use their seat belts. When we needed to get a ride for Elliott to school soon after moving here, we gave his car seat to the driver of the school van. She gladly accepted it but then placed it directly on the back bench of the Volkswagen. There was no seat belt. We both had appointments, so we had to close our eyes and let him go unbelted, something we never would have considered doing in the United States. Despite our admonition, I knew he was about to jump around the van with the rest of the preschoolers.

It is not difficult to see that little children in Rome live in a kind of enchanted never-neverland. We were sitting one day in a nearby park on what seemed like an ordinary January Sunday. The park is next to the Colosseum on the Celimontana, one of the original seven hills, and is a lovely out-of-the-way spot that doesn't draw big crowds and has lots of lawn space for spreading out. You can rent a pony for a ride, buy a helium-filled balloon, or let your kids ride their bikes on a small track that circumnavigates the swings, slides, and climbing frames inside. For the first fifteen minutes, we were the only ones in the park, as it was two-thirty and families were still engaged in *pranzo*. But soon, as Diane and I looked up from reading the newspapers while Julian and Elliott did their twenty-fifth bike lap, the space was filled with distinct clumps of three—*mamma, papà,* and the one child of the family. But these were no ordinary children. There was Batman, Cinderella, Rapunzel, and Zorro, along with the traditional Pucinella, Arlequino, and Pinocchio. Diane and I looked at each other. Our delight at the colorful, flowing costumes and masks was offset by puzzlement. We knew that Carnevale—the Italian equivalent of Halloween, originating in ancient Rome when for a week each year slaves and masters traded places and everyone was masked so as to avoid potential retribution later—was coming up, but not for another three weeks. Not to worry. In Rome, Carnevale, the day of Mardi Gras, is not like Halloween, a dark holiday in late fall when children get to be someone else for one evening. Carnevale is a season, and this Sunday in January was the perfect time for these children to show off their costumes. Within minutes, the park was full of revelers, all throwing multicolored confetti every which way, which got into the clothes and the hair of the Sunday-best-attired Roman mothers and fathers, as well as the occasional grandparent.

Not a single one of them expressed chagrin of any sort. Rather, laughter and merriment filled the air. Dozens of small children squealed in delight as their parents and grandparents looked on and encouraged them to have fun. There were even two or three children with Down syndrome in costume, their unmistakable specialness in no way preventing them from partaking of the shared culture of communal festivity. As soccer balls whizzed by, as a mermaid blew bubbles, and a vendor at the periphery of all this sold cotton candy and caramel popcorn and bag after bag of confetti, as our kids, in jeans and sneakers and sweatshirts, zipped along, we realized that Rome is one big party that goes through different phases as the months pass and the earth makes its yearly visits along its inevitable course. We were merely in the Carnevale phase. The scene was festive, medieval, a fairy tale come alive.

Before long, as the brave but ultimately weak January sun slipped behind the pines, the families began to filter home in the deepening dusk. The entire Celimontana was covered in kaleidoscopic confetti, but the kids kept throwing it, like mad farmers sowing a magic field, assured that no one would even think about asking them to clean it up.

15

What Makes Romans So Sexy?
Close Encounters of Every Kind

The encounter took place not far from home, and it wasn't until I had had the opportunity to think about what really occurred that I realized once again what it means to live in Rome, how the city, despite its considerable size, provides you with intimate situations that are as much a part of the landscape as ancient ruins, magnificent churches, and plates of steaming pasta.

I had just crossed the Tiber from Trastevere to the other side, where Via Marmorata—forming the border between the quite different neighborhoods of the chic, elegant Aventino and the gritty, earthy, dense Testaccio—begins. On the side of the river whence I had just come, not far from the bank, is the Porta Portese, which in these days each Sunday morning houses the most intense, extensive outdoor market you could imagine. Every item under the sun is available in a bazaar that winds for miles through the streets off the Via Portuense. It more than anything resembles the Middle East, and on more than one occasion I have heard people remark that the best way to visit the market is *da solo,* alone, because if not, you spend the whole time making sure that the people you came with are in sight.

It was a beautiful spring morning, and I was waiting for the light to change to cross the Lungotevere and continue along the fabled Via Marmorata. Just thinking about this street is enough to take you back a few thousand years. The name comes from the word *"marmo,"* marble. In ancient times, shiploads of it were brought from Tuscany and the far-off shores of the eastern Mediterranean, unloaded at the dock right there on the river and sent along the thoroughfare to disappear into the building of the city. It is not for nothing that the first emperor, Augustus, was said to have transformed the city from one of brick into one of marble, a material still used by some artists, including our friend Augusto Ranocchi, who goes to Carrara to explore the same quarries Michelangelo did. Remains of the unloading areas are actually still visible down along the river, but you can't climb all over them, as you can, say, at Ostia Antica, the Roman port town that stood where the Tiber meets the sea, which is such an extensive ruin that you feel as if people are still living there as you wander about.

As I was waiting for the light to turn, various motorists were driving past and turning left almost directly beside me onto the bridge I had just crossed. The last car was about to go into the turn, and the window was wide open. I could plainly see the driver, a woman, most likely in her thirties. She was well attired, nothing out of the ordinary, but, of course, in Rome that means "decked out." Her thick hair was done in a modified flip, hennaed a startlingly compelling shade of red. She had spangled earrings that glittered in the sunlight, and a light, open, green linen jacket over a scoop-necked, cream-colored silk blouse that revealed a lot more of her curvaceous bosom than the average woman in America would ever contemplate. For Rome, however, especially in warmer weather, a show of cleavage is standard operating procedure. In fact, when summer arrives, life on the overheated streets resembles nothing short of bacchanalia, as modesty can in no way compete with the semi-nudity one sees in a mostly vain attempt to stay cool. When I first came to Rome, I tried to avert my eyes or cover my face, but before long I bowed to the inevitable and gave up. The sheer number of exposed or semiexposed breasts was just too numerous to overlook. For someone who enjoys the sight of feminine corporal splendor, it is heaven.

I was in the process—for just an instant, as that was the time allotted to me before the distaff driver would zip off into Trastevere—of admiring her beauty. It is not the kind of exquisiteness most Americans in fact consider beautiful, which is of the God-given variety, and which is terribly ultimate and therefore mostly oppressive for women—they either have it or they don't—but rather the kind of showy elegance associated with Italian women. It has more to do with what you *do* with what you have—whether you are proud of it, make the most of it, vary it, show it off—than it does with what you start with. Romans are nothing if not realistic, and one of the things they realize is that when it comes to being gorgeous, only one in, say, a thousand makes the grade. But that's not what is important, because Roman standards of attractiveness have more to do with *la bella figura,* a beautiful presentation of self, than they do with perfect features, and in that game anyone can play and most do. In a country where art is upheld as the highest form of human creativity, making a work of art of oneself is one way anyone can be an artist. As Helena Rubinstein once said, "There are no ugly women, only lazy women."

So here I was, slowly moving my head from right to left as her sunglassed visage was darting past. She was cutting the corner even more sharply than usual to make sure she made the yellow. As she did so, her tiny Fiat Panda, passing over a series of small bumps, shook for a few moments, jostling the driver as well. The effect was to provide me with a nanosecond's worth of exceedingly soft-core eroticism, as the tops of her well-developed breasts jiggled ever so slightly above the soft demibra she must have been wearing underneath, a seductive act she might have wittingly performed for her husband or lover in the sanctity of a bedroom but that she unwittingly performed for me as she whipped the Fiat around the curve and disappeared into Trastevere. She was obviously unaware of the thrill she had provided me because, as any driver in Rome knows, a momentary lapse of concentration on the crazed, chaotic streets could mean an *incidente,* and so Romans drive as if they had four pairs of eyes instead of one. There was no way she could have known that the tender curves of her well-formed body were momentarily on display for a perfect stranger who happened to be in the right place at the right time.

That was the first time I was privy to a certain kind of voyeuristic intimacy that frequently takes place in Rome. The second time—*mamma mia!*—I was waiting to cross the street in a different part of the city, but under the same conditions—cars turning left across my path—when the driver of a vehicle slowed down, ostensibly to safely make the turn, a rarity in itself, but in reality to ask for directions. She happened again to be an attractive woman, and even though she had no décolletage to offer me, she nonetheless had to contend with traffic speeding by in every direction, and, because of that, I couldn't hear where she wanted to go. She repeated it, and at that point I realized that in order to ever understand her, I would have to stick my head through the open window of the car and turn it so that my right ear would face toward her mouth. Barring this, all was futile. Surprisingly, and without hesitation, I did so, and even more surprisingly, without hesitation, *she let me.*

I heard the name—Piazza Emporio—but could not place it. This is actually common in Rome, as people know certain spots not by their names but by various identifying landmarks—the street through the archway that ends in a medieval-looking courtyard near Campo de' Fiori or the little alley behind the Chiesa Nuova on the right as you're walking toward Largo Argentina—and so I said I was sorry that I couldn't help her.

At that point I realized—as had happened during the previous occasion—that there was a connection with this woman that was so intimately circumstantial—like being in an elevator with someone to whom you are hopelessly attracted—that I could not help but notice how it was beginning to affect me. My head was completely in the car, and as it was turned to the left, and leaning forward, I was looking directly down at her thighs. They were sleek, lovely, stockinged *gambe,* and they revealed themselves to me in their startling presence, baring twelve inches above the knee, to where the hem of her skirt began. I could not help but stare at them, because if I looked up, I would have been nose to nose with this woman, and would not have been able to bear the impact of the moment. On the other hand, if I turned my head any further to the left, she would have been looking at the back of it, and for one thing, I don't like people to see my little bald spot, and, for another, I wouldn't have been able to hear her.

What made the encounter so intense, at least for me, was that she had to have known that I was gazing directly down at her exposed legs, that I was just inches away from them, yet that very fact did not prompt her, as I suspect it would have prompted all but twenty-five women in America, to step on the gas and speed away. She just stayed there, as if she were really *enjoying* the encounter, and the thought crossed my mind, as she was trying to provide me with more information, that I was half-expected to move my head down and lovingly nuzzle the inner rims of her thighs. The sensation was overpowering. I could literally feel the air in her car—supercharged, erotically warm on a cold winter day—intoxicated with the seductive fragrance of expensive perfume, the heat of her body a palpable presence.

Finally she said the magic words—Lungotevere at Via Marmorata. My resistance now close to nothing, I pulled my head out into the brisk winter air and told her to make a U-turn and take a right at the next light. It was only after she had gone, and I was reliving the incident with the same kind of longing one experiences after a particularly erotic dream, that I realized that she was headed for the very spot at which I had been treated to the jiggling breasts years before.

This is what goes on regularly between strangers. Imagine what it is like between people you run into on a constant basis. Giorgio, the man who runs the photo shop where Diane, who has a passion for photography, is a regular customer, has been conducting a long-running flirtation in which he turns up the heat ever so slightly every so often. It doesn't matter at all to him that he knows me, talks to me, that on occasion I also go into the shop to buy film or have it developed. When Diane enters—she later tells me—he jumps from his chair behind the counter and greets her, blushing, by putting his hand lightly on her shoulder or elbow and asking what she is going to do that day, where she will be going to take pictures. He makes jokes. He is solicitous beyond the needs of a genial *negoziante,* a shop-keeper. When Diane told him that we were going to the States for most of the summer, he responded by saying, *"Cosa farò"* "What will I do?" His flirtation is unabashed, unapologetic, out in the open. On occasion Diane has talked to his wife in the shop, but even that does not deter him. It is easy to see what his strategy is. He is in no hurry for anything to happen. He will continue to flirt with Diane (he recently asked for a kiss after making a minor camera repair) in the hope that one day she will come into the store, ask for two rolls of color slide film, and say to him, *"Facciamolo,"* "Let's do it." Giorgio has no illusions about his chances. Although I've never spoken to him personally about this, he must know that they are slim. But he courageously plows on nonetheless. He has nothing to lose and everything to gain, because he is enjoying the flirtation in and of itself. In the like-lihood that he cannot coax Diane into bed with him, he still has something to look forward to every time my wife's lovely face and figure appear in the shop.

Giorgio might not be Diane's type, but Matteo certainly is. The father of one of Elliott's classmates, he looks like Boz Skaggs, drives a *motorino,* and has the kind of devil-may-care attitude common to many Roman men. He and Diane first met while the kids were taking a ceramics class after hours at the school. She went to pick up the boys, and, after going back and forth to the restroom to help the giggling kids wash their hands, Matteo suggested they take a shortcut through the basement and out to the front of the building. Diane was skeptical, but the kids, of course, insisted. Before long, they were all walking through a long corridor toward the exit in total darkness, the only evidence of the existence of the *gruppo* the sound of Diane's heels click-clacking on the tile floor. In a dark corridor with a strange man in the United States, she would have been scared, but somehow being in Rome reinforces the notion that flirtation is OK because first of all, everyone does it and therefore it doesn't *necessarily* mean more than what it is, and two, it is part of the complicated erotic dance between men and women that goes on all the time and keeps—even without a *tradimentino*—things fresh on the home front. When they all emerged from the corridor and into the outside darkness, Diane noticed how cute Matteo's *motorino* was, to which he replied that since the kids were straggling, perhaps they should take off for a *giro,* a ride around town.

Does this mean that Matteo wants to sleep with Diane or that he just wants to have fun and spin her around on his *motorino?* She doesn't know, I don't know, and probably he doesn't know, either. What I do know is that it is a reflex response that occurs beneath the level of conscious thought. At the end-of-the-school-year dinner one June—with temperatures in the mid-eighties at 8:00 P.M., the humidity high, and the sun still an atmospheric force—we all found ourselves seated at long banquet tables with red checkerboard tablecloths at a private club along the Tiber, eating pizza, ten, twelve parents—mostly *mamme*—on a side. The jazz drummer Ettore, across from whom I was sitting, turned and asked no one in particular toward the end of the table if someone could pass him the pitcher of wine. I'll never forget the response of one of the mothers, who must wake up at 5:00 A.M. every morning to make sure she looks the way she always looks the rest of the day. Without skipping a beat, she cocked her head, put her elbow on the table, and placed her chin on top of her hand. *"Dipende,"* she said. "It depends." Let's leave it at that.

I don't want to leave the impression that it is only Diane who has live flirtations while I must confine myself to fantasies with *sconosciute,* unknown females. Antonella, the afternoon cashier in a neighborhood bakery, is an accomplished flirt. She sits at the register in her three-inch heels, plunging necklines, and fur coat (in winter), quizzing me about California and asking my children if they realize how *simpatico* their father is. One day she had to come out from behind the baked goods counter to assume her station at the *cassa* and furtively squeezed my hand as she went by. I didn't know how to respond. I almost blurted out *grazie,* but held my tongue at the last moment. Then one day she was talking with Anna, who was briefly Elliott's substitute Italian teacher in school. I greeted both *signore* and was my usual cheerful self. A week later I encountered Anna near the Testaccio market. She was carrying two plastic shopping bags (large paper bags being all but unheard of in Rome) and after exchanging *buongiorno,* she immediately cut to the chase: *"Ma, Lei, dove abita?"* asking me where I lived but being careful to use the formal *Lei* instead of the informal *tu.* When I told her and she instantly realized that I was part of the neighborhood, she said through her lip-glossed smile that we were then *destined* to run into each other from time to time.

There was something about the use of the word "destiny"

that made the ten-second interaction stay with me. It was so poetic, so romantic, so laden with possibility. All these machinations, these encounters, these brief but pregnant pauses in the day, remind me so much that the fine art of flirtation, the freedom to intrigue one another without fear, still exists in some parts of the world and is vibrantly alive and well right here, *grazie a Dio,* in my own adopted neighborhood.

What makes Romans so alluring? It's their availability, their readiness—whether real or imagined—the charm and ease with which they move in and out of highly charged situations, how smooth, glib, and unafraid they are of the opposite sex. When our friend Clelia, at a birthday party in the country in the spring, slapped the bench next to her in the garden while summoning me with the words *"Vieni qua,"* almost what one would say to a dog, or at least a child, and then said, *"Tutti i mariti sono uguali,"* "All husbands are alike," when I obeyed, I couldn't help but think, although I didn't say anything, that they are when they are being beckoned by Clelia.

16

The Smallest Big City in the World: The Intimacies of Daily Life

Piazza Venezia is arguably the most intimidating place in Italy. Pretty much ground zero, the absolute geographical center of the *centro storico*, it takes its name from the Palazzo Venezia, which sits proudly on its west side, the first Renaissance palace built in the city, in 1467, which later became the Venetian embassy. The piazza is threatening because it is a huge expanse of cityscape, a meeting place for five major streets and various smaller ones, providing the site with an effervescence of traffic and noise, enough to make even Romans avoid the place if they can help it, which they mostly can't because it gives access to so many different parts of the center of the city. When Jean-Paul Sartre wrote that hell is "the other," he must have had Piazza Venezia in mind.

At a strategically placed point in the square, where three of the five roads converge, and where there is no traffic light to guide motorists because in truth it would be almost impossible to coordinate all aspects of vehicular comings and goings with the familiar, red, yellow, and green bulbs, sits a low stone pedestal on which stands, at the busiest times of the day, a *vigile*, a policeman, who has the unenviable task of directing the flow. The training for the job must obviously be intense, for the impeccably uniformed, white-gloved official moves with the kind of grace and elegance one usually associates with the conducting of an orchestra. All the moving elements—buses, taxis, cars, *motorini,* pedestrians—must be acknowledged. But somehow, through all the chaos, the seeming impossibility of passage, the competing subjectivities forcing each individual to plan his route with great precision, including even the driver or occasional pedestrian tourist who courageously finds his way to the platform to ask directions, the wait is never more than a few minutes at a time. The feat is so remarkable in itself that you begin to wonder whether it is all being done with mirrors, or whether a veritable law of physics—that no two objects can occupy the same space at the same time—is being defied.

I have passed this spot and seen this ballet performed countless times, but the most memorable incident occurred on a day when the piazza was almost deserted—Christmas Day—when the delicate light of the midmorning winter solstice showed the elegance and grandeur of Piazza Venezia: the Via dei Fori Imperiali, built by Mussolini during the Fascist era so that he could see the Colosseum at the other end of it as he harangued the crowds from his balcony at Palazzo Venezia, where he maintained his office; the Altar of the Fatherland, Italy's Washington Monument, affectionately known as the Wedding Cake or the Typewriter, the newest, whitest, and some say ugliest monument in the city, completed at the beginning of the century to honor the ruling house of Savoy, whose family produced Italy's first king of the modern era, Victor Emmanuel II, who ruled from 1861 to 1878; and the many streets that lead in every direction.

141

The deserted piazza lent Roman meaning to the word intimacy, as on top of the unoccupied pedestal, in plain view of anyone who happened to pass through this Christmas morning, was a typical culinary offering, an acknowledgment, a glimpse of the feeling that at bottom fundamentally exists between Romans and doesn't take long to reveal itself—even to *stranieri* like us. Over time, it becomes so intoxicating, so invigorating, so indispensable to life, that one begins to wonder how it would be possible to manage without this communal familiarity.

The rhythm of Roman life is marked by certain types of foods, which are eaten only at certain times of the year. The first thing you must consume after midnight on New Year's Day is *lenticchie,* lentils in a soup, which represent wealth (the soup is usually served with *cotechino,* boiled pig's foot, but we usually beg off that part). February Carnevale is characterized by *castagnole di crema o ricotta,* small doughnut holes filled with either of the two delicacies, or *frappè,* a kind of oversize fried wonton that is topped with either drizzled chocolate or powdered sugar. During Easter you see three-foot tall, gaily wrapped chocolate eggs everywhere, which when cracked open contain surprises. Then there is *Pasquetta,* the "little Easter" the Monday after the big one, when everyone in Rome finds a way to picnic outdoors, and where a *colomba,* a cake in the shape of a dove, is consumed. On May Day, the first of the month, the other traditional picnic day, one shares the customary family meal by eating fava beans and pecorino cheese, downed with generous beakers of local white wine.

The end of the year Christmas season brings the arrival of *torroni* and *torroncini,* large and small log-shaped, nougat candies with nuts, and *panettone,* large, puffy, raisin-studded sweet bread, and *pandoro,* similar to *panettone* but eggier, and covered with powdered sugar. These two huge bread-cakes look like chef's hats and are eaten at every occasion during the season, exchanged freely among people as if all is well in the world if only one has a steady supply of these sweet, simple delicacies with which to welcome guests. The ubiquitous consuming of these cakes, which originated in Milan and Verona, respectively, is by now so ingrained in our family that I was beginning to question the natural order of things when, six days before Christmas one year, I realized I had not yet indulged. Not to worry. At the kids' annual Christmas musical recital, the table was laden with all manner of soft drinks for the young musicians, *spumante* for the adults, and *panettone* and *pandoro* for everyone.

It is because of the associations, the meanings, the significance of these elementary items—the way they mark the season and the importance of connecting with another, of letting those around you know that you are thinking of them, acknowledging them—that they form a vital part of your Roman life, even if it is the part that makes the passage from Via del Teatro di Marcello to the Via del Plebescito on the other side of Piazza Venezia possible. For there, glimmering in the sunlight, occupying the place normally reserved for the *vigile* that makes this particularly treacherous stretch of asphalt bearable for so many thousands during the day, was the familiar color and shape of the festive box that encloses *panettone.* It was an offering to the Roman god of traffic, that man who on all other days makes movement through the center of the city possible. Who knows if the customary Christmas confection would ever reach him, or if he would hazard to eat it, not knowing its origin (in fact, this year there was a scare, as animal rights activists managed to inject rat poison into several *panettone* belonging to the brand manufactured by Nestlé, which they claim sacrifices animals for testing purposes). But that is completely beside the point. One of the citizens of one of the oldest metropoles in the world took it upon himself to gift someone he probably sees every day, but with whom the intimacy goes no further than complete obedience to the skill and power of his elegant arms, hands, and head. There the package stood, as cars and *motorini* occasionally moved around it, as pedestrians out to celebrate the holiday with a brisk *passeggiata* pointed to the blue box and chuckled to themselves or their partners, as the familiar confection stood where princes, popes, and dictators once walked. It was yet another tiny reminder of the way in which, at its best, all of Rome is one great big family, including even someone who in the United States represents aggression, who is a figure removed and distant, "other" and feared; a person whom one tolerates as a problematic but necessary part of the community, whose role it is to keep in check its most violent elements, those elements that sadly make impossible the kind of intimacy that takes place regularly between Romans, and is, in fact, the standard by which people judge the livableness of the city.

Our Christmas stroll through Rome, through the very heart of Roman Catholic Christianity, continued. The season is marvelous. It casts a spell as glistening lights peer through ancient alleys, stylish heels clatter on crooked cobblestones, and countless *presepi,* Christmas crèches, illuminate the long winter nights. The city is a perfect blend of elegance and simplicity, idleness and high spirits. There are festivities. Piazza Navona is filled with throngs of people, stalls, games, sweets, everything to delight the child—and the child within. Stores are decorated, but subtly, and the tradition of gift giving, which induces annual fears of inadequacy and emptied bank balances of many Americans, has not caught on beyond the small sweet or Christmas cake that more than anything keeps the bond between individuals or, more likely, families, strong. Romans cannot decorate a Christmas tree to save their lives—the tradition is a "barbarian" import—and, in fact, the large firs that stand every year in Piazza Venezia and on the Pincio in Villa Borghese are often tilted, lopsided, and underdressed, but one never hears the usual harangue about the number of Christmas shopping days remaining or feels the mad rush to be all things to all people for two weeks out of the year in order to expiate the guilt of the remaining fifty. Romans have no such problem. Their world at Christmas is the same world it is at many times throughout the year—just another excuse to sit down at a long table with one's relatives and feast for hours on end. The relationships are the same, the greetings the same, the faces the same faces one sees at the beach in summer and on Sunday for *pranzo* (except, oddly, for Christmas Eve; our friend Cristina says that December 24 is the day when everyone dusts off the old cadavers, dining with people they haven't seen all year). The *romani* do not send cards—it is nearly unheard of, for any reason—but acknowledge each other by breaking bread, literally in this case, as *panettone* in Italian means the big bread.

The next day, in the Piazza Venezia, both the *vigile* and the traffic are back, but a gesture has been performed by one citizen to tie him to his fellow *cittadini,* and they to him.

17

Hanging the Wash and Other Joys: Romans Don't Trust Technology

My e-mail in-basket was indicating that I had received three letters. As I clicked "receive mail," I watched while the flashing screen kept me informed of the progress of the downloading. The mail had been sent during my night, while I was dreaming of the Renaissance, which was nevertheless populated by various figures of my Roman present, a contradiction in itself because for the most part the Renaissance didn't initially happen here, but rather in Florence, in *reaction* to what was and what had been happening here for centuries. Art and religion, culminating in the fifteenth-century creative explosion, had not been good bedfellows.

But my night is still the waking day of my Stateside friends, and one of them was sending me the latest report of the economic analyst Edward Yardeni, whose dire warnings of the Y2K computer meltdown are enough to make anyone's hair stand on end—airline flight disasters, welfare check nightmares, and breakdown of energy distribution on a global basis, just for starters. I try to open the file. It is binary, the meaning of which still escapes me. I try to convert it from the only three formats my e-mail ISP provides me. None works. It's still all gibberish—crazy shapes and forms that look like something my sons drew when they were toddlers. I make a mental note to call my provider to find out how I can use my computer to learn more about the possible coming breakdown of my computer. Maybe it knows what is in the report and instinctively doesn't want me to read it because it doesn't want to upset me. The report remains gibberish, and I shrug in resignation, knowing that I'll get around to it and that the computer apocalypse of 2000 will not affect me as much as it will my countrymen. As long as the *pizzerie* can get wood to fire up the ovens, Romans will still be able to enjoy the immediacy—about one minute to bake—of a delicious plate of thin, crusted, flat, aromatic bread with oil and sweet, fresh tomato and *mozzarella,* talking excitedly about everything but the technological world while everybody else experiences the breakdown of it. With the exception of motor vehicles and telephones, whose incorporation into the everyday life of my fellow citizens is so ubiquitous that any day I expect to see some well-dressed young *ragazzo* speaking into his wrist—a step beyond the current rage of tiny speakers and receivers attached to a slim cord that make you think someone on the street is truly *matto,* out of his mind, because at first glance he is talking and gesturing madly to no one—Romans don't trust technology.

Evidence is everywhere. The citywide headquarters of the public transportation system, located near the Termini, the main train station, offers the opportunity to buy a year-long bus and metro pass—the equivalent cost of seven month's worth of monthly passes. The three young people at the counter direct you to another table, where the forms are available to be filled out and turned in. Diane and I complete the forms while we get on line. When we reach the clerk at the counter, we see various people on the other side of the metal grated window that one associates with nineteenth-century train travel rapidly but carefully doing all the things necessary to complete the transaction *manually*. His phase completed, the clerk then sends us to another window for payment, which must be made in cash. No checks or credit cards are accepted, and we are about to pay the city of Rome roughly four hundred dollars for the privilege of riding its buses, trams, and subways for one year for two people.

We pay and receive the receipt necessary to go back to the previous window to obtain our passes. The word *ritiro,* or retrieve, is crucial, as that is the password that we who have already paid must utter in order to let the first-timers on line give way so that we can pick up our cards. The clerk has a huge stack of completed, handwritten forms next to him, through which he must look to *ritirare* the correct one, and unlike the California Motor Vehicle Bureau, which provides your photo, you must bring your own, which he attaches to the card and then rubber stamps with a distinct flair.

Here is the city of Rome, dispensing hundreds if not thousands of cards a day, and the system, even in the year 1999, is performed by people, sending the patrons to this window and that, nary a computer in sight. Twenty individuals are doing the work of five, and Romans are at bottom happy about it, even though they must divide the salaries many more ways than they might prefer. At least they are all working, at least they have jobs, at least there is someone else at hand to talk to, as we notice how rare it is for a Roman official to carry out his duties in solitude. Who would he talk to? How could he get on? The

Roman mentality is entirely the opposite of ours. It is better to have twenty people earning enough money to scrape by—have a *caffè,* an occasional meal in the *trattoria,* enough clothes to maintain a *bella figura,* a *telefonino,* and a functioning *motorino*—than it is to have five people living high on the hog—with several fancy, large, gas-guzzling automobiles; formidable mortgages; nannies; elaborate, technologically current offices; and investments in the stock market—while the other fifteen live off public assistance and have no self-esteem. To Romans, machines do not necessarily make life easier. But they definitely do take away jobs and provide less opportunity for socializing with your neighbor.

They also leave Romans with the feeling that they can't quite trust the process. Italy is not a place where you blithely drop a check in the mail to make a simple payment. In the first place, it's hard to get a check. In the United States, after you tick off 100, 200, 300, 500 for the number of checks you would like to receive when you open a bank account, a box of, most likely, 500 will dutifully arrive in a few days with your name and address printed on them. In Rome, when we opened an account, they asked us if we each wanted a checkbook. When we said we did, we were each proud holders of ten checks without any indication of our identities on them. The message was clear: Don't use them unless you really need to, unless you have no other means to attain something. Another message is equally clear: Keep them in a safe place, since anyone can use them.

Recently, the public utility services started to implement a "revolutionary" system. You fill out a form, and the bank will automatically deduct the bimonthly sum from your account, enabling you to avoid the long lines at the *"conto correnti,"* or payment windows, in the post office. One would think that everyone would have rushed to take advantage of the convenience, as it would save a consumer much time and bypass the check-in-the-mail system, which would never catch on. But Romans have not, as I haven't detected any shortening of the lines for the privilege of paying cash to the teller, who will then stamp your receipt, at which you can look with your own two eyes and then hold on to with your own two hands. To Romans, technology is a little like black magic. You see it, you believe it, but still there is part of you that thinks it was all done with smoke and mirrors, and should push come to shove, you would find out that the bank was really not paying your bill to Telecom Italia, but rather that some functionary buried way in the back office of some nondescript building on the periphery was stealing the money, and you would be without that piece of paper that says that on February 22, 1999, at 10:23 A.M., you paid 216,000 lire, about $120, for two months of electricity at window 17 in the Ostiense Post Office after standing on line for thirty-two minutes as the line at window 18 went by significantly faster. (In Rome there is no "single line" concept, where you branch off to the next available employee when he or she is free, but I'm sure it will arrive before the next millennium.) A computer that will automatically transfer just the right amount of money to the electricity company at the precise moment you tell it to, even if you are sleeping or making love or eating *nonna*'s incomparable *sugo di carne* over *tagliatelle,* and then send you a record of the transaction at the end of the month so that if you called ENEL, they would say that your bill is paid? *Ma va. Stai scherzando?* Please. Who are you trying to kid?

When Italian friends of ours were looking for a new place to live in Rome, many apartments we thought were perfectly suitable were rejected because they didn't have an "ironing room," a little place near the kitchen or bathroom where you can spread out, among your clothes, board, and iron, and have at it. Romans not only don't use dryers, they have in some cases never heard of them or seen one. In fact, when we were considering which washing machine to buy when we moved into our *palazzo,* our Roman friends all advised against buying the one model—out of perhaps twenty—that was both a washer and a dryer. "You'll never use it." "It consumes too much electricity." "It'll ruin your clothes." "What, you don't iron?" When we tell them that in the United States no one has a washer without a dryer, that they run really hot on gas and take about an hour to do ten pounds of laundry instead of three, four, or more hours to do 2.5 pounds, as is the case here, they are incredulous. Is there no sun there? Do they not sell irons? Why would anyone want to use a drying machine on their clothes when they can hang them and then go into the "ironing room" for hours at a time after they've dried? Or you can hire a *filippina* to do it. That's an even better idea, a luxury many people we know unabashedly indulge in, especially if their mothers don't do it for them. But regardless of who does it, you often see in the homes of the *romani* the crispest, brightest, cleanest, freshest, most fragrant piles of folded towels, sheets, shirts, even underwear and socks, not to mention an impeccably clean house. It never ceases to amaze me that they will take such fastidious care of the inside of their homes, yet throw garbage on the street without the slightest hesitation, and certainly without guilt or shame.

With all this in mind, my morning is set. I carefully stuff the mattress cover, the fitted sheet, the comforter cover, and four pillowcases into the washer. They barely fit, but I find space, bending over nearly to ground level to accommodate the usual front-loading *lavatrice*. Add detergent. Turn the dial. It's running. I exhort the kids. "C'mon guys, it's ten after eight. Time to go." Elliott needs another new pencil, his fifth or sixth of the week. This means a trip to the *tabaccaio*. Then it's to the newsstand, the *edicola*, for *figurine*, soccer cards. Finally to the bakery for *pizza bianca* for *merenda*, their snack at 10:30. The kids need to be in school at 8:20, and the three stops will add on five extra minutes. It is not a big deal, as the pupils straggle in until 9:00 and beyond, but Julian likes to get in early and trade *figurine* with his classmates, and Elliott uses the first minutes of the morning to look for yesterday's missing pencil.

Fatto. Done. The kids are kissed and wished a *buona giornata*. They disappear into the courtyard garden of the building and are off. I've brought the *carrello*, the two-wheeled shopping cart used primarily by the *anziani*, the elderly, to pick up the items they need for the day's shopping. I stop at Maurizio's charming little bar in Testaccio, and he affectionately ribs me for being the youngest person in Rome with a *carrello*. The young are more inclined to use cars for everything, as doing the shopping on foot is considered an old person's activity.

My *caffè macchiato* is perfect as usual as I hit my three stations of the household—the little supermarket that sells only packaged goods, the *latteria* for bread, milk, cheese, and cold cuts, and the *frutteria* for produce. It is 9:10 when I arrive home. Diane is behind the closed living-room doors counseling a client, possibly another culture-shocked foreigner, or writer or artist seeking inspiration and guidance. There is still time left on the wash cycle. I unload the *carrello,* fill it with empty plastic water bottles, and head out again. Before long I am at the *fontanella,* Rome's public water supply and drinking fountains. They are gray, cast-iron relics from the nineteenth century, looking a lot like old-fashioned fire hydrants in the United States. The street slang term for them is *nasone,* the big nose, for the soldered spout that sticks out of them and pours a continual stream of spring water that comes directly from the extensive system of underground aquifers on top of which Rome sits. Rainwater passes through porous tufa rock until it meets nonporous clay, developing pools of water that are brought up to the Romans through the *fontanella,* which are spaced every few blocks in the city. The iron spout has a hole in the top side bored into it, and so for a drink a person leans over, places one's finger on the bottom, open end of the spout to create pressure, and guzzles the water as it magically spurts out in a glistening arc through the small hole on top. The water is delicious and fresh, so much so that some say it is the best drinking water in the world, and there are experts in Rome who know which *fontanelle* are attached to which springs. In fact, Julian's social studies teacher took the class on a field trip during which they passed a *fontanella* in the Villa Borghese that is reputed to be the best in the city, the one closest to the *laghetto* at which one can rent a paddle boat.

The one in front of which I am standing runs slowly, and so it takes thirty minutes to fill fifteen 1.5-liter bottles. At first, I am impatient to finish the task, but then the proprietor of a small *frutteria* on the street next to the *fontanella* peeks out to see what the unexpected shuffling is. She sees me and smiles. I ask if the water is good, as I have never been to this *nasone,* and she says,

"Ma, certo," "But, of course." Now loaded, the *carrello* is heavy, but the trip home is mostly downhill. Thank God for our elevator, which is not a given in the average Roman *palazzo*.

The washer is still. The sheets and pillowcases are done. I eschew the dryer, as we do on all but a few days of the year, when the weather is cold and wet and the kids want to wear something specific that still has not dried from the day before. Within moments the *biancheria* are in my basket, and I am on my way up the back service stairs to the *terrazza* with an assortment of multicolored clothespins. There are some terraces in Rome that are as beautiful as any gardens anywhere in the world. At this time, ours is not one of them, used mostly for hanging laundry. But Diane and I have promised each other that soon we will adorn the terrace for outdoor recreational use. We will buy a table and chairs, an umbrella, and plants, and we will take advantage of the pleasing Roman climate to eat an occasional meal *fuori*.

It is 10 A.M. The kids are in school. My wife is still counseling. And the shopping is done. We have fresh springwater in the cupboard and washed fruit that has been placed in a ceramic bowl. Our sheets are clean and fresh, and as I drape them over the line, the warm sun producing vapor in the morning light as the damp blue petals and sea green leaves printed on soft yellow cotton begin to billow in the wind, I realize that in Rome time is marked not by sixty-minute intervals for which a watch is indispensable, but by the fact that another week or two has passed since I was up on the terrace hanging the sheets, that the sun seems a degree or two brighter, warmer, higher up in the sky. Winter is slowly turning into spring.

I can see in every direction, 360 degrees of cityscape. There is the Piramide to the south along the street through which the Allies poured into Rome to liberate the city from the Germans in June 1944, light violet cotton puffs competing with the dense blue of the sky to see which will hover over the immense white pointed slab of the monument. I then look north toward the Palatine, a maze of rugged ruins, sitting old, proud, and omniscient. The buildings around me are all about the same level— architecture on a human scale. There is not a single modern skyscraper in Rome, as the height of St. Peter's Basilica takes precedence. To the west, behind me, I see the churches of the Aventino, medieval, brick spires dominating the watercolor sky-line. Immediately surrounding me is a jumble of *palazzi* much like ours, only newer. I see tiled roofs, terraces, antennas, blowing laundry, and the increasing appearance of satellite dishes.

But then my attention is directed in the hazy distance to the east, toward San Saba. The church bells go off again, as they have always done to welcome the flock to mass. I am intoxicated by the smell of the fabric. After only minutes, the power of the wind and the sun has alchemized the beautiful yet lifeless cotton petals into the essence of pure scent of flower. In a few hours the sheets will be dry.

I pause, and it is only after I get my fill of wonder that I descend the stairs to my computer, the one machine I depend on to keep me connected to the modern world. I sit, and attempt once again to make sense of the simpler life I have chosen to live, six thousand miles away from my previous one.

18

For Men Only: Dinner After Eight (and You Don't Want to Be Late)

Manlio, a swarthy, lively, gregarious, fellow *papà,* gives me the sign one day at school that he wants to talk. He uses the Roman hand gesture that signifies that someone wants to have a word with you later—rotating the wrist at eye level in a motion toward the other person, a gesture so natural you wonder why—with the possible exception of a basketball coach wanting to indicate a full court press—you don't see it more in the United States. In Rome it is used constantly, as a way of indicating something to someone you see but can't talk to because you're engaged elsewhere, usually in conversation with another person who is in midsentence. At that point it would be rude to say, *"Scusa, ma potrei avere una parola un attimino col mio amico là?"* "Excuse me, but could I have a word for just a moment with my friend over there?" You know that the conversation, which is often just for conversation's sake anyway, can end at any moment or go on indefinitely, so you briefly use the wrist rotation gesture and continue listening to the person with whom you are conversing.

This sign, Romans tell me, is also the one preferred in church,

156

as Sunday mass is an occasion to wave to all your friends, and since you can't greet them as they enter the door at the back and you're already seated, you use the "Telephone me" sign—thumb and little finger extended outward, middle three fingers folded down on the palm—simulating a telephone receiver—thumb toward the ear, little finger toward the mouth—followed immediately by the "later" sign. The telephone hand gesture is also useful because when the thumb is tilted toward the mouth, head somewhat back, wrist pivoting slightly so that the thumb moves down as the little finger goes up, it is the drinking hand gesture. I know because when Manlio asked if I wanted to join a few of his friends for dinner at a *trattoria* a few nights hence and I accepted without hesitation, I also asked whether the evening would include the *mogli,* the wives. He smiled, shook his head once or twice, and said, *"No,"* and then, as if to offer an explanation, gave the drinking sign. I nodded knowingly. We are in Rome. When guys want to tie one on, they leave their wives at home.

At the last moment, however, the dinner is canceled as tragedy strikes our little group of school parents. Silvia, a mother of three, was hit by a car while crossing the street in the pedestrian strip and is in a coma with possible brain damage. The news has cast a pall on everything, and we are instructed not to tell our kids what has really happened for fear that they will tell her daughter Flavia, who knows only that her mother fell in the street and is in the hospital. Neither Manlio nor I feel much like merriment, as we are all stunned that our safe little world has been ripped apart. It is only when Silvia wakes up after spending ten days in a coma that everyone connected to the class feels that normal life can once again resume, even if it is too soon to know whether she will fully recover. Nonetheless, it seems as if our constant prayers for Silvia's well-being have been answered, and so a festive occasion would no longer be seen as inappropriate, a *brutta figura*.

Felice, which is in Testaccio, where Manlio grew up and where we will be dining, is one of the strangest *trattorie* I've ever been in. Every indication before you ingest your first mouthful of food is that the evening will not meet expectations. The place has no sign, no name, in fact nothing to indicate what it is because you can't see inside. It is small, with perhaps fifteen tables, standard industrial decor that is at least set off by the white tablecloths and napkins. What it mostly looks like is a private club for card playing. There are no menus, no smiles, and no one greets you when you enter. If you don't have reservations, forget it, you won't eat—at least that meal—at Felice. (How ironic that the name of the *trattoria* is Italian for happy.)

The proprietor of the *locale* is a seventy-seven-year-old man with a grizzled face who defines the word curmudgeon. He shuffles by repeatedly with piping hot dishes brought out from the kitchen. He never writes anything down, and if you ask for a menu you might as well leave, because he'll ignore you for the next hour. No, you don't go to Felice for the atmosphere, you go for the food—if you can go at all, because if Domenico doesn't recognize your voice on the phone or your person when you come in and you haven't booked, he probably won't seat you. It's as if he's bought just enough food to prepare for the people who have reserved, and so nothing is left to chance. One time he was huffing and puffing about a couple who came in and wanted a plate of pasta and a *cappuccino*. Domenico was not amused. "This isn't a *spaghetteria*," he said, storming off with a stack of empty plates. The implication was clear. When you come to Felice, you eat a small appetizer, a first course followed by a second course, and a *contorno* if you still have room. There are no desserts, and if you want coffee at the end of the meal, his nephew will go to the bar around the corner and bring it back for you on a tray with a packet of sugar on the rim of the cup to keep it warm.

Manlio, of course, having grown up across the street from Felice, which has been in existence for a hundred years, is the evening's *capo*. There are two tables set up for five, and when he asks Domenico which is ours, I can tell right away that our host is not in a particularly good mood. *"Dove voi volete,"* he growls, looking away and toward the kitchen. "Wherever you want." Five small sausages are already on the table, and soon local white wine, bottled water, and bread appear. Domenico pauses during one of his endless peregrinations around the small dining room to ask what we want for *primi piatti*. The specialty of the house is *tonnarelli cacio e pepe,* twisted thin spaghetti-like pasta with green olive oil, black pepper, and tons of grated off-white pecorino cheese on top. I am the last to state my preference, as the others have all weighed in for *cacio e pepe*. I fall in behind my *compagni* and detect the faintest smile of satisfaction on the face of Domenico, who is pleased that, as a *straniero,* I get it. We are eating *in famiglia,* and everyone—within reason—should eat the same thing.

Manlio's friend Luciano, who grew up with him and whom I had never met before, is feisty. He is a man of the *sinistra,* the left, and his demeanor reminds me a lot of the kind of righteous leftist that one used to encounter in the States in the late sixties and seventies, a man with an agenda. In fact, he reminds me a lot of me—twenty-five years ago. As soon as Domenico moves away, Luciano, who has never been to the United States, begins to pepper me with questions, and he wants them answered. *"Perchè gli americani non votano?"* he asks, "Why don't Americans vote?" punctuating the last word by making a cross with his finger on the thick white linen, as if we still marked ballots with a pencil, rather than pulling levers or punching cards with a blunted point. It has been a long time since I engaged in a political discussion about America with a foreigner, in Italian, and I am rusty. On the one hand I want to be honest about my thoughts and feelings, on the other I want oddly to protect my country from outside attack, as if suddenly all America were *my* family, giving us the right to criticize one another, but nevertheless not open to criticism from others. I respond by saying that people feel alienated from the system, that it doesn't respond very well to their needs, that they feel there isn't much difference between one political group and the other, that it's a game played by people with money for people with money.

My answer seems to satisfy Luciano. In fact, since I didn't argue the point about how undemocratic and dangerous it is that the elected officials of the United States hold office because 25 percent of the eligible voters put them there, it appeared I had disarmed him. Manlio begins to detect that I might be uncomfortable with his friend's line of questioning and tries to change the subject, but Luciano protests that these things are important to know. The discussion closes with my saying that the papers are now reporting a drop in Italian voting, and I say that as people become more prosperous, they often feel that they can buy their comfort, their security, their well-being, and so they drift away from the political system. I say it will eventually happen in Italy. Manlio agrees with me, but Luciano protests, adamantly. In his mind, political alienation is a feature of the United States, not of his country.

The *tonnarelli* are *perfetti, squisiti, indimenticabili,* perfect, exquisite, unforgettable. The tastes are rich, strong, varied, invading the very map of my mouth's palate of taste buds. I look over and see that the others are ahead of me. Talk has suddenly died down, having taken second place to the pleasures of the *gola*. We are all indulging as the Romans do, as heaping mounds of twisted homemade pasta are taken up on the fork and bitten into, letting fall to the plate what hasn't yet made it into one's mouth. The portions are huge, but the taste is compelling, and the *tonnarelli* within minutes are gone, washed down with the wine. Domenico, setting a stack of soiled plates on our table, stops by again to inquire about *secondi*. I opt for the fish, as the typical meaty Roman seconds, often composed of animal organs, do not appeal to my taste, which still remembers my strict vegetarian days of the bygone seventies. Now, years later, I occasionally eat meat, especially if offered, but I happily decline the pig's intestines and beef tongue, opting instead for a grilled *orata,* a kind of flaky, fleshy white flounder, simply adorned with olive oil and lemon.

Somehow, while I was still reviewing for an instant the gastronomic preferences of my adulthood, Luciano has latched on to Nino, whose son is in the same class with mine. Nino is from the mountainous region of the Abruzzo, and although he has lived in Rome for twenty years, he still maintains the *atteggiamento,* the look, manner, demeanor, and values of a man of the hills. He is short, robust, unshaven, friendly, solicitous—and a fascist. Mussolini is his idol, and soon he and Luciano are exchanging barbs as the action at the table is heating up.

Manlio tries to intervene, but his efforts are futile. Nino and Luciano are verbally sparring, their worldviews, values, political beliefs—their very lives—on opposite ends of the spectrum. In Italy the Right and the Left not only have political meaning, they are cultures, and I can tell that Nino's culture—perhaps because it is so out of favor, so anachronistic, which I suspect he himself realizes—pushes him to drop all political talk entirely in the face of Luciano's intensity. As the second plates are finished, we leave Felice to walk a few blocks to the bar for a late *caffè* (Romans insist that *caffè* has magical qualities: it wakes you up in the morning and puts you to sleep at night), and Nino is now practically leaning on his political enemy, trying to sweet-talk him into admitting the ludicrousness of it all by getting Luciano to laugh, at least to smile. But the leftist is unmoved. His distaste for Nino is held in check only by the fact that he does not want to be completely *maleducato,* bad-mannered, so he pulls his arm away from Nino's by-now lubricated grasp and continues with the tirade against everything Nino stands for. The latter, amused and bemused at the same time, looks at me as if to say, "Do you believe this guy?" to which I can only smile in reply. Nino then playfully asks if I would hold his coat, as if he were a schoolboy and this were the yard in which all disputes were ultimately resolved.

I can tell that Nino is joking, but the whole episode is now having an unsettling effect on Manlio, as he realizes that his choice of dinner guests has been a disaster. The matter is made worse by the fact that we are now passing the Testaccio social club of the Giallorossi, the red and yellow, the original colors of the banner of the ancient Roman legions, adopted for modern use by the Roma soccer squad, whose arch rival, the Biancoazzuri, the white and blue of Lazio, happens, of course, to be the preferred team of Nino. Luciano, a major Roma fan, now seizes on this fact to further turn the knife into his rival. "This is Roma territory," he keeps repeating to Nino, gesticulating madly—his hands together in front, fingers touching as if in prayer, rotating up and down in the "Don't you get it?" gesture—"You are a guest in Testaccio," as the two men are now doing some harmless shoving on the street. It is midnight on a Tuesday in February, but there are clusters of people here and there; more, in fact, than I used to see in Marin at any time during the year. Romans love the streets. It is there that their need for privacy is realized. It is said in the city that in order to go in, you go out.

The bar is jammed, but, of course, since we are with Manlio, the young *barrista* finds room and sets up five small saucers and demitasse cups, along with five small spoons. He asks if anyone wants something in addition to the coffee—implying a shot of something strong—but everyone begs off. In my case, I know that I am on the edge, having imbibed my share, and that a shot of *grappa* or other *digestivo* would put me over the top for the next day. *Caffè normale* is fine for me.

Our walk back is calmer, as Manlio puts his arm around Nino (Roman men are physically affectionate with each other; a double-cheeked kiss when meeting and departing is common, as well as walking arm in arm) and walks fifty paces behind me, Luciano, and Stefano. Luciano has settled down, and is, in truth, remarkably well informed with regard to American culture. Of Woody Allen he says that his early films—*Bananas, Take the*

163

Money and Run—were brilliant, but that lately he's become *paz-zesco,* a crazy person. We then get into another slight argument about the Rockefellers, who Luciano insists are Jews. One of the things about being Jewish is that you know who all the famous Jews are, and, in fact, my father will still take the time to say to me, "Did you know that Winona Ryder is a Jew, that Gwyneth Paltrow is half-Jewish, or that Kenneth Starr is married to a *Yiddishe medele*?" I know that neither John D. nor his many offspring are members of the tribe and let Luciano know this. But the Rothschilds are Jews, he retorts. That's true, I say, but that's an altogether different family. They are French. I know, he says. Rockefeller, Rothschild, he repeats in his thick accent, playing with the foreign names, letting them roll around on his tongue to see if they sound alike, which to him they do.

We are again joined by Manlio and Nino, who is in no condition to drive. Luciano, who was born on Via del Governo Vecchio, in the heart of Rome, now lives beyond the *periferia*—a single man in his midforties living with *Mamma*—and is being offered a ride by Manlio, who also wants to take home Nino, who lives a few blocks away. "I'm not getting in the car with him," says Luciano, which starts a new round of posturing and causes Manlio to lose his patience. All the frustration of the evening's discord has finally worn him down. Manlio is letting Luciano know without quarter than he has been out of line, as Nino stands aside and wonders what all the fuss is about, perplexed that a bunch of middle-aged guys out to have a simple good time couldn't pull it off.

Double-cheeked pecks are exchanged among us all, four earthy *romani* and a transplanted *americano*. Everyone rattles off all the niceties—*"Ci vediamo, allora,"* "We'll see each other then," *"A domani," "Arrivederci," "Ciao, buona notte."* Stefano and I walk away, me toward home, he toward his car. He has a pleasing demeanor and works in the center, at a bank right next to mine. "Come find me," he says, "we'll take a *caffè* together."

I assure him that I will and continue my journey homeward, thinking once again of the pain of beautiful, raven-haired, blue-eyed Silvia, of her three small children, the treacherous streets, the attempt to keep the truth of what happened from the kids so as not to "worry" them. I conclude that I have accomplished what H. G. Wells had always dreamed about. I have stepped back in time, for the moment at least, as globalization and euros and modern management techniques compete for the soul of this city with the simple verities of the old world—men and women entertain themselves separately, while both conspire to keep the young in a prolonged state of innocence. I know what will eventually win and succeed in putting the thought out of my mind as sleep overtakes me.

19

Sunday in the City:
An Early Morning Run

How is it possible that on Sunday—really the one day that I have no commitments, no time pressures, that there is no school to get the kids to, no appointments to keep or make—my eyes spring open, almost as if they had been set to go off the night before, at 7:00 A.M.? What force has taken over my body, my consciousness, my past life in Rome, that would compel me to resist the temptation to fall back asleep, or just lie there, or do anything for that matter other than what I know I am within a few moments about to do, which is get up and drag my middle-aged body into the bathroom to brush my teeth and throw cold water on my face so that I can do what every Sunday morning seems to find me doing—jogging through the heart of the city, when all is quiet, peaceful, empty, when I can pass the monuments and narrow streets without jostling crowds, buzzing *motorini,* the distraction of so many people requiring so much getting around them. My Sunday morning run is something I do alone, something that requires no interaction, no acknowledgment of anyone else, no arranging. It's just me and my passion for the city, which manages to look the same and different at the same time. It's therapy, prayer, inquiry, meditation, and forgetfulness all rolled into one. It's Rome as one rarely sees it.

The Sunday morning run is especially *bello* in late spring and early summer, when the light is full and the air so mild it kisses your body without imposing on it as the summer heat does. You feel as if your skin and the air around you were one and the same, no separation between inner and outer, you and time in perfect harmony, as it will be hours before the city will wake from the usual late-night Saturday revelry, when traffic engorges the small streets and arteries and flocks of Romans enjoy the weekend. I, too, am enjoying mine, but I know that a Sunday would not be complete without a run through history.

The first leg is uphill. I climb the Via di Santa Prisca not quite as far as the church. Going left will take me through the Aventino, but I go right, past the United States embassy to the Vatican and the intoxicating fragrance of the municipal rose garden, in full view of the Palatine, just now taking in the first few rays of its daily intake of sun. The traffic on Via del Circo Massimo, along the fabled Circus Maximus, usually so intense that one literally has to step out into the street, even on the pedestrian strip, to stop the speeding cars and *motorini* in order to get across, is nonexistent. There is not a vehicle in sight; I could crawl across the wide thoroughfare and reach the other side safely.

I resist the temptation and jog instead. Soon I will turn right at the Tiber end of the huge, earthy, open oval and head north along Via San Teodoro, the west side of the Palatine Hill, into the quintessence of the city. My heart rate is up and my body has successfully processed the fact that I am pushing it once again by turning up the heat, but, attired in T-shirt and shorts, sweat beginning to pour down my face and back, the still cool

air feels refreshing on my bare limbs, and somehow I know—
as all runners do at some point into their workout—that I have
managed to overcome my own resistance to putting one foot in
front of the other and will complete my *giro,* my trip around
town. At various spots I can see the remains of the Palatine, still
in shadow, as Romulus would have seen it 2,753 years before
me. Soon I am along the side of the Foro Romano, that treasure
trove of stone, marble, and mosaic that basically lay underground
until just over one hundred years ago, and is now trod every
day by those who want to walk the same streets as the *antichi
romani* once did. Ahead of me lies the first real hill, the back side
of the Campidoglio, but by this time my heart is pumping huge
quantities of blood to my limbs, and I am actually looking forward to pushing my body even more.

I bound up the hill, past the two *vigili* who as usual are chatting
away between puffs of cigarettes. By this time they half expect
me on Sunday mornings, and I detect the faintest *nod* as they
momentarily interrupt their recounting of last night's dinner or
their predictions for today's soccer matches to let me know that
they know that I—who must be a *straniero* because no Roman
in his right mind would be up at this hour, in this garb, doing
what I am doing—am noticed. Within moments I have as-
cended into Michelangelo's incomparable piazza at the top of
the Capitoline Hill, the civic seat of Rome, whose city hall,
which is built on top of the registry office of the ancient capital
and which has stood on that spot since 30 B.C., boasts a facade
designed by Buonarotti himself. The piazza also contains the
Capitoline Museum, which is the oldest public gallery in the
world, dating from 1730, and which contains the splendid sculpture of the dying Gaul, an homage to a people Rome's manifest

destiny gave them no choice but to conquer. To regard the figure is to know what it must be like to feel life slowly being drained out of what was moments before a vibrant human being.

To this point, after fifteen minutes of running, I have encountered two, maybe three people, but I am about to descend on the other side of the Campidoglio and enter the hub of Piazza Venezia, where vendors are setting up their souvenir stands and tour buses are disgorging clusters of Japanese, Germans, and English from other parts of the world onto the streets of Rome. I dodge them easily. By now I am in full stride and I elicit hardly a glance from the visitors as I have not been listed in their guide books of things not to miss in Rome. I circle in front of the Wedding Cake, the Monument to Victor Emmanuel II, and cross on the other side of the square, running toward the Via Battisti, where I make a sharp right. I have successfully navigated the most hectic part of the first half of the journey, and suddenly I find myself watching as the bar employees are sweeping the sidewalk, setting up tables, and getting ready for another day in which they will make several thousand *cappuccini* and *caffè*. Some patches of the wide sidewalk are wet, but the sun is busily making short work of the moistened concrete. I turn left into Piazza SS Apostoli and head for the narrow alleys that lead farther north, peeking through sun-cracked stone walls and secluded inner courtyards, where fragments of daily life are sporadically beginning to reveal themselves.

Here, the streets are once again empty, as I jog past the national headquarters on Via Umiltà, the street ironically called humility, of Forza Italia, the national political party headed—some would say owned—by media magnate Silvio Berlusconi. Two policemen sit in an official wagon and guard the entrance, but there is not much to do, and they seem either asleep or bored out of their minds. I find the little alley called Monticello, which has wrought-iron street lamps and a burnt orange wall and is so small and curved that you have to convince yourself that you have not left the twentieth century altogether. Suddenly, I am aware that the only sounds I can hear are my rhythmic, striding footsteps on the cobblestones, which echo off the close-in walls and lend an even more eerie dimension to my reverie. I half expect to see a medieval mendicant emerge from around the bend or to have to dodge bathwater that might at any moment be flung from an upper window and onto the street.

Where else in the Western world can one find such public solitude? In all the time I dreamed about coming to live in this city, I never thought I would be treated to something so serene and pure, even if it only lasts for a moment, as Vicolo Monticello ends and I join a more well traveled street and am immediately hit with the sound and sight of sanitation workers loading garbage into their ultramodern truck. I can bear the intrusion, because within seconds I am past it.

I run up the Via San Vincenzo and before me stands one of the wonders of the world, the fabled Fontana di Trevi, begun in 1717 by Nicola Salvi as an attachment to the Palazzo Poli behind it. There are maybe a dozen people before the sculpted gods and horses, gazing, reflecting, listening to the forceful sound of the water as it erupts from various openings and falls like so many cascades into the large pools below. I permit myself a smile, knowing that within hours, the piazza through which I am now running will be a mob scene, its most striking feature the thousands of people jostling each other to get a glimpse of the fountain, or standing with their backs to it and throwing a coin over their left shoulders, guaranteeing that they, too, will one day return to the Eternal City.

I cross the Via del Tritone, a major thoroughfare, and pass the house in Piazza San Andrea delle Fratte in which my idol, Gianlorenzo Bernini, once lived. I slow down and touch the building, hoping to be struck by the same genius, hoping—against the odds—that I might too be feted, even for Andy Warhol's modernist fifteen minutes, by princes, popes, and politicians. For now it is enough to know that I can say that I lived in the city that he so richly adorned and that my pleasure of it is made possible in no small part by his contributions. I pass a *romano*. He stops when he sees me, first to make sure that I will not run him down, then to check if I am crazy, and finally just to take in the sight of a sweating, heavy-breathing member of his age cohort. He swivels as I pass and meekly responds to my *buongiorno,* not having the slightest idea what to make of me. In gorgeous, perfect, spring weather, I have not passed a single other jogger. Nor do I expect to. The look on his face says, "Now, I have seen everything."

I sneak a quick glance right before turning onto Via Condotti. The so-called Spanish Steps, the other great municipal project of the eighteenth century, are magnificent, an inspired piece of public architecture, sitting immediately to the right of the house in which the young English poet John Keats died, of tuberculosis, in 1821 at the tender age of twenty-five. Piazza di Spagna is the English quarter of town, and the few tearooms that remain in Roma are located here. As I scamper past the Caffè Greco, which dates from 1760 and at whose bar you can still stand and drink a *caffè* for fourteen hundred lire, eighty cents, or for considerably more than that if you sit down at one of the tables, which only the tourists do, I know that the Via Condotti will take me across the Via del Corso, which links Piazza Venezia at its southern end and Piazza del Popolo to the north, and toward the river.

My jog is at the halfway point and the endorphins are kicking in. I feel as if I could run forever, but if I really could, I would choose the direction of the past, into another time about which I can only speculate. What is left to me now are only glimpses, pieces, fragments of other cultures, other civilizations, mentalities, values, habits, everyday sights and sounds. I love the past. I always have. I don't live in it, but I love living with it. I can't see how, after four years in Rome, I could feel comfortable living in a place that did not have a vibrant yesterday, a history with which I could connect myself.

I am jolted back into the present as I pass the chic shop windows, displaying precious few items that nonetheless don't fail to attract—a simple top, skirt, and pair of sexy, strappy sandals. What is it about them? The color? The design? The display itself? I turn left onto Via Leoncino, past a *fontanella* that predates the nineteenth-century cast-iron models, a stone facing that spills water into a basin, and begin to turn toward home. I can now feel the heat. It comes up from under my feet and envelops my body. Thank God the streets are narrow. Thank God the sun can still not yet penetrate, making my effort all the more *faticoso*, rigorous and trying, like Atlas bent forward from the daunting task of holding up the earth. To my left, where Via Campo Marzio meets Via Uffici del Vicario, past Giolitti *gelateria*, I turn left, leaving behind the guy playing "Mr. Tambourine Man" on the guitar as his sidekick holds out a twenty-ounce paper

McDonald's cup. I put out my hands in the "What can I do?" gesture, and he smiles and wishes me a *buona giornata*.

It is then that the climax of the entire one-hour trip stands before me—the Pantheon. At first I can't see much of it, just the light that is pouring in from somewhere, making the two-thousand-year-old columns stand out against the relative darkness of the street in which I am running, a *vicolo* that is host to Da Fortunato, one of our favorite restaurants, an ideal place in which to eat a leisurely meal outdoors, with the hovering Pantheon a guest at the table.

From the brilliance of the light, I can tell it's almost summer, the air heating up by the second. The Pantheon is so old and so intact that it almost looks as if it came from outer space, an ancient UFO with the huge hole at the top of the roof to let in the natural elements, whatever they may be. You haven't seen anything until you see a shaft of heavy rain dropping over a hundred feet through the opening and onto the marble floor, as if the temple had been designed by a brilliant madman.

A left turn past Bernini's elephant under the obelisk in the Piazza della Minerva takes me through the Piazza Collegio Romano, and within moments I am once again navigating the straits of Piazza Venezia, by now packed with people, buses, cars, sun, heat, and noise. I jog in place, waiting for the light to turn, and then cross the open expanse before heading back up Michelangelo's long, ramplike stairway and once again into the Campidoglio on the Capitoline Hill. Bronze emperor Marcus Aurelius greets me, his right hand extended outward in the gesture of clemency, piety, blessing; his bearded visage reminds me somehow of the Latin I studied in high school in the early sixties. Marcus, of course, is a copy, a wonderful copy, as the original

173

sits inside the Capitoline Museum to prevent its certain deteri-
oration. Yet the worn bronze in the waxing light still strikes a
chord. It encourages my eyes to take in the magnitude of his
stoic presence.

By now I am soaked, my T-shirt having gained a pound of
water from the exertion. I see the Colosseum and the Forum
once again as I go down around its back side, acknowledge the
two *vigili* who are in exactly the same spot I left them, two,
maybe three cigarettes earlier, and hit the home stretch. My legs
are still there, so I sprint part of the way, knowing that within
moments the magnificent ordeal will have run its course. I can
hear traffic in the distance, but this stretch is usually quiet. Visitors to Rome emerge from the little-known hotel to my right,
near San Giorgio in Velabro, which was bombed by the Mafia
in 1992 after the government demonstrated its seriousness in the
Mani Pulite, the Clean Hands, campaign. I can now see the
finish line.

A *fontanella* awaits me, this one in front of the Church of Santa
Anastasia. I lean in to drink up the cold wetness. Maurizio at the
bar has told me that a woman taking a drink like this used to be
a target for a pinch, but that kind of stuff is now part of folklore.
No one is around, so I am safe. The walk home, which takes
another ten minutes and constitutes my cool-down, brings on a
high that is unmatchable—an ecstasy of both body and soul, a
relaxation that is particular to the early morning, to jogging, and
to a passion that can be indulged in every time I encounter the
living past of the city of Rome.

20

Outsiders: A Jew in Rome Is Not like a Jew in New York

P*oppi,*" first grader Elliott said between bites of a *cornetto* one morning just minutes before we would head up the hill to school. I could tell he was about to launch into something that had to do with *la cultura italiana* because he started out using the endearing word for father. *"Quando ci si arrabbia con qualcuno, è vero che la luce dentro si spegne?"* His words, so earnest, so inquiring, so close to his core—took me aback. I had never heard my six-year-old speak like this, of these things. "When you're angry with someone, is it true that the light inside goes out?" Nine-year-old Julian immediately knew the origin of his brother's curiosity, but I had to probe.

"Who told you that?" I asked. "Suora Chiara," he replied. I went further. "And what else did she say?" The words spilled out of him, in Italian, as if they had been inked somewhere in his psyche, words that neither Diane nor I had or would ever say, or ever think to say, since they do not partake of our culture. "She said that when you're bad, *Gesù* leaves your heart and you go to the devil."

I already knew that this would not be a conversation I would

175

share anytime soon with my mother, a Holocaust survivor. The youngest child in a Viennese family, she by a miracle managed to escape Austria and spend the war years in London. Her mother, sister, and two brothers were not so fortunate. They perished in the death camps. Her consciousness of her religion fits perfectly the sad plight of Jews everywhere, in every time, but especially the Jews of Eastern and Central Europe in the twentieth century. It is a consciousness of separateness, of persecution, of difference, a consciousness that believes that when push comes to shove—anywhere and anytime—Christians are Christians and Jews are Jews; that several millennia of mutual mistrust are too long to build bridges that will endure; and that even if there are times when the people of the two religions can live together without hurting each other, those times are rare and are always in danger of transforming, even in an instant, into their opposite, as history has repeatedly shown.

Diane and I do not hold these views. We are Jews, but our identification is cultural, ethnic, and ceremonial, rather than religious or dogmatic. We do not keep kosher, go to temple on a regular basis, or observe the Sabbath. In our more ecumenical point of view, we are but one tribe in a world full of tribes, one people in a hodgepodge of people who all must learn to live together in harmony, despite our undeniable differences. In this way, our mentality is very American. To us, Jews are just another member of the melting pot and live in America in more or less accord with the dominant Christian culture, Protestant but secular. Religion is a private matter, and no one foists any doctrines or beliefs onto anyone else.

But we are no longer in "I'm OK, you're OK" America, where thousands of creeds live side by side in basic, if sometimes uneasy, tolerance. We are in Italy, in Rome, in the birthplace and still center of worldwide Roman Catholicism. To paraphrase Lenny Bruce's quip, "In New York everyone is Jewish, in the rest of the country no one is," I would say that in Italy everyone is Catholic, even if you are not. In fact, on our ritual Sunday *passeggiata* the other day, we noticed that every person passing by was carrying a palm branch, commemorating Palm Sunday. When Diane went to pay the cashier at our corner bar, he, noting that something was missing, said, "As soon as you leave, you're going up to the church to get your palm, aren't you?" waving his own green branch in the air. "I am not a Catholic," she replied. *"Chi se ne frega?* Who cares? Go directly up the hill and find yourself a palm."

I know we must do something about my son's budding indoctrination, but it is not easy to figure exactly what. I had briefly spoken once or twice with Suora Chiara, who is Elliott's religion teacher at school, an Italian public school, and she seemed like a reasonable person, but for all I know she could turn into the avenging angel behind closed doors. In the meantime, Diane and I patiently explain to Elliott that we don't believe the things that Suora Chiara has told him. We tell him that the light inside is always on, that even if you're mad at someone and you yell at them or even throw something at them, the light never goes out, that you are still a good person who has done a less than good thing. It is a subtle point, but to us an important one. Next we tackle the devil issue. For me, it is easy to dispense with it because I can pull out all the philosophical and historical information I learned as a historian two decades ago. Since we are not Catholic, since we have no investment in preserving the good without damaging the child, as we see many of our Italian

Catholic friends trying to do, we have no qualms about saying that there is no such thing as the devil, that what Suora Chiara perhaps means when she says "the devil" is just another way of saying "bad," and that she believes you go to the bad place when you are angry. But then we go back to our original point with Elliott. You don't go to the bad place. People do bad things, and some people call that the devil, but we don't. All the stuff of hideous red bodies with tails and horns, all the medieval scare tactics detailed ad nauseum by Hieronymous Bosch that go along with it, should be ignored.

The question of Jesus, to say the least, is another matter altogether.

I must say I was not yet prepared to get to the central religious, philosophical issue of Western civilization so soon with my children. As Jews, we run on a parallel track, occasionally having had to cave in to the dominant beliefs, but basically being able to hold on to our similar but distinct views. Elliott's remarks, however, strike at the core of how much I want my two sons, who are Jewish by birth and who were circumcised in the traditional *bris* on the eighth day after birth, to be Jewish. I am not naive enough to think that they will find their path to Judaism on their own without some kind of impetus from their parents, especially now that we are in Roman Catholic Rome, where the culture of Christ and the Madonna is so prevalent, so dominant, so ubiquitous, that one would think that, in fact, there is no other faith, no other religion, no other way of approaching the infinite. Yes, there are Jews in Rome—fifteen thousand to be precise—the remains of a community that dates back to the third century B.C., before history had ever heard of Jesus

Christ; indeed, it is the longest continuous Jewish population in the world.

So far, however, the Jewish community has been difficult for us to penetrate, except for a generous invitation one year to a Passover Seder for forty people, held in the living room of the hosts' spacious apartment. The Jews seem to be in their own world, and in comparison to theirs, our Judaism—tangential, occasional, underdeveloped—seems to put us in a category in which we could just as well be a family of American Methodists, or atheists, who have set down here in Rome. Beyond that, their culture is so different, so alien from the Eastern European Ashkenazic Judaism of our upbringing, that when we attended another seder in a Jewish community center not far from the Jewish ghetto, the spiritual if not the physical center of Rome's Jews, and we were still waiting at 10 P.M. for the meal that we knew would surely follow the complete seder, I was reminded of my childhood. I could still feel the persistent hunger I experienced as a child when I would go to the home of our Orthodox Jewish neighbors and sit through the interminable prayers before getting to the gefilte fish, the chopped chicken liver, the matzo ball soup, the potato kugel, and chicken. It was only the thought of these delicacies, which I could still smell as if they had already been placed on the table, that prevented me from beginning to nibble on my fingers. Imagine my disappointment when an everyday Italian meal finally appeared before me—the *primo piatto* of risotto, the *secondo* consisting of veal, a *contorno* consisting of the traditional fried artichoke—as if these Jews had never heard of the gastronomic tradition that had been the staple of my youth. It reminded me of the old joke about an American Jew who finds himself in China on Yom Kippur, stumbles upon a synagogue, and asks to participate in the service. The Chinese rabbi looks at him and says, "You're Jewish? That's funny, you don't look Jewish."

Elliott's comments made it clear to me that we had done nothing so far to remind our kids that they are Jews, whether they understand what that means or not. I know full well how easy it would be for them to lose entirely this link with their past, and that although I did not marry outside the faith—as 50 percent of my fellow Jews now do—I did happen to marry someone whose connection to Judaism is even less firm than my own. None of Diane's brothers had a bar mitzvah; she never studied Hebrew; and to her, if Julian and Elliott are raised knowing that they are Jews because every Yom Kippur Daddy fasts, on Hanukkah we light candles and they get presents, and on Passover you make a big dinner and don't eat leavened bread for a while, that would be enough. Somehow, for me it isn't.

So far, with Julian we have been lucky. Although he was the only Jewish pupil at the private English-speaking school he initially attended for two years, the school honored his differences. When he started last year at the Italian public school in the third grade, the curriculum called for the study of the Old Testament, and his teacher was a young, attractive woman with a decidedly ecumenical spirit. She is now gone, and in her place is Suora Chiara. This year, however, together with five other classmates, Julian has opted out of religion and is studying instead environmental education, which teaches respect for the earth and humankind without having to mention the Savior.

Elliott could opt out of religion, too, but the situation is more complicated for this first grader, in that he would be the only one doing so in a class of twenty-six and would thus from the very first days of his school career draw attention to this very basic difference. It's a dilemma. We ask Maestra Maria, Elliott's mathematics teacher, a woman in her forties with long, platinum blond hair, granny glasses, and exclusively black outfits, what she thinks of what Suora Chiara is telling the class. She laughs a little, perhaps in embarrassment, and lets us know that she doesn't herself agree with the doctrine or the pedagogy. She can't really talk to the nun, but we can if we want to. Since no one else is upset, there is no possibility of organizing another class, and so if we didn't want Elliott to be exposed to these teachings, he would have to stay by himself for the two hours every Thursday morning when Suora Chiara takes over.

Christmas vacation intervenes to enable us to think about this further. Even the Roman friends with whom we have spoken about this situation, and who have no particular love for the Church, the nuns, or the doctrines of Catholicism, caution us. Our research among Romans turns up almost universal disapproval of the Church and its teachings. Catholicism, they say, has done more damage to people in Italy than anyone can imagine, and it is virtually only elderly *signore* who still believe it. But when we ask if they would take Elliott out of the class if they were in our position, they hesitate. Maybe it's better to leave him in. In America, which is populated by individualists, and where "doing your own thing" has become standard operating procedure, being different is no big deal. In Italy, it is much more problematic, especially when that difference has to do with Catholic versus Jew. This is a culture of conformity. I remember watching in amusement one day on the beach as three women in black bikinis walked by, each of them holding a pair of beach

181

shoes. I remarked to Diane that in the United States, one would be wearing her shoes, another holding them, and the third would not have any shoes at all. When we left the beach and sat down at a bar to have a snack, there were four men at the next table, each of them sitting in front of a bottle of Peroni beer, each having poured half the beer into a glass.

Most Romans tell us to keep Elliott in the class and just tell him the truth—which in this case is essentially what we believe. It will be good for him to understand the dominant culture, they say, especially if we intend to remain in Italy, rather than to be singled out as being different from the others, and he can rely on us for an alternative picture. There are enough difficulties fitting in as an *americanino* without having to deal with being the only one who doesn't take religion. I know what they're talking about. We are especially sensitive to this potential marginalization, as Julian's first few months at this school the year before were a nightmare for him, even without having to deal with the Jewish-Catholic question. I take solace in the fact that at least it's not catechism.

Being in Italy, you realize what separation of church and state, a bulwark of American democracy, really means. The popes ruled Rome and other parts of Italy for roughly fourteen hundred years. Then, the republican forces of a united country broke into the city in 1870 and forced the papacy to remain in the Vatican, where it stayed—seething—until Mussolini in 1929 signed the Lateran Treaty, making the Vatican the smallest sovereign state in the world. Part of that agreement provided that the Roman Catholic religion would be taught in Italian public schools—with the opportunity to opt out—and that the Vatican would choose the teachers. Italy is the opposite of America.

There is no separation of church and state, only separation of church and individual consciousness. Catholicism is everywhere—except in the hearts and minds of the people.

That's what makes this situation so ironic. For if one combines the pervasive influence, both historically and politically, of the Roman Catholic Church on the lives of the Romans, together with the fact that the overwhelming number of modern-day Romans take seriously their allegiance to Catholicism, one would think that the Church has these people tightly in its grip.

Yet nothing could be further from the truth, and everyone knows it. "People have turned away from the Church because they sense that it's really about power," said Monsignore Aldo Settepani, one night over dinner. He is a seventy-three-year-old retired Vatican judge, having spent forty years on the bench dealing with marital annulments. And Franca Zambonini, who is a dear friend, a great cook, and has seen the machinations of the Vatican throughout her long, illustrious career as a journalist and director of *Famiglia Cristiana,* said to me one evening that "the Romans are naturally skeptical people, and they have reason to be skeptical when it comes to the Church lecturing to them about morality."

The Roman Catholic hold on the Romans of today is a lot like the Church of San Clemente near the Colosseum: glorious levels of both current and historical Roman Catholicism built on a solid pagan foundation underneath. During one of our many city walks together, Nancy De Conciliis, an expert on the history of Rome who has lived here for more than thirty years, says, "I don't think there's any doubt that Romans are still by and large pagans. Practically all the Christian celebrations were lifted straight out of the ancient Roman world."

On all matters that have to do with being a good Catholic: baptism, Communion, confirmation, marriage, catechism, confession, observance of holidays, last rites—the appearances that lead one to believe that the Romans are faithful followers of the ancient traditions of their religion—there is general compliance. The Church is still strong. It is visible. It pervades Roman life to an extent that one would think it was the absolute point of reference for all of Roman society. When you walk around Rome, especially near the Vatican, you see clusters of nuns, and collared priests carrying briefcases: the Vatican equivalent of the bureaucrats of Washington, D.C. In fact, the Church has left its mark to such an extent that there is very little here in the way of new thinking, of an elaborate intellectual life. Unlike London, Paris, New York, and other great cities of the West, Rome does not have an extensive university culture to provide an air of raffishness, of the avant-garde.

But deep down, in the soul of the Romans, where they really live in their most private moments, I suspect that their consciousness is still pre-Christian, still interested in giving free rein to their impulses, their desires, their interest in having their cake and eating it, too. "The Church is like your mother," says Maria Elena Vasaio, a friend of twenty-five years who has lived in Rome since 1980, working for the RAI, the Italian broadcasting service, as a producer-director, and who hosted me during my first, unforgettable visit here. "You only go to her when you need help or when you're in trouble."

I need help, so I go to Suora Chiara, a confrontation I am dreading. When it occurs, however, I am immediately charmed. Dressed in white coif, light brown robes, and Birkenstocks, this unassuming, soft-spoken nun from the Abruzzo, who seems to be about my age, is bemused by our free choice to pick up and move to Rome, perhaps because she lived in New Jersey for twenty-five years and thus speaks English. "I could not believe it when I found out that Elliott is American," she tells me, in Italian, adding that she loves the openness of Americans. "He speaks Italian like a *romano,* not a trace of an American accent." We exchange pleasantries, which leads me to inform her that not only are we not Italian, we are not even Christian. "We're Jewish," I tell her, not knowing how she will react. She does so according to the party line the Church has been putting out during the recent past. *"Ah, nostri fratelli maggiori,"* she says. "Our big brothers." "Yes," I say, thinking, "And I hope you never forget it, either," which I manage to hold back through my smile. "So that's why Elliott keeps saying that he doesn't believe what I am telling the class," she says, shaking her head in amusement.

Suora Chiara responds. As she begins to teach the others about the Old Testament, she tells the first graders about the Hebrews fleeing from the Egyptians and has the children draw menorahs. I begin to feel comfortable with her, despite our initial and still-nagging doubts.

We had told Elliott our version of the story, still, after all this time, the greatest story ever told. We said that Jesus was a Jew who wanted to empower common people, but the ruling-class thought that he was going too far and decided to kill him. Since the prophets of the Old Testament foretold the appearance among the Jews of a man who would also be God, or the Son of God, depending on your particular Christian viewpoint, some Jews thought that Jesus was this figure, this Messiah, and that all the Jews should follow him and become Christians. But most of them didn't, and then after a long time the Roman citizens and slaves, who had never been Jews to begin with, became Christians. The Jews, of which you are one, Elliott, are still waiting for the Messiah, and just don't think that it's Jesus. We don't "believe" that Jesus was really God, or the Son of God, except insofar as everyone is the son or daughter of God.

Elliott seems satisfied. He is now in the bath, and I can hear him splashing around as Julian in his room memorizes a poem for tomorrow's environmental class. Diane is in the kitchen stirring the *risotto con asparagi,* and I am sitting in the living room reading and listening to music. In the relative quiet, after this rather lengthy explanation, I can hear the sweet timbre of Elliott's voice. "Yeah," he says, "just like I don't believe that Bugs Bunny is really a rabbit." *Bravo.*

21

Breakfast in a Bar: The Coffee Culture

As in all unforgettable love affairs, I remember the first time I was seduced: the very first moments I realized that this lover would be different from the others, and that even if I didn't know that she would turn out to be the "one" with whom I'd spend the rest of my life, at least I knew that my senses were on full alert and that I could not imagine being without her. Yes, I remember the first time I felt that I was in love with Rome.

It was in a bar on the Via del Corso. I had been in Rome for one week, had walked through the Forum, had been inside the Pantheon, had thrown a coin into the Trevi Fountain. I had eaten in one fantastic *trattoria* after another, strolled through the Borghese Gardens, and felt the pulse of the city. I had been hosted spectacularly by my longtime friend Maria, who had come to Rome to live permanently the year before, and her sister-in-law Franca, who had grown up here, so much so that there seemed to be a party every night after dinner, with visits to clubs, theaters, and discotheques, all kicked off by a Thanksgiving dinner that Maria had prepared for fifteen *romani* and me on my first day in the city. I can still hear one guest saying, over and over again—as if he were trying to convince himself with the word, while he held up the bottle of Zinfandel that I had brought all the way from California for the occasion (talk about bringing coals to Newcastle), and tasted the rich, peppery, red— *"Buono, buono."*

All this had prepared the ground for the moment when I would look around and say to myself, "I could live here," which soon became "I want to live here," which moved in the inexorable way that love affairs do to "I never want to leave here." Leave I did, but only in body, for my soul never strayed. It was constantly begging me to go back, to experience again the particular feeling that comes over me when I walk these twisted streets, have conversations with these sunny, lively people who know how to do it so well that they could have actually invented the art of idle chitchat, or *chiacchierare* (key-ah-key-ah-*rah*-reh), as they say, an onomatopoetic word if there ever was one, and eat—every day, morning, noon, and night—this amazing food that insinuates itself into your psyche as well as your taste buds to the point where you can tell after the first bite if something is well prepared or not.

But my schemes to get back here just drifted in and out of the recesses of my life, lost among the shoals of career, sentimental detours, and inertia. Single at the time, I had even made a deal with two female friends on two separate occasions that if we were both still unattached on a certain date in the future, we would take the plunge—at least as roommates—and move to Rome for a spell. But somehow these pipe dreams never materialized, and it was not until five years after my unexpected infatuation, five years after the moment in which I had fallen in love with Rome, that suddenly a plan appeared before me, in the form of a beautiful, unattached woman, who would within the span of eight months become my wife.

Diane also had a passion for Italy, not as viscerally rooted as mine, but planted nonetheless. On our very first date, it came out that a small but elegant farmhouse was available to her in Cerveteri, in the Etruscan countryside west of Rome along the Via Aurelia Antica. Somehow, within the next month, we were already engaged, had set a wedding date, and had decided that we would leave behind our San Francisco lives—for the moment—and go to Italy just after the wedding for travel, adventure, and who knows what else. Our four months in Europe, most of them in Italy and most of those days in and around Rome, only reassured me that I had to live in this country, and slowly Diane was coming around to the realization that I was serious, that we could actually make our fantasy a reality. The hard part—Diane having to learn Italian, improving my own, figuring out what to do next, dealing with the exigencies of shutting down a life in one continent and starting over again in a new one—was yet to come.

But I was committed, not to be denied, having fallen in love with Rome on a cold, drizzly, dark evening six years before. I was in a bar called Allemagna. The scene was nothing short of a dream, an impression from deep within that is only acted upon when you come into contact in your waking life with your true consciousness, which was hidden—even to yourself—until then. Bars are the mother lode of Italian social life, something akin to pubs in England but much more accessible to everyone, both in the physical sense and in terms of what they provide. They are places in which to take a refreshing pause from whatever is going on in your life, places where you can have a *caffè* or drink, either alcoholic or non, have something light to eat like a pastry or sandwich, or have a word with your friend, relative, or stranger, and not spend too much time doing it. Bars are frequently crowded in the morning as Romans are having their usual *cappuccino* or *caffè* with a *cornetto,* at lunch time with those not destined to eat in a *trattoria* or at home (the overwhelming number of Italians—around 65 percent—still take their afternoon meal *a casa*), or in the evening before the *ora di cena,* the dinner hour.

Most Romans do not sit down in a bar, as they see it as a place to stop but not to stay. The usual picture of the American coffeehouse or café, where ten people are sitting alone at ten tables, each of them reading a newspaper or magazine beside a huge mug of steaming java, is not part of the Roman culture. You often find places to sit, some inside, most outside on the sidewalk, but the prices you pay at the tables are usually significantly higher, tourist prices, and Romans make so many trips each day to the bar that no one stop interrupts the flow. Most bars serve the same things, or at least the same kinds of things, and so one's bar of preference becomes a matter of proximity, decor, size, atmosphere, or level of familiarity, for bars can range from pretty basic industrial-looking joints, dim and spare and putting out more shots of *grappa* than coffee, to grand, elaborate establishments with old-time Roman names, hot tables, and little plates of peanuts or pretzels, *salatini* (little salty things) that you scoop out for yourself with a demitasse spoon. (The *romani* have this thing about hands. Food is either eaten with utensils or is held, as is a sandwich, for example, with paper or a napkin. When I first came here, I thought cashiers were rude because they never put the change directly in my hand. I later learned that, to begin with, they don't want any confusion about how much money they gave to you, and second, they have no interest whatsoever in touching your hand, fearing the spread of germs.)

Allemagna was for me the perfect bar. When you walked in, it was like going back in time to the thirties, as the art deco look reminded me of the Europe that once was. The light-colored vaulted ceilings and dark wood strategically inserted gave off a feeling of casual elegance, and there was enough floor space to fit quite a few round standing tables, lit by deco lamps and equipped with a footrest, at which you could pause with a friend and chat about the day's events, or be *da solo,* as I was that fateful evening, and watch the Romans when they are at their happiest—eating, drinking coffee, chatting, interacting in a playful, familiar way with the people who serve them. I had ordered a *cappuccino* and *cornetto,* which is unheard of for Italians at 6:00 P.M., as they almost never have milk after 11:00 A.M. and *cornetti* are decidedly a breakfast item, but, being fresh off the boat, I could not get enough of either of these, and so Allemagna graciously provided them to me.

As I looked around, enjoying the pleasing combination of bitter and sweet, the certainty came over me that this spot was a place I had been looking for my whole life; that here were all these people crowding around the counters that served *dolci, panini,* little *pizzette,* or even more elaborate pastas or cooked meats and vegetables, in a setting large enough to make it worth watching. The people were, of course, all impeccably attired, and even if one were to eat something elaborate and have a drink, the bill would probably not amount to more than five or six dollars. I was love-struck. I knew then that I wanted to have the opportunity to come into Allemagna whenever I chose, that it meant a lot to me not only to know that it existed, but that I could reach it, even if I didn't live particularly close and would not visit every day. Allemagna became my touchstone, and when Diane and I were in Rome in 1987, it became something of our place, even to the point where some of the employees recognized us and began, as Romans are wont to do when they feel comfortable with you, to speak the few words of English they know.

But, of course, we had to leave Rome then, and the events of our lives in northern California took over as we had one child who didn't make it, and then one, Julian, who did, followed by the house we bought in Marin. Then, when Diane was seven months pregnant with Elliott, we realized we couldn't take it any longer, that four years had passed since we had tasted the rich, creamy, blend of the *cappuccino* at Allemagna, along with the light, delicate, slightly orange flavor of the *cornetto*. We had to be there. We *had* to be there.

We managed to find a reasonable flight, booked a small *pensione* close to Piazza di Spagna, asked my parents to watch Julian for ten days, and took off, knowing the whole time that the first thing we would do would be to head straight for "our" bar. Suddenly, it seemed as though our dream of one day living in Italy was to be put to the test. Would Allemagna satisfy as it had done before? Would the coffee taste as good, the people look as elegant, the decor seem as rich and satisfying? We had heard that Italy had gotten "expensive." What did that mean? We would soon know.

We dropped off our luggage after an all-night trip and practically ran down the street toward the Via del Corso. The place, the people, the food all looked the same. It was midmorning. I did what I had always done: went to the *cassa,* the register, and ordered our usual: *"Due cappuccini e due cornetti, per favore."* The cashier rang it up, saying the number of lire as the machine spit out the *scontrino* that I would have to put down along with the small tip on the bar. Two dollars and fifty cents did not strike us as expensive for this delicious breakfast. In fact, it was just what we had paid many times before; what I had paid eleven years ago. The caps were so good, the *cornetti* so light, the whole experience tingling both of us without end.

From that point on Diane and I stopped at nothing to live in Italy, initiating a three-year project that helped us know where to live, how to manage, all this so that I could be closer to my favorite bar, to Allemagna. We had even considered two beautiful towns in Tuscany—Lucca and Siena—but in the end rejected them because we feared that they would ultimately be too small, too provincial, too insular for *stranieri americani*—and too far from Allemagna.

Three and a half years later, we passed the bar for the first time as residents of Italy, just outside Rome. We were living at that time a twenty-five-minute train ride away and were dismayed to see the place under construction, everything closed. It was impossible to know what was going on behind the boarded-up site. "Not to worry," I said, "they are only going to make it even nicer, maybe put in a real toilet instead of the hole in the floor, shine up the marble, polish the wood, get new lamp shades on the art deco pieces. We can wait," I told Diane, as the sign said that they'd be finished in the spring.

The sign was right. They were finished in the spring. But

what now stands in the place where I once fell in love with this city is an abomination. It is a garish redesign, an ultramodern, bright, pastel-colored cafeteria that could serve as a food stop on any turnpike. There are huge slices of pizza under a heating lamp here, a yogurt stand there, and a bar that looks like it was designed in Disneyland. It is infinitely more crowded than it ever was, mostly with youngsters whom I suppose spend more on fast food than their parents and grandparents ever did on little pastries or *tramezzini* sandwiches with tuna and tomato. I have never set foot in it, not even to use the facilities. I am disappointed beyond redemption.

It is true that nothing much changes in Rome, at least on the surface, but then every so often something gets hijacked by modernity, mostly to appeal to the tastes of foreigners and the young. There still exist several bars with a certain particular, not necessarily old-world, charm—the Taverna del Campo in the Campo de' Fiori, Ciampini in San Lorenzo in Lucina, Tazza d'Oro near the Pantheon, and Caffè Farnese in Piazza Farnese— but, for some reason, there are few others that satisfy me the way my old *amante,* Allemagna, used to.

22

Calcio: *The Only Game in Town*

Try to guess the quietest time in Rome. The calmest calm, the most tranquil tranquillity. Certainly, Sunday morning, when I take my weekly run, contends for the honor. During the *ora di pranzo,* there's not a lot going on outside—unless the sun is shining and the café and restaurant tables have been set up—but you can still tell that you are in a big city, as people move to and fro and some kind of purposeful activity is taking place. Anytime between 7:00 P.M. and 2:00 A.M., you can forget about, as the night owl Romans are often out, in bunches small and large, until the wee hours. And when I wake up at 3:00, 4:00, or 5:00 A.M., as I do more often than I'd like, I can hear cars, trucks, *motorini,* the first daily trams, and the occasional alarm sounding nearby, reminding me even in the darkness that I no longer live in quiet, you-could-hear-birds'-wings-flapping Fairfax, California.

Yet there is a specific time when Rome is never more still, when cars are parked, shops are closed, and the random pedestrian you encounter, if he is both male and native to this country, has a transistor radio glued to his ear. The *ora di tranquillità* is

2:30 to 4:30 P.M. every Sunday between September and May, for it is during this time that the quasi-competitive nature of this country comes out and engages in its national pastime, its game of games, the sport that is played all over the world, by more people than baseball, football, basketball, and ice hockey combined.

The game is a simple one, carried out by twenty-two men dressed in colorfully designed jersey shirts and shorts, kicking around a medium-size round ball. There is no equipment—no bat, no glove, no helmet, no stick. There is also no attitude, as the slightest exaggerated transgression or disrespect for the officials or the game will result in immediate expulsion from the match, crippling one's own team, as there is no substitution for the remainder of the *partita*.

It is the only game in town, in fact, in the entire country. It is soccer.

As a young boy growing up in sports-mad Philadelphia, I was prone to all the agony that comes from hoping against hope that my teams would win. Sometimes they did, mostly they didn't, but as I grew older my interest in the major United States sports waned, for the games were gradually taken over by the media, which hyped them so much that the simple, naked competition between athletes—the element that drew me into being a fan in the first place—got lost in contract disputes, multi-billion-dollar television deals, and hundred-dollar autographs. It got so that by the time I came to Italy, I was watching only the championship events on television, my regular-season viewing having shrunk ever so slightly year by year.

This is one thing I miss about not being in the States, as much because my sons are old enough to understand my allegiances and I would have liked to share my earlier passions with them. When we were in America in the summer of 1998, we got totally caught up in Mark McGwire's pursuit of the home run record for a single season. In fact, the three of us were glued to the TV the last night of our stay, rather than being out and about, soaking up our final few hours of native American culture. We watched intently to see if we could say that at least we saw him hit one out of the park during the splendid season of his pursuit. And suddenly, there he was again, his last at bat, our final chance to be part of history—at least baseball history—and we were all hypnotized by the beauty of one of the greatest moments in sport: the flight of a well-struck baseball as it sails in the warm summer night air into the deep, dark recesses of the stadium, the outfielder doing only what we can do: watch. It made me feel good that the kids erupted as shamelessly as I did; that even at their ages, with not much baseball in their experience, they could still sense the drama and feel the rush along with everyone else. But not to worry. Within hours they would be on their adopted home turf, where their sport, their pleasure, their pastime, their *passion,* reigns supreme. Julian and Elliott are both soccer fanatics. Their minds are taken up not with home runs or touchdowns or three-pointers or slapshots. Rather, they are consumed, as is every other male and many females in Rome and all of Italy, by penalty kicks, angle shots, headers, and GOOOOOOOOAAAAAAAALS!

This country is soccer crazy. It is one of Italy's three religions—along with eating and the Catholic Church. Walk down any street in Rome at three o'clock on a Sunday afternoon, and if you didn't know better, you'd think that everyone had fled the city in advance of the plague. The only time you are certain that everyone hasn't, in fact, disappeared is when Roma scores a goal, which is rare, not because Roma is a bad team, but because goals are rare in soccer. When Delvecchio or Totti hits the net with a perfectly placed kick or a go-for-broke *colpo di testa,* the city erupts in a kind of collective ecstatic release that one associates with New Year's Eve or the ending of a world war. Horns blare, red and yellow streamers fly from windows, and fists are raised by the men who happen to be out while others are at home. Like so many other aspects of the culture in Rome, in Italy, people behave as if they were all one big family, all following soccer, even if the country has dozens of professional teams and loyalties are divided among cities, neighborhoods, and occasionally relatives. As a parent, I'm there. Julian is a *romanista,* following his hometown team, while younger Elliott, whose on-field manner has become a carbon copy of the pros—begging the refs with his hands, raising his fists as he runs in an airplanelike motion after a goal—is a fan of Inter Milan, for the simple reason that the most famous soccer player in the world today—The Phenomenon, the Brazilian Ronaldo—plays for Inter.

I thought I was a fanatic baseball card collector in my youth. That was nothing compared to the intense interest the kids give to their *figurine,* their soccer cards, which are purchased to be mounted in an album designed to contain all 635 players in Series A, B, and C, and every manner of fact and figure about the history of Italian soccer, which goes back to the end of the nineteenth century and which has a lore that is the equal of baseball. When you grow up in the United States, you think of soccer as a kid's game, evoking images of the moms who shuttle them to and from the fields in their Volvo station wagons. In Italy soccer is anything but a child's activity, although kids everywhere play, and the ease with which any *ragazzo* at any time could wander through a park or a piazza and join in a pickup game with other *ragazzi,* using a trashcan and a wall as one goal and two *pini romani* as the other, is truly astonishing. When a ball cannot be found, a pine cone replaces it.

Soccer is everywhere. Walk through the imposing Roman splendor of Piazza Farnese—where the monumental French embassy stands guarded by armed Carabinieri—any evening and you will see teens running for all they are worth to make a move and score. Cars, pedestrians, the cute electric bus line 116, and *motorini* must go around them, as the area directly in front of the Palazzo Farnese, with the frescoes on Michelangelo's ceilings looking down approvingly from inside, is theirs. The most venerable newspaper in the country, the *Corriere della Sera,* publishes an edition devoted strictly to sports—which means soccer—*daily.*

Everyone is a fan. Everyone roots. Everyone has associations that partake of their fathers' and grandfathers' and which they pass on to their kids. In the park one day I saw a man, around my age, with his one-and-a-half-year-old daughter. She was occupied, so he picked up a stray ball that was lying nearby and began to kick it in the air—one, two, three, four, five, ten, twenty times he kicked with both feet, without once letting the ball touch the ground. He was obviously skilled, obviously someone who had played a lot of soccer in his day, so much that although he has lost his step, he hasn't lost his touch. It was as if I were watching someone who had played high school baseball twenty years before and who was now taking his cuts in the batting cage without having lost his eye. When they meet at parties, Roman men do not ask what kind of work they do, as that is considered too personal and boring. More likely is the brief and to-the-point query, *"Di che squadra è?"* "What team do you root for?"

One time I was taken to the Stadio Olympico in Rome to witness a Serie A (major-league) match between the Roma and Milan teams (the other Milan team, not Inter). At that time I didn't know beans about soccer, but I knew one thing—I would be rooting for Roma. We were sandwiched in backless benches high up in the stands, and when Roma scored—which it did five times—the place erupted, not in high fives, but in kisses, embraces, the kind of emotion that most American men would not show if they had won the lottery. The group I was with (the only person I knew was Mats, who worked with these *romani*) understood everything about the game, and I had the impression that they would not have missed being in the stands with the other *tifosi,* the fans, had it been the day of their son's confirmation. Nothing would have kept these guys from being just where they were, not even the less than faithful behavior on the part of their wives, as statistics show (Italy keeps track of this kind of stuff) that the preferred time for women who have lovers to be with them is during soccer matches, and so last summer, when the quadrennial World Cup was being played in nearby France and perhaps fifty matches were televised in a one-month period, the media was speculating that there was probably going to be a lot more extracurricular activity than usual.

The 1998 World Cup was so all-encompassing, so overwhelming, so pervasive, that even Diane got into the act. Not that she had more time to visit her Italian lover (although I am always teasing her that it is the surefire way to nail down Italian once and for all), but that she is someone who is mostly put off by the macho quality of American sports. Nevertheless, she was right there with me and the kids, rooting for the teams but especially the individual players, as the tournament progressed. Julian was for Italy, Elliott (because of Ronaldo) rooted for Brazil, and I rooted for both, depending on which of the boys' teams was playing. When both squads advanced, it seemed like our household had taken on a guest who would stay as long as there was rooting interest. Then, in the midst of the tournament, we took a trip first to London, and thence to Paris, of all places, where the late-tournament matches were being held.

Italy had played defensively all series and yet had done well with this strategy. They came undone, however, when they played France. We watched the *partita* on television in London. At the end of regulation play the score was 0–0, and after an equally scoreless extra period, the game would be decided by free kicks: five tries for each team with no one on the field but the kicker and the goalie. With the game on the line, Roma's Luigi Di Biagio, who actually hails from Testaccio, hit the crossbar, sending Italia home and France into the quarterfinals. Julian's tear-streaked face was one side of the coin, but Elliott's cat-that-ate-the-canary grin was the other, as he realized that the tournament had dispensed with the tougher team, France now moving ahead against the predictions of the experts.

Meanwhile, with style, verve, and sambalike rhythm, Brazil was mowing down its opponents. We were back in Rome to watch the final match. Diane had by this time also become enamored of Ronaldo. A twenty-one-year-old, head-shaven kid from the wrong side of the tracks of Rio, he was cute and cuddly and shy, the kind of boy you could see yourself making a milkshake for. But could he run, and could he kick, and his speed, skill, and uncanny ability to be in the right place at the right time were surely going to carry Brazil to victory over the upstart Frenchmen.

But with all the pressure on Ronaldo—with 1.7 billion people watching all over the world; with his countrymen expecting that Brazil would repeat its 1994 World Cup victory over Italy, leaving Ronaldo with only one more win before he would join the legendary Pele as someone who led his Brazil teammates to three World Cup victories; with all the money riding on this, as Nike had already signed him up to push its products and paid him so much money he could finance a few small countries—something was bound to give. After watching him play on the field for five minutes, all of us knew that what had given out was Ronaldo.

What we saw on the screen was the ghost of the player who had thrilled all Italy with twenty-five goals in his first year with Inter. Now 99 percent of the country—the Italians who were rooting for Brazil against the unpopular rival French—were slumped in their seats, awaiting the stunning but inevitable Brazilian defeat. We kept praying for Ronaldo to play as we had come to expect, but before long France's Zidane, who during the regular season plays for Inter's bitter rival, Juventus of Turin, knocked home two headers against the shell-shocked *brasiliani,* and the game ended 3–0.

While for Julian this was payback against his brother, a vendetta as only brothers know how to carry out, for Elliott, this defeat meant that his hero, his idol, *"il migliore giocatore del mondo,"* the best player in the world, The Phenomenon, was slowly withering away on the field, and this six-year-old decided he couldn't take the disappointment. We looked over at him, lying on the couch, green, complaining about his stomach. Within moments he was in the bathroom throwing up, as he got his first (literally gut-wrenching) lesson in the inevitable reality of winners and losers. We glumly watched time expire as France won its first ever World Cup, in its first ever final game, in Paris of all places.

We followed the Ronaldo story in the papers, which is easy to do because it made the sports page nearly every day. Ronaldo had a nervous breakdown, Ronaldo almost died, Ronaldo had received a death threat, Ronaldo had a fever, convulsions, you name it. What is clear is that the young *brasiliano* has not yet recovered, that the following season with Inter has been marred by injuries that come from God knows where, and that he has spent more time off the field recuperating than he has playing.

But even the excitement of last year's World Cup was nothing in comparison to this year's Roma-Lazio match, the colliding of the two local teams. This was the Yankees against the Dodgers, from the old days, before the Bums took off for Los Angeles. Talk about rivalry, about history, about tradition. On the day of the contest—it was played at night and was televised on pay TV, which we don't get—everyone you exchanged even a word with was asking, *"Di che squadra è?"* Even Elliott, whose Inter team was not involved, got caught up in the fever, in this case helping Julian by rooting for Roma. At the Grotte del Teatro di Pompeo that glorious spring afternoon, the cute seven-year-old son of the owner of the *trattoria* somehow found us, and after a few minutes we learned that he was a *laziale,* confident of victory as his team was in first place and Roma was enduring a *così così* year. Yellow red or white blue banners were everywhere. This was an event.

We were huddled around the radio later as Roma's Marco Delvecchio kicked in a beautiful goal early and then banged home another with his head. In the second half Lazio's marvelous Christian Vieri (now playing, to the delight of Elliott, for Inter) scored to pull his team close, but then hometown star Francesco Totti, born and raised right here, scored late, sending Roma to victory and starting a city-wide celebration that lasted until 3:00 A.M. We could hear our neighbors screaming and jumping up and down in the *palazzo,* horns blaring and fireworks going off everywhere, and as soon as the match ended, all television programs left their regular programming and showed the delirious *romaniste* at the Stadio, waving banners, sending off yellow red smoke bombs, gesticulating madly for the cameras.

The next day was even more acute. Everyone, everywhere talked about, or at least mentioned, the *partita.* People we had no idea were soccer fans, with whom we had never once discussed anything to do with the game, were ecstatic. Paola, the beautiful young *ragazza* who is the daughter of the owner of our corner bar, swooning as she served us breakfast, characterized the match as *bellissima,* and said that the day before had been *"la migliore della mia vita,"* the best of her life.

Exaggeration? Maybe, but that's how things go in Italy, especially with *calcio,* the only game in town.

23

Retro Romans Still Do It All: Smoking, Drinking, Sex, Fur Coats, and Suntans

Y ou turn the page of the newspaper and the article hits you right away. It is neither prominent nor buried. It just is. There is a photo of the condominium and an interview with the law enforcement official in charge of the case. The story forms a part of the drive for pleasure, for the exaltation of the senses that only a very old soul—or a very young one—would want to achieve, for those in the middle are still locked in the pursuit of perfection, something to which the young have not yet thought to aspire, and the old have long since discarded.

It was just another prostitution ring, although the very term conveys an impression of something so much coarser than it really is. When you read the story, it all seems so innocent, as if what was for sale was not sex but ice cream. The "agency," located in a nondescript building on a nondescript street in a nondescript neighborhood, was set up by a woman in her forties to take advantage of the time of day—the lunch hour—in which some women are free to take on a second job if they so desire, or a first one if they still live at home or are a *signora* and do no other work at all. And so local females—housewives, students, and women who worked in the area as secretaries, teachers, and sales employees in the many shops—were recruited to provide intimate services for a clientele who knew only through word of mouth about the existence of such an enterprise. The roster of escorts reached no more than thirty or forty, but it was a going concern, and it reflected the fact that in Rome, sex is seen differently from the way it is thought of in the United States.

Like sex elsewhere, it can be erotic or not; thrilling or not; passionate or not; worth it or not. But, detached from romanticism, it is not by and large viewed with the same kind of solemn sacredness that all the pieties in America seem to bring to it. It is no more—or less—than a pleasurable fact of life, like eating and sleeping and talking and walking and reading a magazine. Romans do not fall in love any more or less than other people, but they do have more sex, and they are more likely to engage in indiscriminate sex—without either guilt or contraception—than their non-Latin counterparts.

The police knew about this "house" but had no way of getting in, since admission was by referral and Signora Maria kept a pretty tight rein on the comings and goings of the clientele. It was the proverbial small business, a simple, modest enterprise that matched available women with available men for a few hours during the day. Services rendered, services paid for, and then Francesca goes back to typing legal briefs at the law office or Serena pays a visit to *Mamma* before buying food for dinner, and Giorgio goes back to the bank or Alessio makes his last deliveries. But the police were determined, and when they finally hit on the idea of pretending to be the gas company and saying that they had reason to believe that a dangerous leak reported in the building might be coming from Maria's apartment, the *capo* let them in. The police ripped off their fake mechanic uniforms, showed their badges, and one particular Roman house of ill repute was shut down—at least for the moment.

The Romans live as if Puritans, health nuts, and the politically correct never have existed and still don't. It used to be that I—coming from northern California, where the antismoking movement is strong and where smoking in a public place is now practically criminal behavior—would have to gear up for the fact that I was heading for the land of tobacco. Although Italians smoke less than they used to do, they still smoke a lot, and it is only recently that you see nonsmoking sections of trains and other public places and occasionally even find a bar that prohibits the activity. Friends in America who take it as a given that they would not allow a cigarette to be lit in their house, would not frequent a place in which anyone was smoking, would not date anyone who happened to be a smoker, and probably don't know anyone who smokes ask how we endure living in a place where smoking is still considered a pleasure rather than a vice and where heart disease is low and longevity high.

The answer is simple. You get used to it. It becomes part of the daily routine, another feature on the landscape. Although I have never admitted this before, when I am sitting outdoors, occasionally I begin to miss the familiar aroma if no one around is smoking, and there are even times when I have seen a woman light up who handles the process in a such a defined, erotic way—wrist bent at a certain angle, two long, manicured fingers extended upward, head arched and neck exposed as she exhales the white smoke into the atmosphere—that I couldn't imagine thinking that this woman would be as seductive without her cigarette. It is as if it is the most telling part of her. I experience a kind of letdown when she is finished and hope I will be around long enough to see her go through each defined step once again. Our friend Laura, who is *romana* but who lived in the States for more than a dozen years, is an avid nonsmoker, and has a sign outside her front door, *all'americana,* inviting her guests to smoke outside. At a recent dinner party at her house, with everyone sated and comfortable and happy and still around the table, there was a request from one of the guests to be able to smoke just one cigarette without having to leave the apartment. Laura reluctantly agreed. Within moments, five cigarettes were lit, as all the closet smokers and the "I only have one after a meal" smokers were out in full force. Laura could only shake her head and put on a brave smile. If you don't want to have any friends in Rome who are smokers, you will have to be very discriminating, especially since, even if you choose nonsmoking friends, *their* friends will undoubtedly smoke in your presence.

The more you see Romans, the more you think of people who are stuck in the fifties, before medical science and activists came along to tell us that everything we liked to consume or use in vast quantities—sunshine, fatty foods, alcohol, sex, and the skins of animals—was *verboten.* When the sixties hit, everything we thought was good for us suddenly was bad for us. But you live here and you see no vegetarians; no one who politely refuses wine because he or she is a teetotaler or recovering alcoholic; no one who thinks that smoking is a felonious act (*"Fumare?"* a woman said to me in surprise and disbelief one day in a bar, looking at the end of her lit cigarette, when I told her, in response to a query about the greatest difference between San Francisco and Rome, that Californians consider smoking to be a sin); people who may or may not have lovers or extramarital affairs but who don't have any moral judgments about it; hardly anyone who doesn't think that the more sun you get, the better you look and the healthier you are; very few who give a fig about the fact that animals are raised and slaughtered to be made into the most luxurious coats one has ever seen—garments of every shape, length, size, color, and style—coats so sumptuous to behold and feel that they are worn in spite of the relatively mild months of December, January, and February, when daytime temperatures in usually sunny Rome reach the forties—*in the shade*. At a certain point you realize that warmth and comfort and especially making a *bella figura* at all costs are what matters more than anything.

As a kid, I remember what it meant when my mother referred to a certain woman as having a "fur coat": it meant that she was rich. It was the mark of someone who was not like the rest of us. Who can forget Richard Nixon's famous Checkers Speech, when, in discussing his supposed slush fund, he brought his perfectly midwestern wife out on camera to say that she did not have a fur coat, but a "respectable Republican cloth coat"? The reference was clear: "Listen, people, we are just like you, restrained and modest." The Roman excesses of 1999 seem about as far away from the restraint and modesty of Republican America of 1952 as it gets. Almost every woman you see looks "rich," and no one wants to sacrifice anything in the pursuit of making an unrestrained and immodest impression. The only protest against furs I've ever heard about takes place in early December at the opening of La Scala in Milan—not Rome—where animal rights activists organize opposition and even one year did a striptease to demonstrate their displeasure, as women in sexy black bras paraded around the piazza in front of the theater, shouting slogans—and delighting the crowd. Only in Italy.

Try to talk to the average Roman about infrared rays, ozone depletion, or sunburn, and you get the usual blank stare. Romans still love to tan their bodies. *"Abbronzare"* is an activity so indulged, so widespread, so unapologized for, that during the early days of *rientro* in September, when everyone is filtering back from their usual summer break, returning to Rome from the various beaches, mountains, and even from trips abroad, the number of dark suntans per capita boggles the mind. Two out of every three persons seem to have spent the summer absorbing as much of the bronzing rays of the sun as possible. The look is the early Coppertone variety, rather than the revised version of twenty years later, when in the advertisement you could barely see the difference between the young girl's bottom and the brown back above. Here, it is all-out dark. And on the still-hot, hot streets of the city after the long August break, you can see that the preference was for a non-tan-line look, as who would want to have to suffer through having beautifully dark arms, neck, shoulders, midriff, and legs and have winter white breasts that look like they belong to someone else?

Or take the matter of drinking. Romans are, believe it or not, not big drinkers, in the sense that they almost never drink to excess. In the four years that we have been here, I have witnessed only a handful of occasions where a man was obviously drunk, and these were strangers on the street. People drink wine, but it is considered unmanly, almost the worst behavior possible, a *brutta figura,* to be drunk because then one is out of control, unable to act and react in ways that are to his advantage. A man who drinks too much is unattractive to both men and women. There are almost no bars in the city where people go just to drink. There are more pubs now than ever, populated mostly by the foreign and the young, who want an experience different from the norm, and there is the occasional *cantina* where you see clusters of old men drinking wine as a thirst quencher because they never learned how to drink water.

But for the vast majority of the population, wine is consumed with meals, as a way of complementing the taste of the food, and Romans have no qualms about letting their young children and grandchildren have a nip of the *vino* that is being poured all around. Waiters often ask our boys—*directly*—if they would like a drop or two poured into their wine glasses. Hard liquor is rarely consumed, except for *grappa, limoncello,* or *amaro* after a large meal, as a *digestivo,* and you don't run into the type of person who is making a big deal about the wine, either. It's just wine. It happens to contain alcohol, no one denies that. But it is not consumed in quantities high enough to make a problem out of it, and I have never seen any publicity about twelve-step programs or Alcoholics Anonymous support groups. Perhaps heredity bodes well for Italians when it comes to drinking, aside from everything else.

Pleasure, luxury, excess. These people are not Scouts, militants, or Buddhists. Of course, I'm not talking about everyone, but rather about a culture that takes all this for granted, that sees nothing wrong with a billboard of two unabashedly naked breasts with a smiling baby's head jammed between them, looking out at the world. Even in the eighteenth century, travelers from the northern tier of Europe were both astonished and delighted to see how ravishing the women of this city were, how they would look you in the eye and hold your glance as long as they needed to. Rome has always been a place where people have come to have "fun," so much so that there is a book out called *The Sex Lives of the Popes*.

As an American coming to the city from a non-Latin culture, it is truly difficult to reconcile everything, and I can see that my own Spartan and pleasure-seeking sides are in constant struggle for control of my soul. In the seventies I was a vegetarian, didn't consume much alcohol, thought women who wore fur coats were criminals, drank decaf coffee, and considered anyone who smoked a cigarette oblivious and not worth knowing. The current American impulse toward self-denial is unique. It springs not only from the dour Calvinist Pilgrims who left England because it wasn't pious enough, but also takes on the austere attitude one associates in modern times with the revolutionary Left. Robespierre, who instituted the Reign of Terror in France in the 1790s, was a Puritan. Mao's China was repressive, and the influence of the disapproving, politically correct Left in America shows that people who want everyone to behave like them are usually opposed to anyone having a very good time. It is in the ascetic, renunciative ways of life of the Eastern religions and in the militant organizations of the politically active—whether Right or Left—where the dream of a world without bodily pleasure is nourished.

Rome gives the lie to that crusade. People would much rather indulge in the sensual pursuit of *emozioni forti* than dedicate their lives to some abstract ideal of equality or liberation or justice that can never be reached and only, at best, be approximated. When you come here, you succumb to the temptations—adopting some and rejecting others—or you have to leave because you would find this place much too superficial to be bearable. At a talk we gave on how to transform your dreams into reality for the wives of the American embassy dignitaries not long ago, in response to questions that betrayed annoyance if not outright hostility, Diane and I were advocating some kind of accommodation to the dominant Roman culture. One woman objected that it was a heavy price to pay to "go native." She had the expression, although she was more attractive than that, of the Wicked Witch of the West incarnated as the sour-faced neighbor riding away on her bicycle with Toto. It was the look of strong disapproval, which you rarely see here, either on the face of a man or a woman. I am also reminded of the *californiana* I met at a party one Christmas who, when I asked her how it was going after two years here, said with a straight face, "Well, they're nice people, but I know so much more than they do." I smilingly pointed out to her that she might know more than they do, but what they do know is called survival, having built a civilization that still flourishes 2,753 years after its inception, or, approximately, nine times longer than ours. She said she had never thought of it that way.

In the end, the differences between Rome and San Francisco are precisely what makes the expatriate adventure so exciting, what keeps us young and alive and fresh and never bored. I don't know whether it's better to run five miles a day, eat yogurt shakes, have no family within a thousand miles, and work eighty hours per week in a stressful environment year in and year out, with two weeks off (or less) for vacation, or eat shredded beef and bitter greens sautéed in olive oil, drink five or six little cups of *caffè* a day, smoke a few cigarettes, have your entire family and a community of friends within two miles of where you live, take at least four to six weeks of vacation and come back with a deep suntan, and recognize that what you do for a living is not ultimately going to make much difference in the world. Perhaps the fact that nervous breakdowns, heart disease, divorce, and suicide are so much lower here makes Romans think that we Americans are not really focusing on the things that matter.

Ultimately, life comes down to the fact that what works for some does not work for others, and that each culture develops its ways of survival according to a variety of factors that are in constant, dynamic balance. Italy is in an abundant period right now, so people indulge and everyone—after two world wars and centuries in which this country was fragmented and under the thumb of various autocrats who didn't give a damn about the ordinary Valerio or Valeria—wants to consume, consume, consume. Italians are, in fact, pretty much where the Americans were in the fifties: charmed by new gizmos, earning money, and having more market choices than they ever dreamed possible. Many people are, at bottom, still bowled over by the fact that they own a car.

Who knows whether reaction will set in; whether the course of economic development will make the Romans more like us— more cautious, more thoughtful about what they do with their bodies, more circumspect about limits and excess and the consequences of having too much, doing too much, indulging too much. Maybe it will happen. But maybe not. Maybe this civilization is just different, and it will be hundreds of years before everything blends together and globalization will have finally made the world one large village. In the meantime, the Romans will continue to live with a certain kind of wisdom that mocks the American way, that realizes that since death is a certainty, not an option, we might as well have a good time while we are here and worry about the consequences only when we meet our Maker, if, in fact, that is really what's in store for us. There is also, of course, confession, which fewer and fewer Romans are availing themselves of, as if even that were a relic from a Christian past that has relevance only when you are trying to appease *nonna*.

24

Breaking Bread in Rome: Hidden Bakeries

It was a typical, late-night, before-you-go-to-bed conversation one has with a nine- and a six-year-old, talking about what we could expect in the distant future. I ventured to speculate that within a hundred years or so, people won't have to travel anymore because they'll be able to make use of "virtual" travel, basically putting themselves wherever they want just by donning special glasses or going into some kind of personal chamber. "You could go to Paris," I said, "without having to get on an airplane." Elliott, whose first trip to the City of Light was last year and who doesn't forget much, didn't miss a beat. "Does that mean I'd be able to taste a baguette?" Everyone has priorities, and for most people in Rome, not just kids, it is bread.

Although we are not in France, where there is no dearth of delicious, crusty-on-the-outside and light, melt-in-your-mouth-inside kind of bread, in Rome the stuff that comes out of the *forno* is also something to write home about. I have heard a few people who have spent time here say that one of the biggest disappointments in Rome is the bread, but I don't know what Rome they are talking about, because, if you know where to go, you can get all kinds of goodies baked to perfection.

Massimo D'Alema, the former Communist who is now the head of government, said on a recent trip to the United States that one of Italy's foremost contributions to Western culture was pizza, and after living here for years, I know what he is talking about. Pizza has, of course, completely taken over the cuisine of America, especially among the youth, but here it is a different thing. In fact, I noticed a while ago in the frozen food bins of the "supermarket" in which I occasionally shop (I put quotation marks around it because our local supermarket would fit into one aisle of any respectable Safeway in any part of America) the appearance of packaged frozen pizza in a red, white, and blue box called Big Americans. On the box is a picture of a gargantuan, cheesy, drippy pizza with all kinds of toppings. I must say that the height of the stack of boxes varies from time to time, so someone must be buying them, but I've never actually seen anyone pick one up, put it in her cart, and pay for it at the *cassa,* let alone eat anything bearing any resemblance to it. But I can say without hesitation that I have seen fifty or sixty *romani* crowd into a space no larger than a clothes closet, all waiting with *santa pazienza* for something they think is worth waiting for. What could it be?

The *forno* at the northern end of Campo de' Fiori was recommended to me by someone who grew up in Rome, so I knew it would be worth trying. The only problem was that I could never get in. Every time I passed, the crowd was thick inside the tiny space, and so each time I said to myself that I would have to forgo whatever pleasure awaited me and come again. This happened so many times that I finally realized that I would have to brave the masses and both assert and insert myself.

The first difficulty you encounter at a popular *forno* is that you can't get in the door. Since most doors in Italy open inward, the people inside were blocking this one, but I took advantage of an opportunity when one of the customers emerged with a bag. What I witnessed inside was so strange that it took me a while to understand that this wasn't just another exquisite bakery, but one that specializes in a particular thing.

In front of the assembled throng were all manner of breads and pastries. Everywhere I looked there were stacks of round, long, oval, and flat loaves, baked sticks, called *grissini,* of every variety, and the kind of cakes my Viennese grandparents used to make—strudels, round, golden pound cakes that are called *ciambelloni* in Rome, and various fruit and ricotta *torte.* But despite the plethora of choice delicacies, nothing much was happening. The male servers in their white lab coats were behind the counter bantering with the customers, who were milling about on the other side of it. There was an occasional sale, but nothing noteworthy relative to the dozens of people waiting in a space consisting of approximately fifty square feet for something to which they were dedicating half their morning. The employees were actually leaning on the bread counters behind them, arms crossed, smiles on their faces.

But their rest was short-lived, as in the very instant that I could detect the beginnings of actual grumbling among the crowded, waiting *clienti,* now more numerous than ever, another man all in white—with a hat and bandanna tied around his neck— appeared before the crowd carrying a six-foot-long slab of *pizza bianca,* what would be called focaccia in San Francisco. There is nothing on the pizza but olive oil and salt, and the *fornaio* lays it lovingly on the long cutting board that forms part of the counter dividing us from the servers.

One would have thought from the sudden, collective note coming from the patrons that we were all engaged in an intense bout of group sex and had reached the critical moment simultaneously, for everybody seemed to go "Ahhhhh" for a very long time at the appearance of the long-awaited—let's face it— bread. The long length of it—steaming, shiny with a thin coat of oil that had just been brushed on after the baking process, so fragrant and aromatic that one's unconscious was suddenly awakened and all the wonderful memories of childhood were made available to the conscious mind—enabled three or four lab coats to raise their cleavers in unison and immediately go to work chopping the foot-wide thing and divvying it up for the now-salivating customers. One by one the latter retreat from their positions in the front and make their way to the *cassa* with their prizes and *scontrino,* telling them how much they will now fork over to the cashier, and then wiggle their way out the door and into the mercantile, operatic madness of the piazza.

Sixty seconds after its appearance, the pizza is literally gone. I am shut out. Not even a morsel of a corner of an end remains. The crowd is perhaps half the size of what it had been just moments before, and now other kinds of breads are being passed over the counter to the remaining customers. But the aroma lingers, and the *forno* is, in fact, infused with a kind of scent that has an incense-like quality, as if we were all locked in a sanctuary and some of us had just received the Host at Sunday mass.

I leave the *forno* and return after I pick up some swordfish, vegetables, and spices in the outdoor market. My luck has changed. I manage to wrangle an *etto* (about two ounces) of the simple bread and bite into it. It is both crunchy and chewy, light and substantial, tasty and subtle, all at the same time. And I can instantly see why the *romani* wait as long as they do to get it and then become orgasmic when it is placed in front of them. As a *straniero,* I have no trouble understanding why Romans love to talk about food, why they make such a big to-do about it, why they organize their day and plan for weeks around special occasions, and look forward to every meal. Their involvement with food is of another order. It is a worked-out thing.

This *forno* is by no means the only one where you can get top-notch *pizza bianca.* Another is close by in the *centro storico,* across the Corso Vittorio Emanuele on the Via del Governo Vecchio, 29. As I pass by artisans, furniture makers, and beautiful ceramics shops and enter the bakery, I am struck by how different the atmosphere can be from one *forno* to the next, even if the end product tastes pretty much the same. The place has a name—Silvano—but that's not immediately evident, and it's difficult to remember exactly where it is because the streets are so narrow in this particular *quartiere* and you come upon it so suddenly. But on the other hand, you can always sense that you're close from the presence all around on the street near the *forno* of *ragazzi* sitting on their *motorini* chomping away at sandwiches made from some of the best-looking *pizza bianca* one has ever seen.

At lunchtime the place is hopping, and—if this is possible— it's even more crowded than the other *forno* because it's much bigger and has a kind of sixties diner look, with linoleum floors and a big display case containing all kinds of meats and trays of

assorted vegetables that go in the center of a sliced *pizza bianca.*
It also has a small counter at the side of the store where there
are rows of bottles of *acqua minerale* in which one can indulge at
will. Getting to the counter to place an order is difficult, but the
wait is never long. Elliott is a meat eater and has on occasion
delighted the servers by ordering a sandwich of both *prosciutto*
and *salame* with Swiss cheese and various vegetables. Julian eats
hardly any meat and asks for a *mozzarella,* spicy olives, red peppers, *rughetta,* and yellow corn concoction. When I say to the
ragazza serving us that Julian has *"un gusto particolare,"* a particular
taste, she responds by saying, *"Si vede,"* "One can see that."

The *pizza bianca* is baked a little longer than usual and has a
crispy taste to go along with the soft inside, that perfectly absorbs
the overflowing flavors that one has chosen to compose the
sandwich. The price of the pizza—regardless of how many items
one includes—is the same: 3,000 lire, roughly $1.65 for the veg-
etarian, and 4,000 lire for the meat. It is difficult to imagine
anything tasting any better than this, anywhere, anytime.

The *pizza bianca* is also pretty good at our bakery, which is
our local stop every morning for the kids' *merenda,* or snack.
That is also the time when the *bidella,* the woman who wears a
blue smock and serves as caretaker of the school, comes into the
classroom with a *caffè* for the teacher. So many kids eat *pizza*
bianca for *merenda* that the bakery cuts it in advance, weighs it,
wraps it, and prices it so that you can avoid the inevitable morning crunch and just reach into the wicker basket, grab two
already-wrapped *pizze bianche,* and head straight for the *cassa.*
There's usually no definitive line, just a bunch of people milling
about, putting bills and change on the counter, eager not to be

late for school and work, while the harried morning cashier rings it all up and gives everyone the requisite *scontrino*.

The bakery also has wonderful cookies and cakes and even puts out a decent chocolate chip muffin, *all'americana*, for those times when we feel nostalgic for the food with which we grew up. The muffins have a cute American flag on a toothpick sticking out of them, and I usually indicate my preference by saying *due americani*, because when I say "muffin," the *ragazze* who work behind the counter make no hesitation about correcting my pronunciation. *"No, Signore, si pronuncia mah-feen,"* at which I can only say *grazie,* thinking of what it would be like if a Roman should wander into any of the 32,457 Starbucks in the United States and ask for *due biscotti* (bee-scottee), only to be told that it is pronounced "biscoddy."

OK, now try *sfogliatelle* (sfol-yee-ah-*tell*-eh). It doesn't matter, just write down the word and show it to someone in a bakery. You won't be disappointed. Or *sbaciucchiare* (zba-chew-key-*ah*-reh), if you dare.

25

Mi Scusi:
Romans Forgive—and Forget

Crossing the street, I was about to pass two women who were waiting on the corner, turned away from me so that I could not see their faces. From behind they looked like appropriately elegant *donne romane*—coats, scarves, pants just to the right length, low heels, with hair that was clean, brushed, and cared for. The sight of people standing around waiting for something is a common occurrence in Rome, so there was nothing about these women that might have been considered noteworthy. The day, however, was particular—the Festa della Donna, the Day of the Woman—which was reflected all over the streets and shop windows of Rome.

This holiday is one of those events in Italy that has taken on a life of its own. When we first came here, never having heard of it, we were wondering why every woman on a nondescript Thursday in early March seemed to be carrying a sprig of acacia blossom (called *mimosa* in Italian), why flower stands had wrapped them up so beautifully for display, and why the usual street corner vendors who sell cigarette lighters and little packets of tissues throughout the year were suddenly sprouting the fragrant, bright yellow flowers, as acacia in Rome, as is the case in many places with a temperate climate, is one of the first trees to blossom in spring.

We soon found out that the Festa della Donna is a day on which women are supposed to refrain from being *mamme, mogli, e casalinghe,* mothers, wives, and homemakers, and go off on their own to dinner with other women without having to worry about the welfare of the menfolk. Now, of course, women, even Roman women, are much less inclined to be in the kitchen preparing three-course meals every day than they once were. But the holiday has caught on and has even assumed the usual sexy Italian way of doing things, in that it has become customary for women in the evening to visit clubs where males are modeling clothes and doing striptease acts, the whole thing indicating that the traditional roles—at least for one day—are reversed.

So it didn't surprise me that the neighborhood women were holding the requisite sprigs of acacia, but when I reached them and looked into the face of one of the two, her carriage proud and upright, her splotch of brilliant yellow fluttering in the chilly breeze of late winter, I was struck again—as I am every time I witness something like this in Rome—by the basic sense of decency, of humanity, of just plain forgiveness, with which the Romans conduct their lives.

This finely attired young woman had Down syndrome, but it made absolutely no difference to the way in which she stood or held herself. This was a day in which women—all women— were celebrating their place in society in the by-now traditional manner. As in America, or anywhere, one is occasionally confronted by the presence of someone who has this condition, but somehow these individuals in Rome do not seem to be sequestered from the rest of society. There is a difference the foreigner senses immediately—in the same way as one watches the ordinary interaction of the elderly, the handicapped, the mentally disabled with the rest of the people in the landscape who do not need assistance on a daily basis to survive—and that difference seems to me to indicate that one is forgiven for one's flaws, that it is not necessary to be perfect to be accepted or acceptable, that life can be a fairly difficult exercise and that the most angelic— and at the same time the most human—act we can perform is to forgive each other's imperfections, in the same way as this young woman was forgiven hers by having been given the opportunity to carry her symbol of spring, at the same time that she was respected and dressed like everyone else. Thus, she would be noticed in the same way they were, and not marginalized into a living invisibility that would seek to deflect one's attention, one's gaze, one's regard, elsewhere. I have seen many men, women, and children with Down syndrome in the busy streets of this city, and I have never seen one of them who was not *curato,* cared for, put together, presented to the world in such a way as to let all others know that no degree of misfortune or incapacity was going to prevent him or her from feeling beautiful in the way that the ordinary Roman does, even if the standards of beauty here are in many ways far higher, and in other ways far lower, than ours. Anyone is attractive who takes the time and attention to care for herself. The standards in this way are easy. You only have to want to look at someone, as I did with this woman, and she is attractive.

Recently, we were waiting for a table in a busy *pizzeria* in Trastevere on a Saturday night with a group of Italian friends. There was not much room, and most of the people who were

225

standing around waiting their turn were outside. But the kids wanted to watch the cooks prepare and throw the pizzas in the oven, so we stayed indoors and jockeyed ourselves out of the way of the four or five waiters who were going in every direction with swaying mugs of beer, steaming pizzas, dirty plates, and pastel-colored lire. We tried to anticipate their moves, but we were often in their way. They just said *scusate* and continued with their business. Even when a Vietnamese man suddenly appeared in the foyer with a tray full of jazzy cigarette lighters and other assorted gadgets and trinkets and had to be dodged as well, no one ever betrayed the slightest annoyance at the obstacle course at the front of this restaurant, as the vendor disappeared among the crowded tables to try to make a sale or two.

The appearance of vendors in eating places is common and accepted. It is not unheard of to be solicited by men or women—usually hailing from India, Pakistan, Sri Lanka, Bangladesh, or the Far East—wanting to sell long-stemmed roses or spiffy gizmos at your table. I have never once seen a single one of them tossed out by the proprietor, or heard any of the patrons express annoyance at having his or her meal interrupted by a true outsider to whom you have to say no or, more likely, whom you just ignore. *Trattoria* personnel just detour around them, as if they had just as much right to be where they were as the employees and their customers.

Once, when I was dining out with some of the other fathers from Julian's school, I asked Enzo, whose daughter is Julian's classmate, how it is that Romans, while paying money to dine in a restaurant, are so tolerant of these people who are obviously extraneous to the experience they are anticipating. He seemed perplexed by the question, unable to either understand or answer it. "What is the problem?" he finally asked in return. I explained to him that in the United States this would never happen. My guess was that no more than 1 percent of restaurateurs would allow street vendors into their establishments and that there would be a lot of complaining by the patrons if they did. Now Enzo seemed surprised. "Here in Rome," he finally said, "we are used to living with all kinds of people, and after a while you don't notice them anymore, you just accept them."

His answer satisfied me, but when you mix this tolerance together with other habits that seem to be ingrained among the *romani,* you feel that the explanation runs deeper. Romans are forgiving. They do not blame these South Asians for being South Asian, for being of color, for being poor, for being immigrants, for having to come into the *trattoria* to try to eke out a few thousand lire here and there in order to survive. And this applies to the young gypsies who will pickpocket a pedestrian or bus passenger when the opportunity presents itself; or who walk through the metro car announcing that they are poor and need help; or the violinist and accordionist who play a few tunes and then pass around the cup; or the guys who come to your car window at nearly every major intersection trying to wash your window or sell you tissues or sun visors, newspapers, or flowers; or the immigrants who wander around all the major monuments seeking out families with small children in order to sell a small rubber bag filled with flour that can be molded into any shape for a measly *mille* lire; or even the many street prostitutes, hailing mostly from Africa, Eastern Europe, and the Balkans, who work certain thoroughfares during the lunch hour and late at night and will perform for as little as thirty dollars.

Maybe it's the influence of the Church, or the close physical and emotional proximity in which people live, or the way in which the elderly and children are held in such high esteem, but the *romani* are definitely a forgiving people, and the words that you hear more often than any other, from friends, relatives, associates, acquaintances, and especially strangers, are *"scusa"* or *"mi scusi,"* depending on whether you know the person well or not. To excuse, to forgive, to relieve the other from culpability is a form of interaction commonly practiced here. Our friend Sandra, an American expatriate who has lived in Rome with her family for about as long as we have, after spending eight years in Paris, finds the Romans gentle and accepting. She was standing in line at the *posta* to pay a bill one day, and everyone who reached the teller had to deal with a person who was not having a great day. "Not the *anziana* in front of me," related Sandra. "She was shaking and having so much difficulty getting her bill and money together, and the teller was suddenly as sweet and patient with her as you could imagine anyone being."

Forgiveness is even part of the criminal justice system, as the accused are encouraged to be penitent of whatever crime with which they have been charged and to throw themselves on the mercy of the court. It has often made for hilarious circumstances, as the issue of forgiveness can take on almost mythic proportions, but it also makes for a kind of public confessional, as if the cabin in which every practicing Catholic goes to expiate his sins has been expanded into the society at large, creating a social mechanism by which problems can be resolved by one individual relating personally to another, without the need of complex and convoluted legal procedures to adjudicate the dispute. When an American Marine pilot left a NATO base in northern Italy and flew too close to a ski resort, cutting a lift cable and plummeting twenty skiers 350 feet to their deaths, the American ambassador to Italy, the Italian-American Thomas Foglietta, said that the only thing the Italian people wanted to hear from the United States was two words—"We're sorry."

The longer one stays in Rome, the longer one permits the paternal strictures of Protestant morality to be affected by the maternal Catholic sense of forgiveness. You learn to relax about things that would have driven you crazy before. To borrow from the language of cybernetics, you realize that the basic operating system here was designed by a different company and uses a different language from the system you're using. How else could one explain the lack of capital punishment; the lack of long prison sentences for criminals; the fact that married men and women do not by and large divorce or even separate when they have differences, including marital betrayal; the fact that children get away with almost any type of undisciplined behavior imaginable and that parents just do not have it in them to curb their offspring's wilder instincts; that people get mad, let it out, scream and yell at each other—even on the street, in front of others—and then engage in a kind of mutual reconciliation that absolves them both of any real hurt. Merchants regularly try to chisel an extra few thousand lire out of their customers, are caught doing it—as has been the case with us—and yet it does not affect continued patronage of the shop, as long as the merchant is contrite and admits he's guilty by forking over the extra five thousand lire, or even one thousand lire (fifty-five cents).

Everyone here knows that a person who has passed into the age of reason is a sinner, and that no one really has the right to say anything to anyone else because no one is immaculate. Romans seem to take seriously Jesus' injunction to "Let him who is without sin cast the first stone." Of course, stones are cast—frequently, in fact—but people have the sense that if you dig deeply enough into the life of anyone past childhood, there will be acts and behaviors about which one has had to confess, or should have.

Romans know at the most basic, instinctive level that the drive, the quest, the obsession for perfection will lead only to its opposite—disaster. Human beings are not built that way, they say. We may try our best to be good people, and often we succeed, but at least occasionally we will stumble, stray, sometimes in a big way, and it is only the act of forgiveness that enables us to go on, to overlook the tendency to fail—repeatedly—to fulfill the life Jesus called upon us to live, and to reach an accommodation with ourselves and those around us. And furthermore, the Romans say, history, of which there is more here than just about anywhere, proves them right.

Tutto sommato, all things considered, it's hard to argue with them.

26

Exodus:
Weekends and Getaways

All roads lead to Rome. Imagine living in the place where this is not simply a proverb, a metaphor, a way of describing a point that is the source of all other things, but rather the actual, factual phrase used to describe the city that all roads lead into and out of. When the ancient Romans realized that supervising an empire was going to require a lot of travel, a lot of MBWA, "management by walking around," they knew they needed to build roads that would radiate out of the city and into the provinces. Today these roads still cut through the various neighborhoods and lead out in all directions—Appia, Cassia, Nomentana, Anagnina, Tuscolana, Ardeatina, Ostiense, Aurelia, Flaminia, Salaria, Casalina, Portuense—and also provide Rome with the only access roads there are. One of the more picturesque, the Appia Antica, long stretches of it lined with tall, trimmed *pini* ✓ *romani,* providing continuous shade from the hot summer sun, is one we often find ourselves on when we want to go to the beach, *al mare.* The Appia, along with the others, is often a two-lane highway, no wider than it was two thousand years ago.

231

These roads provide Romans with the weekly or seasonal treat of getting out of the city, and then back again.

It is not a pretty sight. There are really no effective freeways or expressways that take you from one part of town to another. The closest you can get to Rome itself on a reduced-access highway is the Raccordo, the GRA, the ring road that is so far out that you are still forced to take one of the ancient consular roads to navigate to and from the center. And this invites nightmarish traffic because of the particular way in which the Roman weekend is configured. It is slightly different from the American variety, and conducive to the weekly exodus.

My friend Mats, who worked just outside Rome, would go crazy every Friday. Coming from Stockholm, where he was habituated to a workweek that roughly approximates that of any big city in the United States, he was accustomed to leaving the office somewhat early on Friday afternoon or evening, and so at 3:00 P.M. he began to look at his watch. Imagine his dismay when he would receive word—after he practically had his coat on—that a meeting had been called for 5:00 on a Friday afternoon. There he would be at 6:00, 7:00, 8:00, sitting with his colleagues discussing another in an endless series of marketing ideas, realizing again that this would not be a meeting for decisions, but only for talking, feeling that one-third of his weekend was being taken up with work, his psychological clock askew, his routine out of kilter, wondering why his Italian colleagues didn't seem to have any qualms about droning on and on when all he wanted to do was get home to take his shoes off, relax with his family, and plan a little getaway. It took him a while, but he finally realized that the Roman weekend begins on Saturday, maybe even Saturday afternoon, as most of the shops are open in the morning and many schools require attendance every Saturday morning until 1:00 P.M.

All of this serves to make Sunday *the* day, the one day of the week that is really devoted to taking time off, when you eat a big meal with your family—eight, ten, twelve, fifteen people—*da nonna* or in a *trattoria,* as the women chat and the men listen to or watch the *partita,* exulting in unison at strategic moments. Workers know they are not expected to be at the office early or to open the shop Monday before late afternoon, so they have the whole day and long into the evening to relax and enjoy, and even, along with countless others, to leave the confines of Rome entirely and get out into *la campagna,* the country, for fresh air, a profusion of deep green, and a delightful meal *all'aperto.*

Rome is not like New York, London, or Paris, where you leave the center and travel for miles and miles and miles through developed suburbs, where the city has absorbed so much of the countryside that you wonder whether you will ever see a grassy field or clump of trees again. You go thirty minutes in most directions from the heart of Rome, past the borderline *periferia,* and you are treated to nothing but pastures and rolling terrain. Sheep graze on hillsides on the way to the airport.

And so the consular roads are clogged with cars going out in the morning and coming back late in the afternoon, especially in good weather, when there is plenty of light and the days are long, and before you have gone very far, you begin to see, to feel, to appreciate the magnificence of the Italian countryside, to realize once again—because it is easy to forget if all you see every day are the close, cramped quarters of Rome—that there is a country beyond the walls of the city, one that you can get to fairly quickly, and that this country contains other worlds, other histories, other satisfactions for the eye and the *anima,* the soul.

In less than an hour's drive from Rome, you can climb over the ruins of the ancient port town of Ostia Antica; walk around the fantasy-like fountains of the Renaissance *palazzo* at Villa d'Este or visit the remains of the largest house ever built, Hadrian's Villa, near Tivoli; or spend time roaming through the towns of the Castelli Romani, where white wine is made from the grapes of the hillsides, and where, scattered among two volcanic lakes, more than a dozen towns—Frascati, Grottaferrata, Marino, Castelgandolfo (where the pope has his summer home), Nemi, Genzano, among them—are each little enclaves unto themselves, and where you can eat, some say, better than anywhere else in the entire province, including even Rome. A short train ride from the Termini in the center of the city to Frascati takes you first past various unattended shacks and assorted homesteads, but before disappointment sets in, you see a glimpse of wilderness. Suddenly, you are struck by the remains of an ancient aqueduct that carried water from the surrounding hills into the metropolis. Your spirits begin to rise as the air freshens and stirs. Silvery olive groves glisten in the light. Bunches of wild red poppies are scattered everywhere. Row after row, acre after acre of working vineyards, in every shade of green, appear almost unreal. Monte Cavo, the sculpted mountain that peers above the Castelli, with the ex–fortress town of Rocca di Papa nestled near the summit, looms in the distance. Within moments you are in Frascati. The grace and grandeur of the sun-drenched Villa Aldobrandini, named for the family that produced Pope Clement VIII at the end of the sixteenth century, looks out over the elegant village, clogged with tiny streets that wind their way to the edge of town, where a view of Rome just as the ancient patricians saw it from their magnificent summer villas fools you into thinking that this Eternal City could be just another small town lying peacefully in a valley surrounded by mountains. Emerging in the dusky distance, like a fine watercolor, is the cupola of San Pietro.

Or, if you like, you can visit the *necropoli,* the burial grounds of the ancient Etruscans in the opposite direction on the Via Aurelia in Cerveteri, where Diane and I based ourselves in a lovely farmhouse during our extended honeymoon in 1987, a place from which we never recovered, out of which grew a desire to come and live here indefinitely, to take in the beauty, the reflections, the aromas, the feelings of the ancient world for as long as the charm and the fascination would keep us in its thrall. In two hours' drive you can be in Tuscany and stay near another Etruscan town, Cortona, in a small villa, with gardens that go on forever, a carriage house made of stone, tree trunks for ceilings, built hundreds of years ago, almost on the very spot where Hannibal and the Carthaginians defeated the Romans at the Battle of Trasimeno in 217 B.C., enabling him to continue his march to the city itself, where the potent, walled defenses finally kept him at bay.

There are people who have no need of Rome, who find Rome too intense, too dirty, who never come into Rome except when there is business to take care of. These are foreigners and Italians alike, people for whom fresh air, open space, rolling hills, and verdant trees are the elements with which one should live, the basic stuff that sustains the good life and makes people forget that the metropolis exists at all in the broad valley between the volcanic formations of the Alban hills to the southeast; the volcanic lakes of the northwest toward Viterbo and the other tiny villages in northern Lazio; the even taller mountains to the north, beyond Tivoli and the first ring of low-lying hills where one climbs into real altitude and can ski for most of the winter at Campo Felice, a miniresort ninety minutes from Piazza di Spagna; and the sea.

Ah, the sea, the fabled, beautiful *mare.* At times it is easy to forget that this country is a peninsula; that it descends from the snow, the cold, and the frozen lakes of the Alps in the north and juts out into the Mediterranean with enough coastline to satisfy everyone. When you live in the city, when your days are spent dodging cars, hopping buses, wending your way through crowds, along narrow streets, past shop windows and stolid, imposing monuments, it is all too easy to overlook the fact that you are just fifteen miles from the legendary sea. You can go where Ulysses went. You can walk along the same shores that hosted the Greeks, the Phoenicians, the Saracens, the Ottomans, all the peoples of the Mediterranean who once dreamed of conquest and empire, and who looked toward the peninsula and knew it was something they had to have—or at least attempt to have. Just ninety minutes south of the city, at the coast, is the town of Sperlonga, sitting high and proud on the promontory of rock that extends itself over the pristine blue water, looking as if you had just arrived in Greece.

Whitewashed stone houses and intricate, ever-climbing streets greet you as you walk to the summit and gaze down at the resorts below, with their multicolored chairs, striped *ombrelloni,* and gleeful participants only too willing to throw themselves into the perfectly refreshing Mediterranean. Sperlonga was the northernmost settlement of the ancient Greek empire known as Magna

Grecia, the furthest the Greeks reached into what eventually became Europe, and although the flat part of Sperlonga has been developed and hosts beach resorts for miles along the shore, the still-intact hill town is cool and tranquil and above the frenzy. You can walk up to the piazza at the summit, as we did, and sit at a table in the shade of an umbrella with the ocean breeze in your face, have a *caffè freddo,* rich ice cream or, late in the evening, a thick hot chocolate, and let the kids run around because there are no cars. You realize that twenty-five hundred years of history have come before you, that you are sitting where the ancient Greeks sat, that you are a witness to their greatness. They gave to the conquering Romans all the ideas necessary to spread civilization well into the wild forested hinterlands of Europe, to the Atlantic, and later across the big ocean to America.

Here in Italy, in Sperlonga, where Romans go to get away from the city and retrace the steps taken by their patrician forebears—only those who were rich enough or connected enough or resourceful enough to be able to avail themselves of the soothing sea air—you are closer to the source of who you are, of what has shaped you, of the values and thoughts and feelings and love of pleasure and sensuality and beauty that characterizes these Latin, seaside people. It doesn't take long to realize that something is lost, is sacrificed, is overlooked in the drive for excellence, for perfection, for ambition, for glory, for power, for status and wealth, that all these things are wonderful and worthwhile and seductive in the right measure but are ultimately an illusion when they become the central focus, the dominant force, the raison d'être of a human being.

Our friend Laura is a perfect example of the need on the part of the Romans to feel the elements, to get close to sand, sea, sun, earth, sky, air, and experience a sense of open space. She craves nature. She misses no opportunity to leave the city. "You know," she reminds us, "my weekends are sacred." What she means is don't count on her to do anything when the weather is nice anytime from Saturday afternoon to late Sunday, for that is the time when she must get in the car and leave the city. (If we want her to come to a dinner party, it must be held on Friday night.) She usually goes north along the coast to an area called Ansedonia, which has the advantage of being less developed than other shores near Rome because it was essentially a swamp for more than a thousand years, after the fall of the empire, and it was dredged only during the last century. The beaches are popular and well preserved, the access to Rome better than other places because there is an *autostrada* that takes you there, and there are tiny hill towns nearby like Capalbio, Tarquinia, and Massa Marittima, and an island close to shore called Monte Argentario where you can eat dinner outside along the street that borders the sea and be back in Rome at midnight.

Two of our single Roman friends want to join us on a weekend jaunt: blond, sweet Cristina, always dressed *a stagione,* who has made a ritual of coming to our house every Friday afternoon for Italian conversation to supplement Diane's formal lessons with her teacher, Alessandro; and Laura, her long chestnut hair and light green eyes set off by a year-round tan, which she counts as one of her prized possessions. The kids are clamoring for our usual southern route, not as far as Sperlonga, but to San Felice Circeo, where legend has it that the enchantress Circe tempted Ulysses, where there are white sand beaches along the coast, and where Laura says we can handle the traffic on a Sunday if we leave early enough in the morning and come back early enough later that day.

We pile everything in the old Mercedes but get off to a tardy start trying to get everyone together. Traffic is light, perhaps because it is late in the season, perhaps because it is late in the day, perhaps because we are lucky. The beach is beautiful— uncrowded, seventy-five-degree water, lots of sand, perfect air. It is easy to sink into the feeling of being privileged, of sensing that one is in paradise, even just at the thought that after the beach we will drive fifteen minutes to the town so that each of us can eat a slice of delicious walk-around pizza with *mozzarella* and *pomodoro,* looking out over the sea, feeling refreshed and tired in that paradoxical combination that only the sun can provide. We find ourselves relaxed and in no hurry to leave. It is 6:00 P.M. before we begin our journey home.

The first half of the ride back takes forty-five minutes. We are on schedule. The passengers are starting to doze off as the Mercedes takes the road easily at 130, 140 kilometers—80, 85 miles—an hour, faster than anyone can go in the States without incurring the attention of a vehicle with flashing lights on the top and a loud siren inside. What a day, what a country, what a life, I'm thinking, as I pass another car and head toward Roma, Caput Mundi, the head of the world, the center of the universe.

Brake lights greet me as I round the bend in the road. We are still thirty miles from home as I see that we will now go no faster than three miles per hour. The snaking red bulbs in the gathering twilight are a reminder that Laura was right when she said early that morning that we needed to leave long before nightfall. The morning ride had lulled us into thinking that there would be no traffic on the way back, as though it were already late September and the notoriously ritual-bound Romans had had their fill of sun, sand, sea, and tans and had forsaken the beach for the golden leafy hillsides of the Castelli Romani, spending their days lost under the pergolas of the many *trattorie* on the roads leading from one bucolic spot to another.

We try to devise alternate routes. Does anyone know anything about the Ardeatina? Is that a good idea? Can we get home through the Castelli? We caucus. That probably won't work because it's out of the way and will probably be just as crowded. The bumper-to-bumper cars feel overwhelming. We are tired and impatient, and the concentration required to basically do nothing but be in the car is an effort we almost cannot bear. We take the next exit and travel a few miles to the Ardeatina, getting lost a few times and asking directions every ten minutes or so.

The traffic moves for a while and then backs up, another red snake, this one through dark countryside. The second half of the trip will take us at least two hours, maybe more, and we all make guesses as to what time we can expect to arrive home. At least we are moving. Cars are making U-turns ahead of us. Do they know something we don't? We stay the course. Little by little we make our way back to the city. The kids—mercifully—are asleep, and we four adults no longer have much to say to each other. At this point I want only to stay awake, be patient, and not have an accident. I will consider that a victory.

Sunday night in the city provides no relief. Everyone is outside in the seventy-degree weather. One would think that a celebration was in progress, that Roma had won an important *partita,* that something special had happened that had drawn everyone out. The guess is true—in part. There is a celebration,

240

but it is nothing special, just life in the summer, the *romani* trying to eke out the last bit of soothing warmth before the cold northern *tramontana* wind sets in to mark the beginning of fall. We make it home—safely—three hours after our departure, twice as long as it took us on our trip south. Along with our fellow *cittadini,* we have endured another Roman experience, the sublime and the ridiculous wrapped in a package that refuses to leave out one for the other. Take me or leave me, the city says, but remember, I am old, and hence you must take all of me, even the parts you would rather leave behind.

27

Latin Lovers:
Real Men Don't Wear Sneakers

The weather was perfect, the meal we had just consumed *all'aperto* in the garden of our filmmaker friend Carl's house—a simple concoction of spaghetti with a sauce made of ripe, tasty tomatoes, tuna, capers, onions, and extra-virgin olive oil, a mixed salad, and some ordinary white wine that you can pick up at any corner grocery store in two-liter bottles—had been sublime. We were just settling into a drop or two of *limoncello,* a sweet liquor made from the lemons of the Amalfi coast, just south of Naples, when Claudia, an actress, started to talk about the subject most dear to her—men. "The reason why men are so happy in Italia," she said, in Italian, "is because we women let them be *permaloso."*

It was one of those statements you had to probe, because it wasn't quite clear to us what she was saying. *Permaloso* means sensitive, not in the emotional sense, but in the "touchy," thin-skinned, susceptible-to-offense-when-criticized sense. To Claudia, it was the key, the way in which, for all the talk about macho and patriarchy and historical repression of women, a female could control a man—and hence the situation—by indulging his proclivity to take offense at the slightest hint of disapproval. Although it was obviously an exaggeration, evidently designed to assert in an off-handed way that women were really in charge of this country even if the culture seems to revolve almost entirely around the power that men exercise in the workplace, in politics, in business, and civic society, what Claudia was really saying is all that stuff counts *per niente,* not at all. What matters is that every man knows what he really has to do—as long as he is not clueless, a *cretino*—and that is to keep his mother and his woman or women happy. All else is nothing, futile, beside the point. All the public posturing, the need to be seen, to be free to roam, to feel oneself a master of the universe; all that jockeying for power in the world of men means nothing to a woman, because everyone here knows that men are really the weaker sex, the ones who could not manage for a day without the resourcefulness, help, encouragement, direction, and guidance of women.

Mammoni. The word is a mouthful, a handful, a concept so Italian that it could only have been coined in the country that invented the cult of the Madonna, elevating her to the status that only Jesus had occupied previously, that looked at the early doctrines and said that only someone who was already God-like could have given birth to God; therefore Mother Mary must be God as well, and must have been born the same way as she gave birth to the Savior. Only then did Mary become the Madonna, the woman of women, the *mamma di tutte le mamme.*

Mammoni. Italy is the land of *mammoni,* the mama's boys. When our friend Mats was still living in Rome, he used to tell me that he would plan his day around the hour or two after everyone had finished lunch. During that time he knew he would have to write or read a report or article, because it was almost impossible to get an outside telephone line. The reason was simple. His male Roman colleagues were all on the phone, talking not to their brokers or their girlfriends, but to their *mothers*. I am not here making reference to kids just out of college in their twenties, in the workplace for the first time. These are grown men, in their thirties, forties, fifties, and beyond, men with agendas, multi-million-dollar contracts, in competition with other behemoths in the world of global telecommunications, men with power to hire and fire, to say yes to deals that affect stock prices and earnings statements, men whose decisions make news in the world's financial pages, and every day after lunch they are on the phone talking to their mothers. Every day.

Mats said to me that it was all he needed to know about his colleagues—that, and the fact that what was most important to them at work was to provide the right answer. In the Italian system of education, the further one advances, from *scuola media* into *liceo* and on through to *università,* the more the requirements become verbal, and so the need to stand and deliver becomes the overriding issue, creating a people so verbally skilled that at times you want to step back and let them go on and on because the elocution is so polished, so smooth, so full of rhetorical flourish. I've always told *stranieri* who feel overwhelmed at having to learn the language that what matters when you are listening to a Roman is the first sentence. Everything after that is merely backup. So here is Mats' colleague Fiorentini giving the boss a particularly brilliant response to a tough question, and when the *capo* has left, standing up and saying out loud—both to himself and to all assembled—*che figura,* or, what a beautiful presentation I just made with those words. An Italian slam dunk.

244

Mammoni are everywhere. You are walking down the street in Testaccio, which contains block after block of *palazzi* that were built in the Umbertine period, just after Italian unification in 1870, and you see a young man in his twenties, long thin sideburns, cigarette dangling out the corner of his mouth, black Nike baseball cap over dark sunglasses. He leaves his *motorino* where he has dismounted, on the street, and reaches up to knock on a set of closed shutters that are at the *piano terra,* the ground floor. Within seconds there is noise, and the *persiani,* the wooden-slatted shutters that are the staple of all Roman windows, designed to keep out the broiling hot sun while at the same time letting in whatever breeze might be stirring on a given summer afternoon, are opening outward as a plump older woman, wearing a much-used apron, greets the young man. They exchange words. It is nearly one o'clock, and Marco is undoubtedly hungry. Mom is obliging. Through the now-open window, Marco receives a steaming package wrapped in a plastic bag, which *Mamma* advises that he hold steadily. Within moments he will zip off on the Vespa and indulge—depending on the day—in the *gnocchi* or the *trippa alla romana,* or the *tortellini fatti in casa* that has been prepared for him. He will not have to phone today. His "visit" was enough.

Some say that the consensus of the world's collective imagination that Italian men are the greatest lovers comes from their attachment to their mothers, that in return for being *mammoni,* for letting their mothers be *premuroso,* doting, they are in return expected to display the utmost gallantry, which then gets carried over to other women, even if what these men are feeling in the moment is simple lust and they have no interest in a woman beyond the one or two hours they would like to spend with them in bed before departing.

There is an old joke that says that in heaven, the French cook, the Germans direct traffic, the English plant gardens, and the Italians make love. It is easy to see how attachment to Mom forms the major part of the masculine culture. Italian men are so used to being solicitous of women because they are solicitous to their mothers that it is nothing for them to talk, to flatter, to compliment, to touch lightly in a friendly/interested way, to flirt, to comport themselves with irresistible ease and grace in the company of women. When I was a professional matchmaker and relationship counselor, the biggest complaint I used to hear from female clients was that men didn't pay enough attention to them, didn't know how to talk to them, didn't have any idea how to make women feel good about themselves by noticing something—anything: the color of their eyes, the brilliance of their minds, the softness of their skin, the fact that they were wearing something new and *a stagione,* how they smelled, the ease with which they conversed, how varied their interests were, how good their lasagna tasted.

Roman men are the opposite. You see them in bars and on the street and in small interactions in shops and markets, and the first thing you notice is how perfectly at ease they seem to be with themselves. You can tell that these are men who are used to being adored, doted upon, indulged by their mothers, their grandmothers, their sisters, their wives, their lovers, and their daughters. Jackie Mason, in his usual exaggeration, used to tell a joke about the difference between Italian and other men. After a long day at work, the Italian husband comes home to his wife, who asks, "Can I get you somethin', Tony? How's the sauce,

Tony, do you like it? Do you need a drink, Tony? Is there anything else I can do for you?" By contrast, the non-Italian wife greets her husband—a master of the universe, a man who inspires fear in all those who work with and for him—when he comes home from the office and opens the front door, with "You know, you forgot to take out the garbage!"

In Rome men walk very slowly. You see them out and about all day, standing around, talking, laughing, gesturing, leaning into their *compagni* and saying the right word, framing the perfect response, acting like they had every right to be where they were, and certain that the entire society has no problem recognizing them for what they are—men. Watch a man sauntering into the bar to take one of his numerous coffee breaks and you see a person at ease, secure in the knowledge that all is right, *tutto a posto,* because he will call his mother after *pranzo,* and the women in his life will continue to make him *feel* as if he were the most important person who ever lived.

And are they beautiful besides! In the early nineties, one of our male clients who had come to us looking for a partner was about to take his first trip abroad, and Rome was one stop on his intended itinerary. He got around to asking us how to dress, no doubt thinking that if he were to be so lucky as to have *una storia,* a sentimental adventure, while in Rome, it would truly make his life. We told him that Roman men dress very elegantly, and that if he wanted to impress a *ragazza,* he might consider getting a few items while he was visiting. "What about sneakers?" he asked. "Do they wear sneakers?" We told him they didn't, that, in fact, you rarely see a Roman man past the age of twenty wearing sneakers, that somehow the Italians have managed to design shoes that are as stylish as they are comfortable.

We advised him—if he was seriously interested in meeting someone while in Rome—to leave his tennis shoes at home. "I can't imagine not wearing sneakers," he finally said. "What about black ones?" Ah, my friend, I thought, not revealing what was really going through my mind, seduction requires sacrifice.

In a city where everyone has a "look," where making a *brutta figura* is about the worst faux pas you can commit, you can't fail to notice certain young men in their twenties and thirties who look like they are fashion models. Their appearance is so put together, so carefully laid out, so *curato,* that you realize that all the wardrobe consulting in the world would never provide you with the stuff to compete with these guys. Everything is in place, down to the three-day growth that somehow looks becoming on them, perhaps because of their dark complexions. I'm not particularly light-skinned, but when I've tried to go a day or two without shaving, I look like a street person. Then there is the hair, which is sometimes quite long and wavy, with a kind of sheen to it that at first makes you think that it's greasy but is really pomaded to look that way. The *ragazzo* sometimes sports an earring, almost always a cigarette and sunglasses, and although it doesn't seem like he's doing much of anything except looking good, he often wears a suit that is absolutely the latest design, cut, and color. This year these guys went in for the gray, three-button variety, sometimes with vests that extended way up the torso almost to the collar, with various shades of blue shirt and boldly designed wide tie, with a knot so wide it seemed to extend from one shoulder to the other. Often the pants are narrow and long, gathering fabric around the shoes, which are heavy, bootlike, sometimes with buckles.

Looking at a guy like this, you would think you have been time-transported back to the Edwardian period, except that suddenly his *telefonino* will go off and soon he is engaged in earnest conversation as he hops on his *motorino* (drivers in Italy are called *centauri*—centaurs, the mythical half man, half horse) and drives off—one-handed—the other hand holding the phone as his gorgeous, helmetless head disappears into traffic. You have to wonder. What does he do? Where does he work? Does he work? Who would hire him? A young stud like that, it's hard to imagine that he has a university education, and yet he is dressed so exquisitely that he either is somebody, or pretending to be somebody. We've heard that some people have fake *telefonini* and others pay people to call them at various times just to make a *bella figura,* a great impression.

No wonder these guys are *mammoni.* No wonder they don't marry, but stay at home until they are thirty-five, forty, and beyond, living off the need on the part of the mothers to coddle them, to wash and clean and cook for them, to treat them as though they were royalty. How could anyone top a deal like that, especially now that most women want to be treated the same way; now that they don't want to cook and clean and wash and be available for their men the way their mothers were available—and still are—for their fathers and brothers? "How's the sauce, Tony?" doesn't seem to be carrying over to the new generation of young women. Women work, have their own lives, friends, and independent existences.

And yet the role of the man has not changed. The sentimental relations between men and women in Italy are beginning to strain, as the people who do marry often do so for convenience, have no children, and take their income and what the family provides them and keep it for themselves. A city that up until a generation ago had only princes now must deal with the arriviste, the princesses, who are just as determined to be spoiled, adored, pampered, and given everything that their male counterparts receive.

But if everyone wants to be spoiled, who will do the spoiling? Is it any wonder that Italians have decided in general to have few children, or none at all, in light of the fact that men are ruled by their mothers and women don't want to give up the role of spoilee to become a spoiler? *"Mammismo"* may be the butt of many a joke here, but people at the same time consider it a real problem, one that is made more complicated by the way in which Rome at the same time is being dragged into modernity, pushed by euros and European Parliaments and globalization to leave its comfortable provinciality to history and become a dependable, market-driven society, with rules that are followed, an infrastructure that works, and a more "serious" attitude toward life. It's as if the whole culture is holding its breath, waiting to find out if it's safe to exhale, knowing that a way of life is changing and not knowing at the same time if the change is for the better.

In times of flux, who can you count on more than *Mamma*?

28

Not Only for Sale: The Artistic Approach to Life

We are late for dinner. But I tell my friends, who are visiting from Philadelphia, that it's not something to worry about, that everyone is habitually late for dinner, and that our hosts are really not expecting us to be on time. The time for dinner is when we arrive.

My visiting friends are inquiring about whether it's appropriate to bring flowers as a token of their appreciation for the invitation and considering whether we should wait to have the flowers gift wrapped, or just take them and be on our way so that we would be "on time." They believe my reassurances, and we consent to have Luca at the flower stand apply his considerable talents to making the fragrant, colorful gifts of nature even more beautiful than they already are.

In Rome almost every store will gift wrap something for you—gratis—and you don't have to go up to the fourth floor, down the hall, around the corner from the personnel department, and past the service elevators and bathroom to have it done, either. Even a small neighborhood bookstore in which we bought a book as a present kept a stack of wrapping paper on the counter, ready to be applied to whatever title was being purchased. I noticed that the proprietor, without prompting, asked the *signora* who was standing next to us, waiting her turn, if the book was intended to be a *regalo,* a gift. Even stores that for some strange reason are not prepared to gift wrap nevertheless manage to gift wrap. They will take your item, deposit it into a colorful shopping bag, and then staple a bow to the top of it, infusing the package with infinitely more gaiety. Any ordinary bar has wrapping paper on hand to turn the smallest confection into something bright and cheerful. A nearby toy store proprietor happily gift wrapped twenty-five party favors for Elliott's birthday celebration. Everybody gift wraps all the time. It is expected.

Luca, of course, is so used to gift wrapping that he cannot conceive of a single sale in which he *doesn't* perform his services for the lovely stems. When he asks whether you want him to *incartarli,* wrap them, he must know if they are for the *casa,* which means simple wrapping, or a *regalo,* which calls for something more elaborate. For Luca, selling flowers is a means by which he can apply his creativity. Merely taking the flowers out of the buckets, putting a few greens in between, and then handing them back to you in exchange for several thousand lire does not inspire him, is not why he decided to do this kind of work.

As he begins to select just the right color ribbons and crepe paper, the *fiorista* clearly has no perception of time. Whether he takes five, ten, or fifteen minutes to give the flowers the accoutrements they deserve, it's all the same to him. He is operating on another level, one that considers making everyday things into works of art to be the highest form of creativity toward which a human being can aspire. Minutes pass. We watch him arrange his materials on the table—first the flowers, freesias and irises, interspersed with gladiolas, then the wrappings, the greens. He quickly folds the *carta* in a certain way, creating a scalloped edge, and carefully takes one flower at a time so that they nestle inside the bouquet in just the right manner, almost as if he were a clothing cutter who was contemplating the cut of the fabric so that it would fall along the curves of the body to accentuate this or that particular line.

Someone pulls up in a car, honks the horn, shouts "*Ciao, Luca*" out the window. He continues his work but begins to engage animatedly with his friend about the day's events. The conversation involves him to such a degree that he stops what he is doing, excuses himself, and saunters the short distance to the car. I have long since given up the notion that we will ever come close to making our appointed hour for dinner, but this last move on Luca's part also convinces my friends Ned and Debby that we will, in fact, be late.

After several additional minutes, *l'artista* returns to the bouquet, apologizing once again for the delay and explaining that he needed to find out what was happening with some flowers he had delivered for a party, and that this was his only opportunity since his friend is going out of town the next morning and won't be speaking with his cousin who knows the people who received the flowers and is the one who made all the arrangements. In the meantime, he has wrapped our flowers—the yellows, purples, and a smattering of reds creating a stunning concentration of color—tied the matching purple bow, and stapled the brightly colored crepe paper. But still, he is not finished. He goes back into his shed, gets several colored adhesive stickers, and applies them over every staple. He has worked for twenty minutes and has created something so beautiful, so unusual, so infused with craft and skill and technique that we know we will never remove the paper, that we will just stick the whole package into a vase with water and let the entire bouquet adorn the table of our hosts.

Ned, who had already entered the world of disbelief, tries to tip Luca, offering two thousand lire more than what we had agreed upon earlier, but the *fiorista* smilingly returns the money, his manner indicating that the work of art he has created and the pleasure we were obviously deriving from it were his payment.

You get the feeling among the Romans that, in the broadest sense, culture and art matter more than commerce. For them, they are categories of life that are intertwined with all others, and cannot be separated, put aside for safekeeping, and trotted out when people feel the need of some soul enrichment or spirit lifting. This country holds 70 percent of the recognized works of art in the world, is the birthplace of the Renaissance, has an artistic tradition that completely permeates civic life. The national minister of culture was recently taken to task in the newspapers because she failed to show up at the annual opening of the opera at Milan's La Scala, explaining her absence with the excuse that she was nursing her five-month-old baby. (Art even trumps family.) When American-turned-English film director Stanley Kubrick died, the news occupied the first four pages of coverage in one of the national dailies, and this went on for days, not because film is the biggest part of Italy's national artistic patrimony, but because cultural expression matters, and as such engenders debate, discussion, and discourse at the highest journalistic levels.

One of Elliott's assignments in his math class was to make little designs out of the squares that were printed in his notebook. He draws a box around ten squares and colors them one color for the number ten, draws a box around nine squares and uses another color for nine, etc. Our concern was that he would select the right number of squares and apply the right color, which he consistently did, but after a few weeks he was being increasingly reprimanded by his math teacher for not making neater drawings. *"Bene, ma più ordine,"* "OK, but more order," she would write. Her wishes were basically ignored by Elliott, who quickly drew the lines by hand and even more quickly colored them, going out of the line, and not fully filling the spaces. Maestra Maria was not amused, and she turned up the heat. Overlooking completely the fact that Elliott was getting the right answers, she wrote *"Che brutto disegno!"* "What an ugly design!" on one of his sloppier efforts and then called us in to inform the *stranieri* exactly what was expected of their offspring. She pointed to Elliott's work and told us that it was not acceptable, that it was not only a matter of knowing nine from ten, but of executing his work in a manner that respected the process. It is *bella figura* again, this time applied to first-grade math. We got the message. Elliott now uses a ruler to draw lines that conform to the printed squares, and he fills the entire space with color and erases the overflow if he goes beyond the borders. He is already being inculcated into a way of life that values the form—as well as the substance—of things; that values the way they look, not only the way they function.

Romans are attuned to beauty, to art, to culture. They are convinced that the way to a satisfied soul, to a life worth living, is through the expression of one's creativity. Even when you go to the local *alimentari* and order turkey or *prosciutto,* the slices that come out of the machine are not piled on top of one another, creating a heap that resembles the loaf off of which the cold cuts just came, but are laid side by side on the paper and rolled into a sort of tube that creates a flower-shaped design, a more appetizing display when you are ready to unfurl the package and regard what you have just that morning purchased. Romans are convinced that beauty is the best investment you can make in life, that just a little extra effort will create something that has value beyond what you can sell it for or what you can use it for. Case in point: The uniform of the Italian air force was designed by the famous Roman *stilista* Valentino.

What matters to these people is that they try to continue the incredible artistic enterprise of which they are the inheritors, that they honor traditions that go back to the Etruscans, the Romans, the Greeks, and were assimilated into the imperial culture. The emperor Hadrian was an architect, and in the design of his villa outside Rome, he incorporated everything he had seen on his many travels throughout the conquered lands. Even the early Christian period, for all its deemphasis of the body and of physical beauty in general, was not without its contribution to the artistic way of life. You need only look at the many mosaics and frescoes that adorn churches all over the country, as well as *cosmati* floors—a type of mosaic made of inlaid stone that reflects prescribed religious patterns—to see that this is the case. They are put together with care, incorporating tiny, perfectly edged colorful pieces, contributing to a feeling not only of the spirituality that is associated with ultimate life and death concerns, but the release of emotion that comes from being in the presence of art, as individuals seek to transcend their own mortality by composing, creating, or building something that leaves their own time and place and touches people of other times, other places.

You look at Italians and on the surface you think they are like us, that their values are the same, that their ambition is to be rich, to retire early, and to be seen by all as someone who has "made it." But they are not like us. Their mentality has been molded by another age, a time when the amount of money anyone could earn was regulated by strict religious and municipal rules that paid heed to the "common good." There were masters, journeymen, apprentices. You worked at a craft, perfected it, and offered your creativity to the community. Becoming "rich" was impossible. Even in the Renaissance, when the genius of individual artists was celebrated as never before, the creators were still seen as craftsmen, paid to execute the commissions of the wealthy in order to adorn their *ville* and *palazzi* with the kind of works of art that once adorned the palaces of Nero, Tiberius, and Augustus.

This principle is not limited only to art, but adheres as well to the prosaic craft of auto-body repair. Within six weeks of our arrival in Italy, we had already undergone three minor accidents and were dealing with two bashed-in doors on the driver's side. In America the doors would have been ordered from Mercedes, replaced, and then painted, and the job would have cost a few thousand dollars. In Rome the doors were banged out, worked over, stuccoed, sanded down, and finally painted—all hand-done work, taking what seemed like forever, weeks at least—but since time is not money here, the tab was much less than half of what it would have been in America. The color is so close to the original I cannot tell the difference, but the *carroz-*

zeria, apologizing, explained that the particular color of our car no longer exists at Mercedes, and the auto-body shop had to *mix it themselves.* As I watched them take all the time they needed to be as precise and creative as possible, I could not help but think of the bygone artistic geniuses: the dedication of Michelangelo, the versatility of Leonardo, the brilliance of Bernini.

It is 9:30 P.M. We are "late," of course, for dinner. Our host Josefina greets us as double-cheeked kisses are exchanged all around. *"Guarda, che bei fiori!"* she says, taking the flowers and leading us into the living room where the chilled *prosecco* is waiting. She wasn't expecting us this "early" (thirty minutes after the time of the invitation). "Make yourselves at home," she says. "Pino will be here any minute, and, *scusate,* I must still go and take a quick shower."

29

James Joyce Slept Here: Everyone Who Is Anyone Has Passed Through

M any Romans will tell you that the Amalfi coast, a tiny spit of land that juts out into the Tyrrenian Sea just south of Naples, is the most beautiful spot on earth. Steep, dark purple mountainside slopes covered with fragrant lemon groves spill downward toward the sea, and tiny villages perched along the grades remind you that life can be lived vertically as well as horizontally.

As you step out onto the edge of paradise, you can feel the golden warmth or misty dew penetrate deep within your core as the clear turquoise ripples merge with sandy stretches far below. Among the small villages that dot the peninsula, Ravello is arguably the most striking. At the top of a hill a few miles from the shore, its cobblestone alleys and comforting small size give way to villas adorned with magenta bougainvillea, perfectly situated so that you feel as if the azure sea is yours alone, as if you have left the human realm and joined that of the gods. At one of these *palazzi*, Villa Cimbrone, set in an exquisite garden, there is a plaque on the building commemorating an event that took place inside, only this occurrence does not date from the thirteenth century, the seventeenth century, or even the nineteenth. It took place in 1937. In that year, in this *palazzo,* says the inscription, Greta Garbo fled the bright, intrusive lights of Hollywood and had a tryst with the conductor Leopold Stokowski.

When you see the marble tablet, your first reaction could be one of surprise, as you normally associate Italy with events that took place in the distant past. But then you look around. It is late May. Sea-foam greens, lavenders, lemon yellows, and flushed pinks intoxicate your vision, and the fragrance of the blossoms gives off a kind of natural aphrodisiac. You can only imagine how this place must have felt to the lovers, far away from the chaos and constant hounding that they must have endured in America, safely out of view of those who would exploit their passion for their own purposes.

Italy is like that. It is a place that has drawn the curious, the religious, the rapacious, the impassioned, and the searching, for millennia. To these shores have traveled people who sacrificed much to come and partake of its vast culture, and no place better epitomizes the ability to attract the best and the brightest—at least for a while—than Rome.

In contrast to the one tablet you see in one of the most charming towns in Italy, you find dozens of such tablets all over the city of Rome. If you walk down the streets of the *centro storico* with your eyes at the level of the second story, you will be introduced to the history of the men and women of greatness who felt the need to come here, to allow the spell to be cast on them, to stretch the mind, to project the spirit back in time to its origins, and you can actually touch the building in which someone who has contributed to the person you are, lived. Per-

haps you have curled up with one of these great writers, been
hypnotized by her prose, immersed yourself in his soaring arias,
or gazed spellbound at his paintings.

You walk down the Via Frattina, away from the American
Express office at Piazza di Spagna, toward the Via del Corso.
The street has little vehicular traffic, but what it lacks in automobiles it more than makes up for in people. Everywhere there
are *romani* rubbing shoulders with tourists, shopping bags of Max
Mara or Alberta Ferretti in one hand, cones of *gelato* in the other;
in all manner of dress, height, looks; everyone coming and going
in an intricate dance that has a rhythm and a timing that only
the *romani* seem instinctively to know. At eye level there are
shop windows displaying everything your heart desires, while
interspersed are outdoor cafés where people are not only nour-
ishing their appetites, but are also watching to see who is wearing
what and how something they saw the day before in a fashion
magazine or in a shop window looks when someone actually
has it on. Over here there is a store selling dinnerware, cande-
labras, shapely glass hand-blown in every shade, and linen tablecloths. Over there one can buy lingerie and stockings in a myriad
of styles and patterns, shoes with the latest toes and heels, luxurious cashmere sweaters.

Another window is so adorned, so elegantly laid out, so feminine, so alluring, so compelling in its startling simplicity, that
for a moment it escapes me completely that these are in fact
products and cosmetics on display that can be purchased inside.
They all have the same theme, all inviting the viewer, the pass-
erby, the potential consumer to come in and participate in the
luxury, the sensuality, the warmth of the overriding bright gold
that comes through the glass and glistens in the early morning

brilliance of the sun. The message is clear. Look at me. Notice me. Enjoy me. I'm here for you. I exist for your pleasure, your enjoyment, your comfort. You don't have to be rich or famous. You only have to have the courage to participate in the glamour that comes from caring for yourself—how your skin feels and looks, the luster of your hair, the scent you leave behind as you pass others on the street. So intoxicating!

But up above all this, partaking of an entirely different world, is a plaque. At number 51 it tells you that from August through December 1906, when the writer-artist was in his twenties and in voluntary exile, dreaming of *Ulysses,* "creating our universe from his Dublin," James Joyce lived in this building, in this very spot that still stands and that looks very close to how it did then. It is a conundrum that reveals the enigma that is Rome. Compared to the way life is lived today, the world of 1906 was another era, when telephones, automobiles, air travel, the trappings of modernity that we take for granted, were in their infancy, and television, computers, even radio, had not yet been invented. There were only two ways to communicate with someone—by message delivered by wireless or the post, or in person.

Yet compared to, say, the third century A.D., when the Aurelian walls that surround the city were put up, a hundred years ago seems as if it were only yesterday, an era in which Joyce could write novels that we can read and live a kind of life that we ourselves basically still live. Rome gives you this perspective—constantly—whenever you see teenagers with metal studs sticking out of their lips, noses, eyebrows, and ears, as you turn from this *Clockwork Orange*-type image and see the column of Marcus Aurelius standing majestically along the Corso, detailing the battles and conquests that led his troops to endure hardship and death for the glory and the grandeur of an idea, the imperial vision, a tribute both to the gods and to the human capacity to sometimes be godlike, something kids with Mohawks know nothing of. They study Roman history in school, but to them it might as well be myth, for all the connection they have to the spirit of the past.

Back to the passersby. Perhaps your subconscious has been infiltrated with the thought of something that will melt in your mouth, sweet and cold. You find yourself heading straight to Giolitti for *gelato,* one of the best in Rome, on Via Uffici del Vicario. You see someone madly licking her *cocomero,* watermelon *sorbetto* with chocolate chips acting the role of seeds, and *sorbetto al limone,* another savoring a cone of *bacio,* rich chocolate and nuts, and *frutti di bosco,* wild berry, as you wait in line to pay and are anxiously trying to decide what flavors to choose.

When you leave Giolitti in a euphoric daze and turn left, making a right at the first street, Via Campo Marzio, past more elegant shops, you are now just a few paces away from the Italian lower house of Parliament on Monte Citorio. On the building at number 1, above Davide Cenci fine clothing, is a tablet that tells you that here in 1859 Giuseppe Verdi—who was from the north—lived in Rome at a time when the ferment for a united Italy was about to peak, and the country was only eleven years away from realizing the dream, when its soldiers under Garibaldi and the head of the House of Savoy, Victor Emmanuel, who later became Italy's first king, were fighting the French, the Austrians, the Bourbons, and finally the forces of the pope to free the country from fourteen hundred years of fragmentation, division, and repression.

What was it that drew the English poets Keats and Shelley,

whose tragically brief lives ended here—Keats in the very building that stands adjacent to the Piazza di Spagna and Shelley in the warm waters off the coast near Rome—or Goethe or Wagner, or the French painter Ingres, who had two long stays in this city in the early 1800s, was greatly influenced by Raphael, and whose sensual treatment of the human figure in turn influenced Degas, Renoir, Matisse, and Picasso? What enticed Michelangelo, Raphael, Caravaggio, and Bernini to come to Rome and display their talents for those in a position to reward and celebrate them? Or Henry James or Stendhal or Edith Wharton? Although today's Rome is a metropolis consisting of three and a half million people, the history of its population has been like an accordion, contracting from two million in A.D. 250 to fifty people in the year 500, as the severing of the aqueducts in the early sixth century brought disease and concerted flight down from the hills and into the Campo Marzio, which had been the training grounds of the feared Roman legions and then became the center of the medieval city. Even in 1870, upon unification, the population of Rome was only 214,000, hardly the numbers that constitute a major metropolis.

Yet in the same way that people would rather romanticize San Francisco, with seven hundred thousand people, than other cities with several million, Rome has always captured the imagination of those who have sought to define themselves artistically, as a place that has kept the historical faith, has carried on the traditions and maintained the vision of the ancient world, when beauty and form and a certain kind of earthly harmony were worshiped as the means by which one partakes of the divine. People are drawn to Rome because it is still the pagan mecca, still the place that beckons those who want to gobble up all that has been done before and turn it into that which has never been seen, never been heard, never been imagined. People whose minds are mired in the modern decry the lack of space here, and in that sense they are right. But what they fail to take note of is the other kind of space, temporal space, historical space, space that opens up in time, that stretches backward and forward instead of across, that gives you a perspective that is at once soothing and frightening, reassuring and threatening. You come to Rome to confirm once and for all that you will meet the same end as everyone else, that although the city will endure, you will not, that you might as well fill your days with whatever life has to offer because your time is limited and you will eventually be recycled, probably without a plaque.

Even the churches tell you that. Despite the most dedicated attempts to convince you that this life is but a prelude to an everlasting one, they, in fact, reinforce a sense of the opposite. They liberate you from the thought of the future because what you see before you, what you hear in the Gregorian chants on a Sunday morning in the Church of Santa Sabina, what you feel as you light a candle in the hopes that Silvia will recover, is so awe-inspiring that it fulfills you on the spot, making you forget about what comes next. Who needs to think about what comes next? Who knows if there even is a next? All you know is that the sounds and images of this city are so sublime that you want to embrace everything to do with the senses and never let go or look back. Artists have come to Rome because for all the "Thou shalt nots," it remains the repository of "Thou shalt."

There is not one, but two plaques dedicated to Federico Fellini. The first is on the Via Veneto, the one that celebrates *la famosa dolce vita* of the fifties and early sixties, as Rome threw a party that lasted for years and signaled once and for all to the *romani* that *la guerra* was finally over, that the comic tragedy of fascism and the deprivation of war could now be *archivati,* put into the archives, buried. At the end of Via Margutta is the second plaque, the one that tells you where he and his wife of fifty years, the actress Giulietta Masina, lived. People think of a master filmmaker like Fellini and imagine him rich and powerful, but he wasn't. His films were not blockbusters, despite the occasional critical acclaim, and so he sweated every project and really never knew where financing for the next movie was coming from. One thing he did know, however, and it made him something of an agoraphobic, is that he hated to leave Rome. For him the city was his mistress and his muse, the place from which he drew ideas, inspiration, and sustenance. He believed— only half-jokingly—that when he was outside the city he was vulnerable, that he could die, that the lack of the ingrained familiarity that characterizes this place would set him adrift and jeopardize his safety. He couldn't wait at one point to leave Los Angeles after another failed negotiation to make films there, because in response to a request to provide him with an office in a building that was "old," his hosts had shown him a place that had been built five years before. He didn't like it because, among other things, the windows didn't open. Romans hate air-conditioning. To them, drafts, especially cold ones, come from the devil. They much prefer the intense heat and street noise of summer to the hermetically sealed artificial environment provided by modern technology. Fellini's reply to the offer of space in one of the choicest buildings in L.A. was to ask to be taken to the airport for a flight back home, *subito.*

Rome does that to some people. It gets under your skin and

tingles you with sensations that are often more imagined than real. But that is its charm, the ability to let you picture yourself as anything you want to be. Rome is a small place, small enough to feel like a stage, where everyone is acting the role each has imagined playing, a place to which artists have been drawn, their inspiration overflowing like the fountains one sees everywhere, its beauty and contradiction distilled in song, in words, in color, and in light.

30

Rome at the Crossroads: Natives and Immigrants Through the Eyes of an Expat

At first, he seemed to be just another part of the landscape of the neighborhood. There are people, many more than one would imagine, whom you somehow manage to see all the time, and these encounters form the backdrop for your own everyday life. Although the Romans, when all is said and done, tied by the daily routines of life to their families, are not wont to take you in and become your best friend within fifteen minutes, as is, or seems to be, the case in northern California, they nevertheless are open to amiable daily exchange, even if it is merely to say *buongiorno* or *buona sera* or *salve,* once you have had even the most minimal kind of interaction with them. And since there are so many people living in such small areas in little neighborhoods throughout the city, with so much of life taking place outdoors—in the streets and shops, bars and *piazze*—you generally find yourself feeling rather quickly as if you have become an addition to a community, even if the Romans have assigned you the role of *americano.* It was rather amusing when, for instance, Diane found herself at the local hair salon, seated between the pharmacist, her hair full of curlers, on one side, and the woman from the *alimentari* who breaks off pieces of *parmigiano*, rich red dye settling into her fussed-over head, on the other.

Part of our community is a man who is obviously different from the others, but to whom I had begun to nod and smile and politely greet in my daily comings and goings, and he, after a few responses that seemed somewhat guarded, began to nod back. Then one day, as I was leaving my *palazzo*, I saw him peering at the intercom, looking at the names. When I asked him if he needed any help, he replied that he was trying to find some kind of "psychological center." I knew right away he was looking for Diane, and since he looked harmless, I told him that my wife was a professional counselor. He nodded, more definitively this time. I had met the Professor.

He was dressed in the same manner as I had always seen him— his compact, well-fed frame encased in a long woolen overcoat and Russian hat to repel the less than frigid Roman winter, freshly pressed shirt and tie showing through the folds of his red silk paisley scarf—holding the old wooden cane that I had never seen him without. We spoke for a few moments in Italian before it dawned on him—as it always does before long with the natives—that I had grown up with a different mother tongue. "Do you speak English?" he suddenly asked, in perfect, accented English. "Yes, I do," I said, to which he responded, smiling for the first time in the frequent street contact we had had, "So do I," which was obvious and made us both laugh. "The therapist is your wife?" he repeated, confirming what I had already mentioned. "And what is your name?" he continued. "Epstein," I said, suddenly not knowing where we were headed but feeling safe enough to continue down the road I had already embarked with this obviously fascinating character. "So you are Jewish," he then said, in a way that all Jews instinctively know when they want to reveal their own identities. "So am I," he said, obviously by this point delighted.

The first thing I had already noticed about Professor Ferruccio di Cori was the fact of his age. This was a man who had lived. I could see in his eyes that they had witnessed much, that he was like the city in which I was meeting him—advanced, mature, experienced, a little sad at the thought that there was much, much more behind than ahead, yet still eager to live on, to not give in just yet to fate and call short the adventure.

In a few minutes of Sunday morning conversation, I learned the contours of his life. Raised in an upper-middle-class family in the Prati section of town, near the Vatican, he fled the imposition of the infamous racial laws directed at Jews by the Fascist regime of Mussolini in 1938, and, at the still-tender age of twenty-six, fled Italy, arriving in the United States on Thanksgiving Day, 1939. He stayed for fifty-six years, attending Harvard and becoming a medical doctor and psychiatrist. And then, responding as he so poetically puts it, "to the call of the wild," he returned to Rome in 1995 to live out the rest of his life on familiar ground, in the territory that had witnessed his beginnings.

The Professor looks like he was found by central casting to play the role in which he has chosen in life to actually cast himself. He is a poet and playwright, a still-practicing psychiatrist and university teacher, an *appassionato* and scholar of Pinocchio. At a birthday party for Diane, he held the dozens of guests enthralled as he read his exquisite poetry in both Italian and English. Although by now his gait is slow, it is easy to feel his intense physicality, that there still exists the mind and heart of a twenty-six-year-old boy in his considerably older body.

But for all his primordial intentions, he is living proof that you can't go home again, as his frustration and disillusionment with Rome, the Romans, and Italy in general are evident and undeniable. He has already been subjected to a shell game in which his condominium apartment was almost swindled from him by a famous Roman icon and her boyfriend, whom the Professor claims was not even the man who was brought into the courtroom and convicted of having plotted with the actress to divest the Professor of his property. "Don't worry," said his lawyer when di Cori protested that the man under accusation was not the swindler he had hosted in his apartment when the phony deal was struck, "somebody is going to jail. If it's not the guy you met, then it's the guy you are looking at now." Justice—Italian style.

Like each and every Jew who survived World War II and is old enough to remember it, the Professor has stories. They are replete with frequent flights from town to town, country to country, including a period when his family—mother, father, brother, sister—was being hidden in Rome by his wet nurse. He tells us the tragic tale of the president of the Roman Jewish community, having fled the city in advance of the Nazis, leaving behind in plain view in his office the list of all the Jewish families in the city. The eventual roundup and deportation to extermination camps was only too simple.

Each day I gaze out our windows, admiring his lovely *palazzo* and courtyard, sitting proudly adjacent to ours. As I enter Professor di Cori's penthouse apartment, it is just what I imagine Freud's house to have been like on Berggasse 19 in Vienna—

dark, labyrinthine, floor-to-ceiling bookshelves stacked with volumes, sculptures and countless objects strewn about, a huge portrait of Dante staring down at you, dozens of antique canes in one corner, old maps and photographs of Rome every-where—so much to see that you realize when you are there that, like *la città eterna,* you could spend a lifetime in his place and not exhaust the opportunity to immerse yourself in the end-lessly captivating world of the id. "My place is like the uncon-scious," the Professor jokes as he sees Diane and me looking around in awe and astonishment, neither of us having ever seen a place like this before, "everything thrown together."

Every time I am with the Professor I feel as if I am communing with the twentieth century itself, the very last chapter of this bloody millennium, with war once again tearing at the otherwise delightful landscape and mended fabric of Europe after more than fifty years of blessed peace. Is Milosevic another Hitler? Does the failure to stop the Nazis at Munich in 1938 apply in the case of Kosovo, or is the major mistake of thinking we could intervene in a civil, nationalist war in Vietnam the lesson we should be living? Once again we are wrestling with history, fail-ing to understand a mentality different from our own. All the questions we thought we had answered are back in play as bombs fall, women and children are massacred, and people are driven from their homes in the name of an ethnic ideal that seems to hearken back to the beginning of this thousand-year period. It was in 1054 when the then unified Catholic Church split into two distinct parts—Roman and Eastern Orthodox—and was then swallowed up in the East for centuries in the maw of the Muslim Ottoman Turks, who occupied the Balkans for more than five hundred years. They advanced as far as the gates of

Vienna in 1683, when they were turned back for the last time, their legacy yet with us as Orthodox Serbia still dreams of avenging its defeat in 1389 at the hands of the Muslims by exterminating the Islamic Albanians in Kosovo five hundred years later. Will we ever be free of the ghosts of the past? Is it really possible to dream of a technological future that finally lays to rest the ancient passions that still plague us? Although life in Rome leads you to believe that the answer is no, somehow, as the Professor has done by returning, you have to put aside the supposedly ameliorative magic of the modern world and try to make peace with the ghosts.

The Professor loves America. For him, it is *the* place. "The horizon is broader there," he says. "I arrived with two suitcases and no money, and I made something of myself. In Rome you can't do that." He is fond of quoting Bob Hope's famous line, "I have a tuxedo, I can go anywhere." For him, the joke typifies the respect for the ability of the individual that he feels is difficult to find in Italy. Rome is not the same place he fled as the clouds of World War II and the Holocaust were gathering. I continually probe to see if there is any part in him that shares my enthusiasm and passion for Roman life. "The language is beautiful," he says, and then, rolling his eyes toward heaven, "and the food . . ." He lets the thought go, choosing to let his face do the talking.

The Rome to which Professor di Cori has come back bears little resemblance to the even more intimate small town he left. *"Sta cambiando,"* the natives say, it is changing. Even in the relatively short period of time in which we have made this city our home, we have noticed the difference. In 1872 Henry James wrote, "Could Rome after all *be* a world-city?" no doubt referring to the hopelessly provincial, preserved quality of the place that still reigns in the center even though the concentric rings have been inexorably built up all around it.

And the tidal wave of immigration in just the past few years has contributed to the changed look of the city. Just the other day as I was riding the metro I glanced around, and for the first time I thought I had been transported to New York or Paris. The passengers seemed to resemble the United Nations as I looked in vain for a face and a way of dress that was undoubtedly Roman. Crime seems to be on the increase as the wave of foreigners that have been welcomed in Italy recently has produced a number of assaults in cities that had for years not witnessed this kind of thuggery. Once again a person with a liberal, open mind and humanitarian impulses faces the fact that the immigrants come from cultures that have different ways from the natives of dealing with situations. Their habits are in general rougher, unmannerly. Some are less inclined to ask permission to pass rather than to barge ahead in a way that almost every Roman considers *maleducato,* rude and impolite. The beauty and verdant splendor of certain passageways in the Villa Borghese have been overcome lately by people who have all manner of tchotchkes to sell, laid out end to end on white sheets, for next to nothing as the placid *romani* stroll by in that nonchalant way they have done for centuries, mostly oblivious to the intrusion and seemingly unmoved by its pecuniary insistence.

To me it is an eyesore. I do not deny the need for people who end up in Rome to make a living and feed themselves and their families, and, in fact, an entire community of Filipinos has made itself indispensable, as their members smilingly, willingly, gratefully clean the homes, watch the children, and take the aged parents and grandparents of the suddenly *impegnati romani,* busy

Romans, on their walks, but I can't help but think that the street vendors are here because of the notoriously lax law enforcement of the authorities. I wonder whether the gendarmes of Paris would tolerate such blatant trafficking in the Luxembourg Gardens or the bobbies of London would allow this to go on in Hyde Park.

The signs in Rome are pointing in a certain direction, and that does not bode well for *la dolce vita,* the leisurely way of life that has characterized this city for a long time. I have been observing this place for two decades, and it is clear that though my experience of Rome often feels like a throwback to an idyllic childhood I enjoyed in Philadelphia in the fifties, which I now experience again here forty years later, the links to the old ways are diminishing. A life based on family and modest income in exchange for lots of free time is being shown the door. The liberalization of the marketplace, stores that are now open continuously, fast food and sudden disinclination toward an elevated cuisine, immigrants—however useful and necessary—flooding the economy with cheap labor and unassimilable customs are all conspiring to erase the doubts that Henry James expressed about the city more than a hundred years ago. In its movement— typically Roman, which is to say slow and deliberate—toward modernization and globalization, one of the last places in Europe that is both authentic and indifferent to the world of the digital, the cookie-cutter, the instant, and the bland, Rome is nonetheless on its way to becoming just another big city that is open for business all the time and as such destroys the family and forces its members to conform to the requirements of the market. Italians have wholeheartedly embraced the idea of a united Europe, and that will eventually mean the end of the Rome of the afternoon siesta, the consistent local cuisine, stay-at-home mothers, and people who enter a store with a greeting and who talk to each other, saying *buongiorno* and *come va?* and who are responded to not only by the shopkeeper, who is more than likely the owner or at least a member of the family, but by the other patrons as well.

The Professor knows this, which probably accounts for his disappointment. He cannot turn back the clock, and, looking into his sharp, sparkly but fading eyes, I realize that—while I can appease myself with the thought that at least we have chosen to live in Rome while it still partakes of an older, more intimate way of life—neither can I.

31

The Many Faces of Rome: Getting Ready for the Party of the Millennium

For the moment our odyssey through the vicissitudes of Roman life must wind down, and we are back where we began—on the Via Veneto. Here, a few minutes by foot from the Church of Santa Maria della Concezione, where the bones of the monks come alive to remind you that mortality is your only fate, sits the Hotel Excelsior, a stunning example of the kind of transformation of which Rome is capable, and which provides a message different from the one monks want to emphasize. In the hustle and bustle of arrivals and departures, the sheen of polished glass, brass, and marble, the sensual allure of expensive clothes, perfume, and plush carpets, the message is all about the here and now, and the results have the effect of underlining the fact that Rome is so old and so varied that it never fails to show you many faces, intertwined threads that sinuously wrap around each other in a kind of tapestry of the whole of human history.

The Excelsior has a certain fascination, for at last report, Steven Spielberg and the sultan of Brunei were still going at it, locked in a ferocious bidding war to see who would acquire the rights to spend New Year's Eve, 1999—the absolute ultimate stop before the dawn of a new age—in the freshly redesigned Villa Cupola suite at the Excelsior, which includes, among lots of other floor space, the building's original cupola that faces onto the Via Veneto. The suite normally can be had for five thousand dollars per night, but the last day of this one-thousand-year period is undoubtedly a special occasion, and so two of the richest men in the world have both decided that it is worth the effort and are sparing no expense for the opportunity. As of this writing, the issue still had not been decided, and the bid is currently up to ten thousand dollars for the evening.

What could be so precious? Even to people for whom that kind of money represents nary a dent in their personal balance sheets, there has to be some kind of attraction, some measure of charm or power or cachet that would make possessing it worthwhile. We had heard that the clientele is mostly Arab sheiks, sultans, and princes. In fact, when one unnamed sheik takes the Villa Cupola, the six remaining rooms on the floor are usually taken at the same time for his extended family, assistants, and perhaps his many wives, the entourage of any respectable traveling Arab nabob. In this world, the world of five-thousand-dollar hotel rooms, even my *landsman* from Hollywood, Steven Spielberg, is an interloper.

The work of restoration of the cupola has been done by our friends Karen and Michael Stelea, who are the hosts of a party in the suite. It was easy for us to accept their invitation, especially when Karen told us to bring the kids. They would be joined by a half dozen other children in a special section of the suite while the adults celebrated Michael's birthday downstairs. When we arrived, Karen welcomed us and began a tour of the premises that lasted twenty minutes. They have re-created a Renaissance palace within the confines of a hotel on one of the choicest streets in the world. The ground floor of the penthouse suite has two completely appointed bedrooms, several antique marble bathrooms, a formal dining room with an elaborate Venetian glass candelabra, and a very presidential-looking office where I sat at the desk for a moment or two imagining what it would be like to be a head of state, perhaps a throwback to my youthful infatuation with politics, and a formal living room with a ceiling that used to be normal Roman height, but that instead has been opened up to reveal the startling splendor of the fifty-foot-high cupola, which was a storage space until just months ago. It has now been turned into a work of art by a young *romano* who has rendered frescolike paintings on canvas and then mounted them in the arching dome. Every touch, every building element has been devoted to the re-creation of a time long since past to suit the tastes of people who possess the means to consume a culture and a history that has been brilliantly re-created for their diversion.

Rome has for millennia connected the historical dots. It was always the crossroads of the ancient world, the stopping-off point between east and west, north and south. Now, even though its days of strategic importance have long since been assigned to the pages of dusty academic tomes, it still stands at a kind of cultural junction that welcomes all faiths, races, religions, peoples, and types. It has seen so much, lived so long, endured every kind of deprivation at the same time as it has enjoyed all manner of pleasure that it long ago lost the impulse to judge. The Via Veneto is as hospitable to the chadored women and white-robed princes of the desert as it is to the schoolteachers and their kids—

decked out in T-shirts, shorts, and sneakers—who hail from Minnesota and emerge from the air-conditioned freezer that is the Hard Rock Cafe and into the sweltering reality of Rome in summer.

Our host leads us out of the Renaissance and into the future. The suite's second floor contains only one room—the movie theater—outfitted with the latest video technology, the DVD. The eight kids who have been invited to the party quickly scurry to the red-cushioned seats in front of the huge screen, settling in for an evening that begins with *George of the Jungle*. The kids are a mix of Americans, Italians, and half-and-halfs, but within moments the adults realize that the language of the silver screen is international. The movie starts out in English with Italian subtitles, but when we realize that some of the Italian kids are too young to read and don't understand English, we switch to Italian with English subtitles. It's better for us as well, as Diane and I are constantly fretting about Julian and Elliott's lack of formal education for the last few years in their mother tongue.

We continue up the stairs to floor three. The views of the city are spectacular, but all eyes are on the Jacuzzi set into the floor, tiled by Tunisians who were brought to Rome for this very purpose, to set down tiny pieces of naturally colored fragments in just the right way to make the correct patterns. We move into the next room, a small gym complete with Nautilus weight machine, treadmill, and a Bang and Olufsen sound system. Down the hall is a shower, Turkish bath, and sauna, and all around are canvases that depict the Roman baths of another era, when all the city came to cleanse their bodies and refresh their spirits at the same time.

Karen and Diane descend the stairs as I linger to walk out onto the terrace in the darkening gloom of a spring evening that sees rays of dramatic sunlight alternating with sudden showers. The American embassy to my left—the stolid successor to the Villa Ludovisi, whose grounds covered this area with vast fields and vineyards until the end of the nineteenth century and which now forms the core of the American quarter of the city—is surrounded by guards and barricades, another tragic reminder that history, which is taking place in the form of a bloody, hateful war just a few hundred miles from here, is something from which we still have not figured out how to escape. Just to the right, at the top of the hill and the street, are the northern remains of this part of the city's third-century Aurelian walls, pointing out once again that I am still within the protective confines of what was once an integrated world, a place that could shut itself in from all those who—and there have been many—had heard of its mythical riches and wanted to grab a handful or two while they lasted. Now, in another era, where guided missiles, launched from airplanes so far up in the sky they cannot be seen by the naked eye, can strike targeted bridges on the ground, the walls are no longer a barrier with the power to decree life or death, but merely another part of the cultural patrimony of the city.

Yet they are a psychological fact, and they remind me that in Rome there are people who will never see the re-created Renaissance that exists two floors below me, or use the gym and the Jacuzzi, or watch a film in the theater, and yet from their point of view, they would no doubt employ the shrugging Roman expression *chi se ne frega*—what does it matter to me—because their own lives are full and rich and partake of their own ancient rhythms that create a feeling of power just the same.

This idea of power brings me back again to the Renaissance, to the Florentine mercantile attempt to create a world in which art, creativity, beauty, and free (well, almost free) expression were let loose after centuries of dour repression by the Church. Diane and I had recently been to another party, at the Circolo della Caccia, in the Palazzo Borghese, which is a true Renaissance palace. The dinner was given in honor of George McGovern and Gore Vidal and was situated in a room that looked like it actually could have been designed by Michelangelo himself. Frescoes adorned the walls and vaulted ceiling of the dining area, as thirty people at three tables were served French-style by waiters wearing white gloves. Diane was seated between the senator and a journalist who was married at one time to a daughter of Gianni Agnelli, the industrialist owner of FIAT, and I sat between a baronessa and a contessa from Venice who used to live in the city but who now comes into town only for special occasions. When I asked her if Rome had changed much in thirty years, she said that it hadn't. "Rome never changes."

The sight of San Pietro from the terrace suddenly carries me out of my recollections and brings me to the indisputable authority of the Church. Something Gore Vidal was once quoted as saying reminds me of the year 2000, and the thought that Rome would be celebrating the event by hosting a Jubilee, a holy year, the first having been called in 1300. The year 2000 would be an especially significant time for Catholics from the world over to come to Rome and make a pilgrimage to all the important basilicas in the city so that one's spiritual debts could be forgiven. Gore Vidal said that the reason why he liked Rome was because it was the best place from which one could watch the end of the world. With the year 2000 upon us, his ironic wit forces one to stop and think, for the word "millennial" not only refers to chronological time, but to biblical time, a time that some say corresponds to the Second Coming of the Lord, and as such takes on a decidedly more apocalyptic significance.

Not to the cynical Romans, however. Not even to Church prelates, for whom the Jubilee is one large pain in the neck. "It's all being done for business," says Monsignore Aldo. "It's nothing but a big party. People could just as easily stay home and receive the same kind of benediction." Nevertheless, the city has been preparing for the invasion of millions of tourists. *"Disagio oggi, una città migliore domani,"* says the huge billboard in Piazza Venezia. Discomfort today, a better city tomorrow. Romans are not impressed. The city is being ripped apart and obscured by scaffolding to create a spectacle that will be the talk of the world. Museums are adding new wings and updating their infrastructures, streets are being torn up for the building of underground tunnels and new parking facilities to handle tour buses and the expected 20 percent increase in traffic in the already-crowded streets, and monuments, churches, historic *palazzi, ville,* and other significant points of interest have been under wraps while they undergo serious face-lifts, dotting the landscape with the familiar red-painted wooden construction sites that seem to sprout up almost daily, like spring wildflowers after a downpour. Vehicles are being diverted everywhere, as new signs appear at every turn, telling thoroughly confused drivers how to reach what were once familiar spots in the city, spots to which they were so accustomed to going that they could almost get there with their eyes closed. Now they must follow routes they do not know, as if they had become strangers in their own city. "We shouldn't have to pay any taxes this year," says our friend Maria, "while they're making this big mess for an extravaganza that nobody really wants."

But if the *romani* are cynical, the expats are not so universally opposed. "I think all the work for the Jubilee is fantastic for Rome," says Sandra Craig. "When we lived in Paris, the city was so clean you could practically eat off the streets. Maybe this will make Rome a tidier place, without taking anything away from its charm and character." I don't know. Rome is being pushed by the Jubilee into being more organized, as utter chaos would reign if it functioned as it normally does. The question, as always, is this: Is modernity an unmixed blessing? Is life "better" now than it used to be, apart from the fact that people do live longer and have more freedom, more "control," over their lives? Will Rome sacrifice itself for the tourist buck and become a place, like many others, that runs on the clock rather than on an approximate notion of time that tends more toward hours or even days, instead of minutes and seconds?

Downstairs, back in the Renaissance, the party is in full swing. Conversations among the clustered adults are interrupted now and then by manic youngsters scrambling to fill plates of pasta with tomato sauce, eager to return to the theater for the double feature. Diane is stunning in her emerald green *tailleur,* long streaked-blond hair, and black high heels. She is often mistaken for a *donna italiana,* but not on this occasion. Every Italian guest, as if he or she had been handed a guidebook at birth, is in serious, dark, evening attire. Diane is deep in conversation with a petite woman wearing a ruby red suit—obviously another non-Italian—whose manner and accent seem all too familiar. She is a Jewish doctor from Philadelphia, married to an Italian. She has been here for ten years, and her obvious cultural familiarity with us is both intriguing and puzzling her. "You live in Rome and you're planning to stay?" she asks. "You mean you chose to come here on your own?" she again wants to know, shaking her head at Diane's and my assent. She is incredulous. Her only response is "Oy."

I know exactly where she is coming from. It is obvious that she is in Rome because she fell in love with a Roman, not with a city. For her, like many expatriates who for one reason or another find themselves here, Rome is an obstacle to be overcome, not a relationship to be lived and enjoyed.

I became infatuated with this city twenty years ago, and over time my feeling for it has only deepened, blossoming into true love and touching my core, the place within to which I respond the most. To me, Rome is like a *bella donna,* aging but still vivacious and exquisite. The years have only accentuated her true nature, which also, of course, includes the flaws. She can be infuriating, maddening, even cruel, and certainly cannot always be trusted. And it's hard not to worry about her coming years. She will be tempted, as has been the case so often in the past, by foreign strangers. Will she try too hard to accommodate them and lose her soul and leave me behind in the process? *Tutto sommato,* it is not easy to live with her, but I couldn't imagine living without her, either. For where would I find a more charming, challenging, sensual, fascinating partner with whom to reside?

After the party, a swift cab ride through the ancient streets deposits us close to home. It is well past midnight. The boys run ahead of us, kicking a pine cone back and forth as Julian sings the *romanista* anthem, "Alé, Forza Roma, Alé," to the tune of Verdi's "March of the Elephants," from *Aida*. As we approach our *palazzo,* familiar figures emerge from a sleek, stylish car. At first glance, they seem to be dressed for a wedding, but as we draw closer we see that they are coming home from *comunione,* one of many we have witnessed this season. As our eyes adjust to the dark, we recognize the *bella famiglia,* and realize immediately that this has not been just another *comunione.* It has been celebrated for Flavia, the daughter of Silvia.

The *ragazza* is the embodiment of white—long, lacy dress, shimmering bows, patent leather shoes—and walks hand-in-hand with her little brother and sister. *Papà* comes around to open the door. *Mamma* emerges, without her well-worn cap. She exudes a cautious radiance that lights up the dark street. Her styled short hair, lipsticked smile, and lovely dress, stockings, and heels are striking, and the way she expresses herself—not only with her voice but with her movements as well—reminds me of the Silvia we knew before the accident, impeccably attired every morning to accompany the *bambine* to school. But it also brings to mind the anguish we all felt upon first hearing of her misfortune. At that time, her chances of recovery were by no means assured—in fact, they seemed quite bleak—and we struggled to pretend that everything was normal in order to keep the children ignorant of the shock and disbelief that had descended upon us. Silvia is living proof that prayers not only make you feel that you are doing all you can to ease a dire situation, but can be answered as well. In fact, her mere presence is nothing short of a miracle.

Our paths cross. We exchange the usual pleasantries— *"Che bella!"* *"Auguri, Buona notte,"* *"Ci vediamo domani al bar"*—and continue our separate ways. But the brief, neighborhood encounter has the effect of restoring my balance, and I am reminded, once again, why I have chosen to live in the Eternal City.